CYBERLAW

CYBERLAW

What You Need to Know
About Doing Business Online

David Johnston
Sunny Handa
Charles Morgan

Published in 1997 by Stoddart Publishing Co. Limited
34 Lesmill Road, Toronto, Canada M3B 2T6

Distributed in Canada by General Distribution Services Inc.
34 Lesmill Road, Toronto, Canada M3B 2T6
Tel. (416) 445-3333 Fax (416) 445-5967
E-mail Customer.Service@ccmailgw.genpub.com

Distributed in the U.S. by General Distribution Services Inc.
85 River Rock Drive, Suite 202, Buffalo, New York 14207
Toll-free tel. 1-800-805-1083 Toll-free fax 1-800-481-6207
E-mail gdsinc@genpub.com

01 00 99 98 97 1 2 3 4 5

Cataloging in Publication Data

Main entry under title:
Cyberlaw: what you need to know about doing business online

Includes index.
ISBN 0-7737-5926-3

1. Computer networks – Law and legislation – Canada.
2. Internet (Computer network). 3. Business – Computer networks.
I. Johnston, David L.

KE452.C6C93 1997 343.7109'944 97-930317-6
KF390.5.C6C93 1997

Cover design: Bill Douglas @ The Bang
Text design and page composition: Tannice Goddard

Printed and bound in Canada

We gratefully acknowledge the Canada Council for the Arts and the Ontario Arts Council for their support of our publishing program.

For
Sharon, Debbie, Ali,
Sharon Jr., Jenifer, and Sammy;
Danielle and Rish;
and Valérie and Chloé

Contents

PREFACE

Three years before the third millennium our global society is undergoing a profound economic, social, and cultural shift. This results from two four-letter words: code and chip. The first refers to DNA and the human genome project, which seeks to understand the architectural plans from which human beings and other forms of life are made.

The second, the chip, symbolizes the information revolution. This in turn is driven by dramatic changes in computer and communication technologies. Electronic commerce in the new digital economy manifests this change — and presents fundamental challenges to the law. How quickly and comprehensively can form (the law) adjust to function (the new economy)?

This book is written for the general business reader interested in how the law is responding to business concerns in the digital economy. How are businesses coping with the digital age? What are the tensions imposed on the rule of law? We tackle these issues by comparing existing law to the new technologies and new forms of business spawned by the information revolution. Technology and business are dynamic. Like two intermeshed gears in a mechanical transmission, the speed of change in the one engages and enhances the acceleration of the other. But the law is static and its institutions adapt slowly — and this creates a dilemma.

Business's basic goals in the digital revolution are efficiency and flexibility: the capacity to adapt quickly to a rapidly changing global environment. Business's expectations from the rule of law are: (i) predictability, (ii) fairness, (iii) enforceability, (iv) cheapness, and (v) speed. How well does the rule of law satisfy these needs? Not well. Moreover, the level of dissatisfaction is increasing as the "mismatch" intensifies.

But there are reasons for this mismatch. First, the information age's pace of change is unprecedented. Second, law is intended to be reactive and soberly deliberate. Third, law is often a last resort, to be applied when other, more flexible and market-related solutions to problems have failed. Finally, some of business's expectations of law may mutually conflict, e.g. the goals of fairness, cheapness, and speed (often summarized as "flexibility") may contradict the goals of predictability and enforceability (summarized as "certainty").

In these pages we describe the changing nature of business and technology in the information age; identify the expectations this creates for the rule of law; and explore the law's response. We examine particular categories of law: privacy (security, communication), regulation, intellectual property, contracts, torts, and private international law. These aren't exhaustive, but they do illustrate the tension areas between new technology and business and old law. Finally, we examine how "informal law" (alternative customs and standards) is emerging or being crafted by the players to resolve the tension.

As the measuring rod for law we use business's expectations: predictability, fairness, enforceability, efficiency (cheapness and speed), and adaptability. We encourage the reader to apply these measures (or another suitable judging standard) throughout these pages, and to consider what law reform initiatives are desirable and possible to ensure a "better fit" or a more appropriate "delicate balance."

The book's organization is simple. In Chapter 1 (The Digital Revolution) we consider the transformative effect of new information technology on business practices, and their legal consequences. The chapter puts the digital revolution into a historical context in order to highlight the similarities and differences with other periods of epic change in commerce. We underline a principal theme: the tension between stability and change. We ask what business leaders need to know about where the law is going in the digital age, and how to encourage leaders in law to show the wit, wisdom, and nimbleness to engineer the adjustments.

Chapter 2 (Digital Technology) is a brief primer on the technology of cyberspace commerce. We examine the networks and software of cyberspace, how businesses get into and navigate through it, and what material is out there. We also anticipate some of the areas where electronic commerce exposes the law's fragility.

Chapter 3 (Businesses in Transition) examines the process of business change. As the computer becomes as ubiquitous as the telephone — and the Internet becomes a business tool even more important than the telephone — they transform how we inform ourselves, how we buy and sell, and how we transact and interact. We explore how this shift affects relationships between companies and their trading partners, corporate clients, individual consumers, and the law, which purports to provide a safe haven for this business turbulence.

Chapter 4 (Electronic Privacy) explores the increasing anxiety that the information age's intrusiveness creates for citizens, consumers, and companies. We evaluate the technological and legal methods that business may employ to provide assurance and protection; and the legislative and self-governing "rules" that governments and businesses may apply to enhance the rights to be left alone and to know what is known about oneself.

In Chapter 5 (Security) we examine such basic protective questions as what security do individuals and firms need in order to do business on the Internet, what are the risks they face, and what technological and legal safeguards currently exist.

Chapter 6 (The Regulators) looks at government and the referees of communications law. We raise questions about whether and how rule makers and rule enforcers are necessary. We depict their difficulty in keeping up with quickly accelerating and changing patterns of traffic on the information highway. More formal and traditional regulations are contrasted with more flexible and rapidly developing alternate regulations and alternatives to regulation. And we pose the question of whether "top down" or "bottom up" approaches are best suited for information highway regulation.

Chapter 7 (Intellectual Property) explores a difficult and emerging area of law. This law deals with the protection, use, and expression of ideas and innovations. Normally viewed as a form of property law, it's captured under such titles as copyright, patents, and trademarks. We deal primarily with copyright, which governs the expression of ideas, because it's the most difficult and prominent intellectual property law for cyberspace — and is under the greatest strain. In examining its classic balancing function — to encourage creativity by private property protection and ensure dissemination of knowledge and entertainment for maximum public gain — we see digital communication as presenting a unique challenge. We also examine the conflict between trademark law and domain names, a topic that is of great concern to businesses operating in cyberspace.

Chapter 8 (Contracts) deals with a seductively simple issue: a promise made between two parties to do something for value, creating legal obligation. What kinds of contracts exist in cyberspace? How do we enforce them? Are the old legal forms up to the new obligations created by electronic commerce?

Chapter 9 (Tort Liability) discusses what happens in law when something goes wrong, and injury occurs to someone who isn't a party to a transaction, or the event isn't dealt with in a contract. For electronic commerce the traditional tests of negligence, nuisance, damages, and foreseeability operate with less reliability in establishing right and wrong, and rights and responsibilities.

Chapter 10 (Conflict of Laws) looks at what is sometimes called private international law. Here we explore such classic questions as which court and which jurisdiction's laws should apply when the laws of two or more jurisdictions conflict in electronic commerce, and how to enforce any resulting judgment. The increase in speed and the collapse of space in digital communication guarantees that these problems will occur with greater frequency and complexity. What are the best approaches to reducing these chaotic trajectories?

In Chapter 11 (Where Do We Go from Here?) we briefly explore the future of digital law and electronic commerce. Can we keep up with the fast-changing technology? What happens if we can't? "The future is now" or almost now; we look scarcely further ahead than three years to the next century. (And by that time it will be appropriate for us to look back on the journey taken in this book, humbly confess how wrong we've been, and try harder on the next leg with another business and law road map.)

The glossary at the end of the book lists definitions of frequently used cyberspace and electronic commerce terms. These, too, will surely change.

Despite its segmented chapter treatment, we've attempted to create a simple two-part evolution in the book. The first part focuses primarily on how businesses are dealing with a digital economy, and the second part illustrates how well or poorly the law is managing. That said, these two themes interweave throughout. While our attention is primarily on business interests, we introduce a variety of other perspectives on various issues of public concern, including those of the employer, employee, consumer, government, and private citizen.

Finally, we take a comparative approach to the law. The initial orientation is Canada — the law we know best. But we frequently treat U.S. law, where the issues under discussion are most dramatically and frequently illustrated; and we make some forays into European Union law. Our intent isn't to describe the business and law of any one jurisdiction. Rather, in tune with the global reach of the information age, we preview the digital transformation of twenty-first century business and technology as one that affects the law of each nation and all peoples.

We are all products of and live in the Faculty of Law at McGill University. Here Canada's two legal systems — civil and common law, the two great legal traditions of Western civilization — are studied, taught, and reformed under one roof. We bring unusually varied perspectives to the task, as influenced by different generations, ethnic origins, education, experience, and philosophies.

For David this book is a return to first interests. His first book as a young law professor in 1968 was *Computers and Law*, an effort to taste the new wine of technology in the old bottles of law. He followed that in the early 1970s with several empirically based studies on electronic commerce and the law. These explored legal change to accommodate first the replacement of paper cheques as evidence of money by electronic signal (laws for the chequeless society), and second the immobilization of the paper stock certificate and the electronic registration to transfer and signify title to stocks and bonds (laws to immobilize securities). Alas he retreated into university administration for several decades. He has only recently emerged, like Rip Van Winkle, to see the landscape dramatically changed. But the questions exhibit an uncanny tenacity. His experience is a blend of public administration, business, and science and technology policy and law. He was Dean of Law at the University of Western Ontario for five years and Principal of McGill University for the next fifteen until 1994. He has chaired the Government of Canada's Information Highway Advisory Council since its inception in 1994; chairs the Canadian Institute for Advanced Research and the Neuroscience Centre of Excellence; and is president of the Board of Overseers of Harvard University, his first alma mater. He serves on a number of corporate boards, including three (Seagrams, Canada Trust, and CGI) with significant information highway interests. He is a professor of law in McGill Law Faculty's Centre for Medicine, Ethics and Law. He was recently awarded the Canadian Advanced Technology Association I-Way award for public leadership.

Sunny is a lawyer (Ontario) and law teacher specializing in high technology law, and is legal counsel to the Montreal law firm of Martineau Walker. He is completing his doctorate of laws at McGill, where he presently teaches courses in *Computers and the Law* and *Copyright Law*. He holds a Master of Laws degree (McGill), a Bachelor of Laws (University of Toronto), and a Bachelor of Commerce (McGill). He has written extensively on intellectual property and copyright law as well as on issues of privacy and security in the information age. In addition to the law, he's kept his hand in the business of cyberspace as co-owner of a Montreal-based Internet service provider, ZooNet Inc. Sunny is a frequent speaker on issues of high technology law to law audiences, industry associations concerned with these issues, and the media. Although he began his legal career concentrating on the area of software protection (copyright and intellectual property law), Sunny quickly realized that a convergence of once disparate legal fields was occurring. Accordingly, he adapted his pursuits to include telecommunications law and regulation, free speech issues, licensing, and privacy matters. Although he began this journey as one skilled in computer technology (he started programming on key punch cards at the age of thirteen), he's the first to admit that more often than not the problems raised by technology are ones that are fundamental to humankind. Their solutions may be just as easily found in the writings and thought of the eighteenth and nineteenth centuries or earlier as in those of the twentieth century.

For Sunny and David this is a second opportunity to collaborate on a book explaining the information highway to the general public. In *Getting Canada OnLine: Understanding the Information Highway* (Stoddart 1995) we crafted a road map for the information age. We sketched out how modern communication networks have reduced time and space, dramatically expanded access to and manipulation of information, and raised challenging legal and policy questions for societies around the shrinking globe. In this book we continue this exploration with a road map that highlights business in the digital age and the strain and stress created for and by the rule of law.

Charles completed his undergraduate studies in philosophy at Trinity College, University of Toronto, and went on to do a "Maitrise" in philosophy at the Université de Paris IV-Sorbonne before beginning legal studies at McGill. He graduated from the "National programme" in June, 1997. The programme combines study of both the civil and common law. At McGill he served on the editorial board of the *McGill Law Journal* for two years. He will article with McCarthy Tétrault in Montreal in 1998. His first connection to this project began from his discussions as a student in Sunny and David's seminar on *Copyright and Information Technology*.

We celebrate the remarkable efforts of Ann Brodie, who manages the office from which the book springs, and her thoughtfulness, tenacity, and tact; and Elaine Quinlan and Patrick Shea, who have deciphered and rendered clear many mysterious manuscripts with persistence and patience. We thank Deborah Johnston, our co-author in our earlier book, who helped astutely with early drafts of this book and whose duties with the Department of Justice kept her from co-authoring this one; Lindsay Morgan and Peter Martin, who commented on early portions of the manuscript; Danielle Miller, who lent her time and expertise to the editing of the manuscript at various stages; and Blaine Baker, who generously reviewed the complete manuscript shortly before publication.

We salute our partners at Stoddart Publishing — Don Bastian, Kevin Linder, Stephen Quick, Greg Ioannou, and Karen Alliston — for their wise counsel from beginning to end of this project. We acknowledge the contribution of Marc Branchaud, who along with Sunny co-wrote an earlier article that has formed the kernel of the Security chapter. Both Marc and Sean Sofin of ZooNet Inc. have faithfully served as sources of information and advice regarding matters of technology. We thank them for their patience and input.

We finally thank the McGill Faculty of Law, our colleagues and students who give us a wonderful stimulating and collegial environment in which to think and work.

CYBERLAW

1 THE DIGITAL REVOLUTION

TRACKING THE WHIRLWINDS OF CHANGE

Suppose I'm one of those people who can never find a pair of jeans that actually fits. I hear of a service offered over the Internet. It's a dream come true. Using my home computer, I log on to my local server, then connect to a brand-name jeans company based in California. It promises a custom fit. The manufacturer's Internet "home page" carefully explains how to take my measurements, fill out the online purchase request form, and send it off at the click of a button. Simply using my computer's mouse, I can choose among an assortment of styles and then customize according to my body shape. The click sends the purchase request over the Internet to the jeans company, its custom-fit clothing manufacturer, and a courier company, which three days later delivers the jeans to my door.

Perfect. A win-win-win situation. I'm a satisfied customer. The jeans company and its partner in manufacturing establish a broader customer base, involving premium products (with premium prices). There's no inventory, no paperwork, no costly interaction with a retailer or wholesaler, no discount pricing for unpurchased jeans. Moreover, the courier company expands its catalogue clothing delivery business substantially.

But what if something goes wrong? What if a friend fills out the Internet purchase request form in my name as a prank, doubling my actual measurements? What if the customized jeans, intended as a gift for my friend leaving for France, arrive two days late and hence are useless to me? What if there's a glitch in the ordering software, or in the hardware of the robot that actually cuts the fabric at the manufacturing plant?

Despite the fact that "nothing was signed," was there a contract? If so, who are parties to the contract? The jeans company? The courier company? The manufacturer? All of them? How can I remedy the situation?

Welcome to the digital age. We're in the midst of a revolution: the information revolution. This book considers the transformative effects of new information technology on business practices and their legal consequences. What new forms of business processes has the digital age made possible? How does electronic commerce enhance efficiency, creativity, productivity, and customer satisfaction? How might it alter relations among employees, business partners, competitors, and customers? What are the legal implications of these changes? Is there any regulation? Should there be? What can business expect from government regulation? What legal pitfalls should business leaders anticipate when considering the implementation of new information technology? Is the law evolving? Is it becoming a relic? Will the digital age revolutionize the law, just as it's revolutionizing such institutions as health care, education, and commerce?

Consider this scenario: an American airplane manufacturer, struggling to compete with a European consortium, decides to overhaul its entire design and manufacturing process. It incorporates the latest in new information technology. It creates the first "paperless" airplane using digital design. No paper drafts. No mock-up models. No test flights. Every aspect of the design and manufacturing process is computerized. The aerodynamics of the wing shape, the ergonomics of the cabin chairs, the responsiveness of the airplane under a barrage of weather conditions — these are all tested using a computer with 3D design and flight simulation software. Even more revolutionary, the potential customers for the new plane, as well as the mechanics who will service it, participate in the design process. The shape and location of the instrument panels in the cockpit, the size and weight of the airplane, the design of the landing gear, the accessibility of parts that require frequent replacement: every aspect of the design is both collaborative and paperless. This collaboration also occurs at other levels. Two different software companies provide the essential custom software. Japanese subcontractors construct the fuselage; Europeans, the landing gear. So many different companies are involved in the manufacture of the airplane's various parts that it's dubbed a "collection of parts that fly in close formation."

The new technology has many advantages. This airplane revolutionizes the aeronautic design and manufacturing process. It catalyzes a seminal shift in the enterprise's business process structure. Time to production and production time are reduced; so are costs. Customer satisfaction climbs because of their early involvement. Former rigid hierarchies and compartmentalization practices within the company collapse. New forms of cooperation crystallize between contracting parties.

If ever the plane should crash as a result of a design flaw, however, who would be held liable? The airline that owns the plane and that participated in the design? One or all of the manufacturers of the parts? The software companies? Moreover, which law would determine the answer to these questions? American? Japanese? The country over which the plane was flying at the time of the accident? And if a court judgment is obtained, where and how is it to be enforced? Less calamitous but still costly, if certain parts don't fit or arrive late who's liable and for how much? To whom do insurers look for risk minimization?

Permit one final example, this time from the realm of intellectual property — the epicentre of legal and commercial transformation in the digital earthquake.

A long-established and well-respected encyclopedia publisher is rapidly losing market share to a computer software company! The newcomer has launched a flashy, multimedia encyclopedia. The text entries are accompanied not only by photographs, but also by video clips and audio files that can be played over a home computer. The publisher decides that its only chance for long-term survival is to launch a new product of its own; one that will leap-frog its upstart rival. It produces not only a multimedia CD-ROM version of its encyclopedia, but also an Internet-accessible version, available on a pay-per-use basis. The advantages are numerous. In its thirty-volume print version, the encyclopedia could be revised and updated only once a decade (or yearly, as a CD-ROM). Now it's updated daily. Moreover, rather than a fixed or static multimedia instrument, constrained by the amount of information that fits on a laser disk, the encyclopedia can now be any size. Using the Internet linking language known as HTML, it can be linked via the Web to files held in databases all around the world. When a user looks up an entry on the fine art of making Scotch whisky she may find not only a textual description, but with the click of a button she may also take a "virtual" tour of the Glenlivet mill. In the sampling room she can almost smell the oak casks. Suddenly a collection of dusty books has become a "user interface" to the world's collective knowledge.

But how has the meaning of "copyright," and the ability to enforce its laws, changed in this virtual world? The text, video, and audio files, and even the HTML markup language once obtained, may be "cut and pasted" by any computer and sent halfway around the world, virtually for free, in virtually no time, virtually undetectably, and in virtually infinite numbers of perfect copies. The text of the encyclopedia as well as the video and audio files may be original works. But can the publisher claim a copyright in the choice of links it made to other Web sites? Does it make sense to call the maker of such a "virtual" encyclopedia a "publisher"? Are the copies of the encyclopedia "pages" sent over the Internet as bits of ephemeral electricity really "copies" for the purposes of copyright law?

Science fiction? No. This is happening now. Although the legal issues in the three scenarios above are hypothetical, the examples themselves are case studies from Don Tapscott's *The Digital Economy*.[1] The companies in question are Levi's, Boeing, and Encyclopaedia Britannica. And these examples are only the beginning.

The Big Picture

Look at the scale and significance of the changes currently taking place in society. The computer is often compared to the printing press in the magnitude of its social impact. The information revolution is compared to both the agricultural and industrial revolutions. These analogies might seem like hyperbole, but both are legitimate.

The printing press wasn't merely a time-saving tool that eliminated the need for laborious manuscript copying. It helped to alter in a fundamental way long-standing sociopolitical structures. The press spread literacy throughout Europe: for the first time the Bible was translated from Latin into the vernacular to be widely read and distributed. The press also fuelled the Protestant Reformation. Priests and cardinals were supplanted as intermediaries between man and God; nation states and city states shed the uneasy but pervasive authority of Rome. Individuals began to use the printing press to interpret and discuss their own condition. The rule of law began to be developed and interpreted on a more rational and function-related basis, increasingly free of the canons of the Church.

So too, the computer today has handed powerful tools of information technology to a broad cross-section of society (though access is still an issue). The computer's effects aren't merely, or even principally, related to its timesaving features. Rather, the computer alters the way people interact. It provides a catalyst to democratic reform, changes in business processes, and the free exchange of goods and ideas across national borders. But this revolution has only just begun.

Like the agricultural and industrial revolutions, the information revolution is producing deep and wide changes in our economic, social,

---

The computer alters the way people interact. It provides a catalyst to democratic reform, changes in business processes, and the free exchange of goods and ideas across national borders. But this revolution has only just begun.

---

and cultural institutions. Certain traditional sectors of the economy have withered; other sectors, all but unimaginable only twenty years before, have produced wealth beyond the telling. An astonishing degree of creative energy has been unleashed, both constructive and destructive. We marvel at all that is novel; we lament what is lost.

The current revolution contrasts remarkably with its predecessors. First, the agricultural and industrial revolutions evolved over years, decades, and even centuries. The information revolution is erupting in a matter of weeks, months, and years.

Second, the information revolution doesn't just provide society with new tools of production. It does the previously unimaginable: it conquers time and space. Virtually any amount of information can be sent almost anywhere in the world in the blink of an eye. Whether my working partner is in Manila or Montreal becomes largely irrelevant. We

The Return of the Enlightenment?

John Perry Barlow — songwriter for the Grateful Dead, co-founder of the Electronic Frontier Foundation, and current Internet guru — wrote a seminal article on the anachronistic nature of current copyright laws called "Selling Wine without Bottles." Finding inspiration in the Enlightenment for his vision of the "new frontier," Barlow cites Thomas Jefferson:

> If nature has made any one thing less susceptible than all others of exclusive property, it is the action of the thinking power called an idea, which an individual may exclusively possess as long as he keeps it to himself; but the moment it is divulged, it forces itself into the possession of everyone, and the receiver cannot dispossess himself of it. Its peculiar character, too, is that no one possesses the less, because every other possesses the whole of it. He who receives an idea from me, receives light without darkening me. That ideas should freely spread from one to another over the globe, for the moral and mutual instruction of man, and improvement of his condition, seems to have been peculiarly and benevolently designed by nature, when she made them, like fire, expansible over all space, without lessening their density at any point, and like the aire in which we breathe, move, and have our physical being, incapable of confinement or exclusive appropriation. Inventions then cannot, in nature, be a subject of property.

can use the computer to interact in "real time" as easily as we converse with or pass a document to a colleague in the next office.

Third, in contrast to the Industrial Revolution, where business was an early user and the most immediate beneficiary of the new technology, business is one of the later groups to discover and use the Internet — though the "take-up" rate is dramatic.

Fourth, unlike the commodities that stimulated the economy of earlier ages, information — the principal commodity of our age — isn't diminished when it's shared. Rather it's often refined and enhanced when spread, ideally leading to the general acquisition of knowledge to the benefit of both giver and recipient.

This last characteristic is what transports us back to the Enlightenment values that have infused much of the latter development of the Internet, and provide much of the inspiration for this book. Surfing about the Net, one is struck by its civil libertarian atmosphere: ideas — all ideas, even "dangerous" ideas — are shared, debated, and bantered about for the general education and edification of society. We believe that if we can understand electronic commerce and the law that governs it, we shall better manage it — and ultimately use the remarkable tools of the information age to the mutual advantage of all our societies and the individuals in them.

THE INTERNET'S IMPACT

The Internet may prove to be one of history's most dramatic examples of turning swords into ploughshares. Remember the Internet's origin. In 1969 the U.S. Department of Defense created the computer-linked communication system as a fail-safe system for the U.S. President, the Commander in Chief, to give the signal for war in the event of nuclear attack, and to conduct that war "safely" should traditional means of communication be knocked out. From that intended, and almost certain never-to-be-used situation, it was extended into a secret, highly organized communication system between the Pentagon and university researchers conducting classified research around the country. Gradually these university researchers began to use it for communication of non-classified research, as did their students and their students' families and friends around the world, giving new meaning to that old Latin term *universitas* — "applicable everywhere." Most recently business has discovered the Internet, with consequences still too early to anticipate and describe faithfully.

Thus, in approximately three decades, the Internet has evolved from the most secret, hierarchical, controlled, and seldom used technology to the most open, porous, flat, uncontrolled, ungoverned, ubiquitous, and "heavily trafficked" system imaginable. The fact that it spans the globe puts it largely beyond the control of any one nation state, or in particular the U.S. Pentagon — history's fiercest focus of force — which gave it birth.

Accordingly, despite its brief existence, the Internet has already reinvented itself several times. A military tool, an academic tool, a democratic tool, and now an economic tool.

The Legal Conundrum

Herein lies the conundrum that the digital age poses for a legal — and business — mind. The fundamental challenge of the rule of the law is to prevent war and promote peace. The rule of law is based on the orderly development of principles that govern all members of a society equally and in the same manner. Ideally, changes in the law are incremental, organic, and evolve as much as possible so as to clarify, rather than alter, existing law. Certainty of result is sought, often above justice itself. Given such a conservative predisposition, the law is ill-poised to address revolution. Revolution and the rule of law are at antipodes.

Look at the Internet itself. Many describe it as chaotic, anarchic, amoral: some even decry it as a land of "hackers" and perverts. Is there room for the law in such a land? Is there room for business? For many years, most business leaders implicitly said no.

It's not surprising that the Information Revolution has left many business leaders flat-footed. Lawyers and business leaders are generally uncomfortable with orderless states. They wait for the Mounties or the Cavalry to go out there and "civilize" things before setting up shop.

Anarchy is a fragile state. Human beings, it seems, have an inherent need for order. "Netiquette," the often unwritten rules of acceptable interaction on the Internet, provided the first indication that structure and order could find a place on the Internet. Because most users of the tools of new information technology value security of transaction and privacy in their interactions, such structure and order will probably increase.

Now that they've hung up their signs in the virtual world, business and the law must respect the fact that they're late arrivals. For a period of several years commercial activity of any kind was met with severe censure on the part of Netizens. Similarly, attempts by law enforcement agencies and legislators to control the content of Internet exchanges have experienced enormous resistance and have proved to be virtually pointless. The Internet has instead developed its own rules of interaction. Thus, as players, the business and legal communities must recognize that they've only recently sat at the table and that the welcome has been frosty. This is simply a matter of good common sense. Before launching a new product it's always been essential for business to know the market culture it is engaging. And as many have since discovered, business techniques developed for the "real-world" economy will not always work in cyberspace.

Conclusion

We've introduced the book's subject matter and posed several key questions that it will explore. We began with three concrete examples of how the digital revolution is transforming business and the law. We then considered these changes in a historical context, reviewing how the digital revolution differs from previous economic and social revolutions, and less abstractly, how the Internet's origins are influencing its present and future. Finally, we raised one of our principal themes: the tension between stability and change. Business looks to the law for stability, consistency, and predictability on the one hand, and efficiency, flexibility, and responsiveness on the other. How does the law respond to these conflicting demands? How is business coping with dramatic change? We explore these questions throughout the book.

2 Digital Technology

Get On Board for Cyberspace

William Gibson first coined the term "cyberspace" in his popular science fiction novel *Neuromancer*. In Gibson's novel, cyberspace represents a psychedelic virtual world where hackers and corporations do battle. He paints both a bleak and invigorating picture of technology gone mad; one is reminded of the nineteenth century allegory of Frankenstein. While neither technology nor the people using it have yet attained the sophistication envisioned by Gibson (and probably never will), battles in cyberspace do occur, and at many levels. Hackers and organizations, both corporate and governmental, contest. Tales of teenagers who penetrate sensitive military installations aren't mythical; we've all heard the news stories. Then there's the relentless race to secure and re-secure vulnerable computers — an entire security industry exists to address these problems. And yet another, much larger struggle also dominates the arena: corporations go head to head for consumer dollars in the virtual marketplace.

Cyberspace, or the information highway, for which the Internet is the most prominent technology, refers to networked environments in which digital information travels. Cyberspace communicators (e.g. computers) must be able to connect to this network and communicate in digital form. We're all familiar with the telephone network, cable television networks, and some of us with local area and wide area computer networks. In physical terms cyberspace is these networks interconnected: a network of networks. Human information is converted to digital information, represented by 0's and 1's, that pass seamlessly from one network to the other through various gateways. The human information is reconstructed in as little as a few seconds.

Here we discuss the networks that make up cyberspace, how one gets into and navigates through cyberspace, and what material is out there. For a more detailed review of the supporting science, refer to our book *Getting Canada OnLine: Understanding the Information Highway*.

It's increasingly important for businesses to understand cyberspace. Why? First, tariff and non-tariff barriers continue to fall, with international trade agreements such as the General Agreement on Trade and Tariffs (GATT) and the North American Free Trade Agreement (NAFTA). Trading blocs such as the European Union (EU) allow goods and services to flow freely between member states. Cyberspace is a key setting for this global marketplace, where deals can be made, products bought, and money transferred.

Second, cheap access to up-to-the-minute information has miniaturized the business world. Comparative advantages of companies in any one geographic area have magnified as sales barriers shrink. The Internet is the ultimate in comparison shopping! A vendor seeking a product for resale may exploit cyberspace for the best price, since he or she isn't limited to local or regional distributors. Where the foreign cost plus associated transaction costs (such as shipping and costs of returns) are lower than the domestic distributor's price, the vendor will purchase from abroad.

Third, economies of scale in manufacturing and distribution to meet and beat competition increasingly require wider and deeper markets. This is especially true in less populated countries like Canada. Access to a global marketplace filled with potential customers allows new industries to emerge. Consider beach wear. While Canadians may purchase these products, access to tropical countries where such goods are in demand twelve months of the year allows Canadian firms to produce higher volumes domestically, driving down the cost per unit. Cyberspace is both a tool and a target to achieve these economies.

Where the product is informational, e.g. computer software or financial information, the effect is further magnified. Costs of transportation, often a deterrent to importing foreign goods, have largely evaporated. Large multinational software companies (and now even smaller firms) facing high employment costs in industrialized nations can relocate the development parts of their operations to countries such as India, with its high skills and cheap labour. Cyberspace reduces the costs of dealing with distant suppliers.

Communication Networks

Several technologies form the information highway. It mixes older technologies, such as the telephone and cable networks for which there is considerable infrastructure investment, with newer technologies such as

What Makes the Information Highway Possible?

The digitization of information, regardless of its type (text, audio, or video), is driving information highway development. We're converting networks into digital carriageways. Once information is converted into digital form (by a computer or other device) and broken down into packets (like putting different pages of a book into envelopes and mailing them), it doesn't matter which roadway it takes, since it's all 0's and 1's. Upon reception, the receiving device reconstitutes the digital information into its intended form.

The use of a new enhanced digital packet-based technology — asynchronous transfer mode (ATM) — creates uniform digital data packets for travel through digital networks. It also minimizes overhead, e.g. information regarding the destination and reconstruction of the message. Newbridge Networks of Ottawa is an ATM pioneer. It has marketed and sold its ATM products primarily to telecommunications companies (e.g. telephone companies), which are now able to achieve greater efficiencies by putting more information on their networks.

Remember: *if it's digital, it can travel on the information highway.*

the computer. While the technologies remain in flux, some trends are emerging. For example, the interconnection of communications networks, both new and old, as carriageways for digital information will likely remain the cyberspace backbone for some time.

The Telephone

The telephone system is far and away the most ubiquitous of all communications networks. It's also the most popular on-ramp to cyberspace. But although the telephone network may be used as the roadway, it's the personal computer that serves as cyberspace's interfacing device. A personal computer, a modem, and a telephone jack are all the hardware one needs. Modems convert digital data into analog signals that can travel over the phone line, and reconvert the analog data into digital form for use by the receiving computer.

At the other end of the phone line one needs a connection or port of entry into cyberspace. Internet service providers (ISPs) provide this service, usually for a monthly fee. Universities and some organizations, such as the Freenet movement, may provide this service for free to

CONNECTING TO CYBERSPACE VIA THE TELEPHONE NETWORK

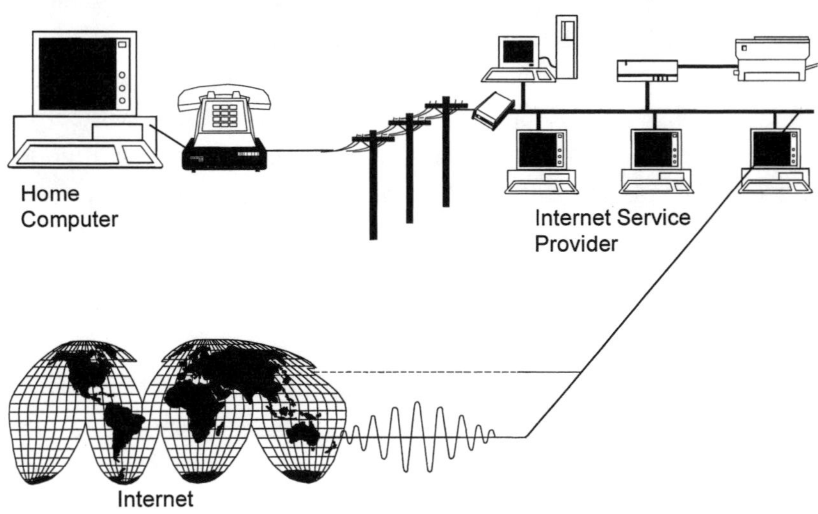

members. These organizations may receive government funding, corporate sponsorships, or raise their own funds. The traditional wired telephone network isn't the only way to get onto the information highway. With a cellular telephone account and the proper modem one can just as easily log on to an ISP. A wireless connection increases mobility, even though its cost is currently higher.

Is the fax machine, so heavily relied upon by business, a cyberspace communicator? Not exactly. Fax machines do communicate digitally using the telephone system, but the Internet can't use the language that fax machines speak without some computer assistance. Local computers may be set up to receive faxes. The fax information may then be sent over the Internet to a computer located in the local calling area of the fax's intended recipient. The recipient computer calls the recipient fax machine, which transmits the document. While this system saves on long distance telephone costs, fax information can't interact in cyberspace to any greater degree.

Cable Television

Three out of four Canadian homes subscribe to cable television, and many more homes and businesses are cable-ready or can be wired up with little cost or effort. Since cable connection provides yet another potential entry point for cyberspace, cable providers are gradually enhancing their services to compete with traditional telephone ISPs. Because of its broad *bandwidth*, more information can be pushed through cable over a given time period than through the twisted-pair copper telephone wire. High-quality interactive audio and full-motion video require substantial bandwidth. Because they're in increasing demand, cable's current advantage is commercially opportune.

Cable is traditionally one-way; it sends out a signal without receiving one back. But cable can be modified, at considerable cost, to accommodate two-way communication. This transformation is already taking place in many major urban centres. Cable companies are beginning to offer high-speed Internet access to their customers at rates comparable to telephone Internet access. Nevertheless, full Internet cable deployment will take several years to achieve.

Telephones are *narrowband*, but have two-way switched communications already in place. The telephone shouldn't be dismissed simply because it can't currently provide broadband services. Why?

Newer Technologies

First, much of the phone system — referred to as trunk lines — transmits at rates comparable to cable; the bottleneck occurs at the last length of telephone wire into the home or business. This can be upgraded to higher bandwidth wiring, such as the integrated services digital network (ISDN). ISDN wiring transmits digital data at speeds capable of handling audio and video signals with remarkable clarity or resolution up to 128 kilobits/second. This compares with speeds of 33.6 kilobits currently achieved by computer modems. But modem speeds are in fact deceptive, because they require time to convert the information from digital into analog form and back again.

ISDN has been available for several years. Customers have largely been businesses, which can afford ISDN's current high costs ($800/month with a hook-up through an ISP). Telephone companies are gradually introducing it at more affordable prices ($150/month) to residential customers with comparatively lower usage. Prices continue to contract as ISDN expands.

Second, compression technologies — which allow more information to travel over existing wiring — are developing at accelerating rates. Predictions of future developments are precarious, but it's likely that we'll soon be able to transmit some level of usable real-time video over existing twisted-pair copper wire. Already there are video conferencing technologies that employ one or more ISDN connections. While the motion remains slightly jerky, the technology is highly usable. Often these systems allow the use of more ISDN connections to achieve greater clarity (three connections will normally provide an excellent full screen video conference).

Finally, the telephone's strength lies in its ubiquity. Regardless of capacity, its connections allow information of different types — sound, video, or text — to travel to the remotest of regions, whether the route be footpath or super expressway. This use of lower bandwidth connections on networks that can handle higher connections perfectly illustrates the information highway paradigm. Cyberspace is about communication. It's not about a specific type of communication, and it's not limited to a specific group of people communicating with each other. It's about providing a virtual space available to and accessible by all.

The Internet

This brings us to the Internet, which is currently cyberspace's prototype and still evolving.[1] Definitions of cyberspace typically draw from the Internet experience. The Internet is a global computer network of networks. Smaller computer networks, single computers (whether personal, mini, or mainframe), telephone systems, cable television systems, and cellular telephones all form part of the Internet. At its lowest level, the

---

People meet; ideas are exchanged; companies compete for consumer and corporate dollars. The Internet is increasingly becoming a public marketplace.

Internet is nothing but a set of standards. It allows devices, typically computers in the conventional sense, to communicate with one another. It speaks a common language. At its highest level, it's a public virtual space. People meet; ideas are exchanged; companies compete for consumer and corporate dollars. The Internet is increasingly becoming a public marketplace.

How did the Internet evolve? To expand on the preceding chapter's description, the Internet grew out of ARPANET, run by the U.S. Defense Department's Advanced Research Projects Agency (ARPA; the NET stands for network). In 1969 the U.S. military created a decentralized secure command system. Computer networks, holding more and more vital information and responsible for coordinating military tasks, had previously operated in a centralized fashion like the hub and spokes of a wheel. If the central computer, or hub, was attacked and destroyed or disabled, military operations relying on that network would be hopelessly crippled. ARPANET employed a decentralized, spiderweb structure of interconnected computers whereby the destruction of one or several nodes would no longer sever the remaining nodes' ability to communicate with one another.

Over time, academic researchers working on military projects became interested in using the ARPANET facilities for their own research. As academic use grew, the ARPANET was placed under the jurisdiction of the National Science Foundation (NSF). Its mandate was to extend network usage widely to educational institutions conducting research projects.

Contemporaneously with ARPANET's rise (later DARPA Internet and eventually just Internet) was the rapid proliferation of personal computing and local area networking. In the 1980s academic institutions developed increasing appetites for inter-institutional communication. The elegance and strength of the ARPANET standard encouraged its adoption by newer network facilities. Eventually the number of relatively isolated computing facilities reached a critical mass. Since each had implemented the same communications standards, communicating with one another as a virtual network was merely a connection away.

During the late 1970s the NSF had set up several geographically disparate super-computer research facilities. Since dedicated connections between them were extremely costly, a new system was developed whereby each facility connected with other academic and research centres within its geographical region. These institutions in turn connected with others in close proximity. The ARPANET standard, designed for decentralized communication, was perfectly suited for the task. Once these institutions were interconnected each had a virtual link with the National Science Foundation. Each academic centre was also linked to the others, and each acted as a node by forwarding communications traffic toward its ultimate destination. Over the past fifteen years this network has evolved enormously in capacity, users, and content.

Equipment upgrades allowed higher bandwidth transmission, which accommodated increases in network traffic. So did software changes to the programs controlling the traffic. Furthermore, great strides in computer processing and memory technology gave Internet users real-time multimedia content.

Internet user upsurge has been remarkable. No longer are users solely scientists or academics; they come from all walks of life. They use the Internet for everything from entertainment to information, from chatting to conducting business. One can read the *New York Times*, research Egyptian bread-making, chat with a friend, or order a T-shirt. And Internet use continues to grow exponentially and globally. Estimates of Internet users can only be approximated: 5 million in Canada and 16 million in the U.S. So too for estimates of computers linked to the Internet

Estimates of Internet users can only be approximated: 5 million in Canada and 16 million in the U.S.

(30 million in July 1996), given the proliferation of personal computers and local area networks.

Business has recently discovered the cyberspace consumer — but it's also learning that "good citizenship" may be even more important in the virtual than in the real world. For example, Web sites providing content, such as technical support for products, are visited more frequently than those that merely advertise a product. The consumer is demanding that business add value to cyberspace and not simply use it to advertise. (In fact, such a solution still allows business to increase profits by reducing many of its costs, for example by reducing its technical support staff.) Netizens will visit only those business sites that provide information they wish to receive. Placing advertising even on frequented sites is tricky. Pictures and animation slow down the loading time for browsers, which may be enough to dissuade them from visiting again despite whatever content the sites contain. Netizens pass judgment quickly, and bad experiences are easily shared with other users through modes such as USENET news.

Travelling through Cyberspace

Forms of Internet communication are best thought of as modes. Typically, specific software tools are required for each, although the user

The following section contains detailed descriptions of the technologies and workings of cyberspace. Some prior use of the Internet, though not essential, will prove helpful in understanding this material.

may employ a single comprehensive computer program and may be unaware of the nature of each mode used. Today's most popular modes include electronic mail (e-mail), World Wide Web (WWW or Web), USENET news, Internet relay chat (IRC), file transfer protocol (FTP), and telnet. These modes permit a variety of communication. One can use e-mail to chat with a friend in Switzerland, post the company newsletter on a Web home page, get quick answers to almost any question via USENET news, play a game of poker using IRC, transfer the latest satellite weather photos using FTP, and connect to a computer halfway around the world using telnet. Many other, less popular services are available. Here we explain the technology and provide some tips on how one may begin using it. We discuss why businesses might want to establish a presence in cyberspace, and how they can do so.

E-Mail

Electronic mail, or e-mail, is the most popular cyberspace communication form, enabling the user to send textual messages to a specific recipient. Messages can be transmitted instantly, regardless of physical distance between sender and receiver. E-mail is analogous to the postal service: computer programs that talk to one another replace human collectors, sorters, and carriers. And as with the post, e-mail poses security problems. Where messages are not encrypted, i.e. coded, messages may be (though rarely are) intercepted and read. Thus, e-mail is often likened to sending a postcard. One may receive the communication without ever knowing whether its contents have been read along the way.

E-mail is delivered using an address scheme specific to computer networks. An address contains several components: first the user, then the @ sign, then the mail server to which the mail is being sent, e.g. sunny@zoo.net.

Mail is sent to the user "sunny" at the computer address "zoo.net." This computer is also known as a mail server. Once the zoo.net computer receives the e-mail message, it's held until user "sunny" picks it up.

The computer address, here "zoo.net," is a *domain name*. A domain name is an address that refers to a particular service or cluster of services, e.g. WWW, USENET, or e-mail, that are run on a computer or network of computers. These services may each have their own name within the domain, e.g. the Web server may be called www.zoo.net, whereas the USENET server may be called news.zoo.net.

Domain names are registered with a central authority that manages the Internet domain name system. There are several "managers" of domain names, each of which is responsible for a given set of suffixes, in our example ".net." The Internic (INTERnet Network Information Center) organization, an American non-profit group, is responsible for the .net, .com, and .org names and others. These are known as top-level domains; they constitute the right-most portion of an address. Domain name managers such as the Internic also issue associated underlying numerical Internet Protocol (IP) addresses. Each domain name identifies a unique IP address. These numerical addresses, often hidden to users, are what cyberspace computers use to identify one another. The name system was developed because of the difficulties human beings have in remembering number combinations.

The top-level domain name may or may not represent geographic location. It does for certain suffixes, such as .ca (Canada), .fr (France), and .ch (China). But for others geography is irrelevant. The zoo.net in our first example points to a computer located in Canada. In this case .net is a suffix used to denote Internet service providers (ISP). Similarly, the domain name zoonet.ca also points to a computer in Canada that may or may not be an ISP. The most popular suffix by far is .com, which identifies commercial enterprises. Names are generally flexible. Given basic parameters, the user has some range in determining what name suits his organization best. For example, an ISP in Canada may choose a name with a .net, .ca, or .com suffix. This decision may depend on whether a name is taken in one domain, e.g. zoonet.com. One may also choose to register it in another, e.g. zoonet.ca.

The name before the suffix can be anything, as long as it's approved by the managing organization. Different organizations have different rules. In the U.S., Network Solutions Inc. administers the second level domain names ending with .net, .com, .org, .edu, and others. In Canada, the CA Domain Registrar administers domain names using the .ca suffix (representing computers located in Canada). Network Solutions Inc. has typically been more permissive in what it allows as a name. This is changing as more names are accepted and as disputes between registrants erupt.[2] By contrast, in Canada the CA Domain Registrar requires that organizations adopt names reflecting their geography. An organization with only one office in Montreal will choose a name that ends in "montreal.qc.ca." An organization with offices in more than one city but within the same province can omit the city but not the provincial portion. An organization with offices in more than one province can omit both the city and province parts of the address.

Once a name is registered it can only be used to identify the registrant's computer services. As mentioned above, a domain name may refer to more than one computer, depending on the services being offered, e.g. WWW or e-mail; it's fully within the control of the registrant. Once spoken for, the name can't be chosen by another. This is a function of the technology, not the law. The name appearing to the right of the @ and to the left of the suffix may have several segments, often identifying an organization's sub-departments, or particular Internet services such as the WWW. For example, handa_s@falaw.lan.mcgill.ca is the e-mail address for user "handa_s" at the Faculty of Law's local area network at McGill University in Canada. Internet addresses may not, however, always be as logical. It depends on the registrant.

NEW ADDRESSES IN CYBERSPACE

As a result of the surge in demand for cyberspace addresses the domain name system will be expanded later in 1997. New top-level domain names will be added that largely target business use in cyberspace. The new names include: .firm (for businesses), .store (for retailers selling in cyberspace), .arts (for cultural activities including entertainment), .rec (for recreational services), .nom (for individuals), .web (for Web-related material, such as how-to manuals), and .info (for informational services). For example, a business named ABC Inc. may choose the domain name abc.firm. A retailer may choose abc.store.

Enterprises seeking to establish a presence in cyberspace may either use an ISP with an established name or register a domain name. ISPs are private firms that for a fee operate computers connecting their customers to the Internet. Since many ISPs allow their clients to register names that identify the ISP's computers, a firm doesn't require a complete mail server (a task best left to network specialists) in order to have a personal address. As more organizations establish their presence in cyberspace, the list of available names will diminish.

For businesses deciding whether to register their own domain name (most ISPs will do this for a nominal fee) the choice is clear. Registering a domain name costs very little — usually less than $100 combined with a small yearly fee, depending on which top — level domain the registration is being placed under. Network Solutions Inc. charges $50 U.S. per year for a .com registration; .ca domain registrations in Canada are free. For businesses using an ISP for their Internet access, registration of a name can be done by the ISP for a fee or directly by the business. It involves filling in a few forms.

Creating a cyberspace presence without one's own domain name, however, can be more costly in the long run. Without a registered domain name, switching ISPs also means switching the address, which can result in customer frustration. With a registered address one can switch ISPs without any difficulty, since the Internet will redirect information accordingly. This also allows one to shop around for the most cost-effective ISP, and to continue to do so. Further, businesses want to be easily found. Using an address with one's name makes a great deal more sense than using a combination of one's ISP address with one's name. Users expect business Web sites to use the www.businessname.com addressing scheme.

The World Wide Web

The World Wide Web ("WWW" or simply "the Web") is the Internet's most rapidly growing mode. Text, pictures (graphics), video sequences, sounds, and animation can all be conveyed. The Web grew out of two older technologies: Gopher and wide area information service (WAIS). These were ways of organizing text and files for the user's easy search.

The Web subsumed these technologies and added a vital feature: multimedia hyperlinks. This system links information and allows users to click onto active or "hot" portions of text (or graphics). Once a hyperlink is selected (clicked), the user has more information on the subject matter contained in the link, and in any of the aforementioned forms. For example, a magazine's Web site might consist of a table of contents. To read the feature article, the user would click on the title of the article or its corresponding icon, automatically linking the user to the feature file. Although a Web site is typically a one-sided communication (unlike e-mail), this is changing. Interactive Web sites are coming online with increasing frequency.

To place information on the Web (known as building a Web site or home page) one needs two items: a Web server (computer), and content. Because cyberspace is a world without physical boundaries, it's irrelevant whether an organization manages its own server computer or uses a third-party web server, e.g. an ISP, to hold its content.

Content is easily prepared using the simplest of personal computers. Text files must be translated into the computer language known as hypertext markup language, or HTML. Some programs, including Microsoft Word and Corel's WordPerfect, can translate existing documents to HTML automatically. In its simplest form, the language articulates textual information preceded and/or followed by markup tags. Guides on how the language works are abundant. For those already using the Internet, many are freely available online.

Web addresses are similar to e-mail addresses, with one exception. A Web address is simply the computer's address where the Web information is located. There is no user identifier. Another name for a Web address is universal resource locator, or URL.

Furthermore, in many cases "www." is added as the left-most term of the address. For example, www.zoo.net is the address for the zoo.net Web page. It's not always sufficient, however, to key the address into a Web browser — the program used to navigate through the Web. With many older browsers, one must precede the entire address with http://. The "http" stands for hypertext transport protocol. It prepares the Web browser for Web information. Other prefixes exist for different services, since Web browsers are capable of accessing a variety of information modes or services. For example, http://www.mcgill.ca must be keyed into the browser to access McGill University's Web site. But gopher://gopher.mcgill.ca is used to access McGill University's Gopher site. Gopher is an information service that's similar to the Web but more rudimentary in its features. Nevertheless some institutions continue to use Gopher to distribute information. Software browsers that work on the Web also work on Gopher. Note the use of "www" and "gopher" as part of the address name in each case. This isn't a function of the technology, but rather has developed as an ad hoc standard for naming addresses.

USENET News

USENET news, or simply news, is a distributed global message base currently featuring over 20 000 various subjects, or *newsgroups*, for discussion. This number should grow dramatically over the next few years. Users connect to a local USENET news server. They can read messages that have been sorted both by newsgroup and within the newsgroup into *threads*. A thread is analogous to a conversation, but with two differences: anyone can respond to it, and it doesn't take place in real time. Messages may be posted on the news server. They're then spread by the server throughout the USENET system to all points on the globe. After some delay, a message could be available on all USENET servers. Some servers may choose not to carry certain topics. For example, a newsgroup that has bilingual messages of items for sale in the Montreal area, entitled mtl.vendre-forsale, isn't generally carried by servers outside the Montreal region. A newsgroup such as misc.legal, which discusses miscellaneous legal topics, may however appeal to a wider audience and be carried by many servers around the world. Generally, USENET services are carried by one's ISP. There are, however, also some free USENET sites available on the Internet.

Other Services

There are many other Internet services. Some have gained wide popularity, such as Internet relay chat (IRC) and Gopher (described above).

Others are less known. Some are proprietary to one company's technology, meaning that its technologies are incompatible with those developed by other companies. This may be a result of choice (other firms might not want to employ the technology), or legal protections, e.g. a patent that prevents others from using the technology. Often, however, proprietary technologies simply indicate the development of new products in an area where standards have yet to emerge. Each company tries to get its technology adopted as the standard in order to become the initial dominant player in the market. This is pure competition. Trying to keep a technology proprietary over a long term, e.g. through legal means, may cause the technology to fail by creating an artificial barrier (e.g. steep royalties) to its use. The home use SONY Betamax video recorder, now largely extinct, is an example. The Apple Macintosh computer is running into similar problems.

Software allowing use of the Internet as an audio telephone is a good example of proprietary technology. Although standards are gradually emerging, there are many products that employ their own protocol or language. In other words, these products may only function when connecting to a product made by the same company. The Internet's most popular products don't employ proprietary technologies; rather they use existing standards or develop technologies that are freely available for use by their competitors.

Examples of other popular, non-proprietary, Internet services are file transfer protocol (FTP), Internet relay chat (IRC), and Internet talk. Many of these services can be found as parts of a single user interface, such as Netscape's Navigator, which started primarily as a Web browser. FTP, e-mail, and USENET news are currently built into the Netscape product, which has since become a general navigation tool handling many of the standard services.

FTP is a standard by which users can transfer computer files to one another. Businesses with networks can make files available to the world at large, e.g. technical specifications or advertising brochures for products. Or they may restrict FTP use to employees who transfer files between home and the office, allowing staff to work at home. Today's Web browsers generally have FTP capability built in.

IRC, or "chat," is a textual form of real-time communication between two or more users. Servers that handle IRC are generally set up for public use at no user cost. Once connected, a user is presented with thousands of topics, or chat rooms, to enter. A user may also set up his own room. Once inside, a multi-party conversation can be initiated. Private rooms may also be obtained. Chat used for sexual gratification is often referred to as *hot chat*.

Some entertainment companies schedule live online discussions with celebrities who promote their products; the film industry has done this with actors and actresses. Users are free to connect to the company's server and ask questions to which the company may directly respond. While IRC for business is limited to applications such as advertising or customer support, it may also present a product itself. The most popular such use currently consists of hot chat rooms run off of a *pay server*, i.e. a server restricting access to paid members provided with a password.

Talk, similar to chat, involves a textual conversation between two parties. But the connection is made directly between the parties' computers; no server is required. Only two parties participate in the conversation.

Many other forms of communication are developing. Some improve on existing technologies, while others are entirely new. For example, higher bandwidth connections have made available real-time multimedia communication, such as Internet-based video conferencing. Similarly, "white board" notation systems, which allow people at distant locations to view and draw on the same virtual white board, are coming online. Broad deployment and acceptance of these technologies at affordable prices are only a few years away.

Private Systems and Networks

No treatment of cyberspace is complete without reference to private systems and networks, some of which are Internet-linked. (We discuss below a related topic, Intranets, under "Open Network EDI and Intranets.") Private systems were in use long before the public had affordable Internet access, and many are still used today. These systems are popularly referred to as bulletin board systems (BBSs). They may consist of a single computer or a local area network of computers that users may dial directly into via modem connection. Some BBSs charge a fee; others are free. Typically, BBSs allow users to read and send messages, engage in discussions (both real-time and atemporaneously), and upload and download files. On more modern systems, there's usually a connection of some type, possibly intermittent, to the Internet. Often this allows private BBS users to send and receive e-mail globally. One example is FidoNet, a standardized system whereby BBSs phone one another and relay e-mail. Although it may take up to a week, the e-mail will eventually find its way to its destination. FidoNet currently consists of about 30 000 systems worldwide.

The Internet's relatively free and open access to information and services means that private BBSs are decreasing. The remainder cater to particular groups with specialized subject matter. Most businesses that used to run their own BBS systems (primarily for information distribution and communication with customers who had computers) have switched over to the Internet. This has eliminated the administrative costs of BBS, which included computers and modems for direct connections and often required specialized equipment. Using an ISP to house a company's material is a cost-effective alternative, currently priced at roughly $30 per month.

Private networks are the bigger brothers of the aforementioned private systems. The main difference is size and power. Private networks such as CompuServe, America Online (AOL in Canada), Genie, Prodigy, and the Microsoft Network cater to thousands of users, and are often available globally. These networks may seek corporate sponsors and partnerships with consumer-oriented organizations such as airlines and retail stores, which set up services accessible to network members. The cost of connecting to private networks is higher than that for connecting to the Internet, where many services are free. Private networks generally offer users an Internet gateway via their connection, and may make certain commercial services uniquely available. With the gradual linkages between networks, primarily through the Internet, private systems and networks all constitute cyberspace.

Other examples of private network systems that are used frequently are electronic funds transfer systems. We're all familiar with automated teller machines, and with the PLUS, INTERAC, and CIRRUS systems that allow us to do our banking at electronic kiosks throughout the world.

Establishing a Presence in Cyberspace

When establishing an Internet presence many organizations choose to set up both e-mail and Web services. A personal e-mail address is generally assigned to each employee and a general company Web site is set up. Several questions must be answered before this can occur.

First, what (if any) domain name will be chosen? A business can use an ISP's name but, as discussed above, it is more prudent to register the company's own name. The domain name typically includes the company's name, e.g. ibm.com or microsoft.com. Simplicity is best, since users can find the company's address intuitively. Once chosen, the name must be registered with the proper authority (Network Solutions Inc. for .com and CA Domain Registrar for .ca; there are many other choices as well).

Second, what's the suffix or extension? For commercial organizations the .com suffix is a good choice. But if a name is already taken, the company may have to choose variants on the preferred name. For businesses in Canada, the .ca extension is also a possible choice. Firms preferring to mask their geographic location should avoid country-specific extensions such as .ca. It's best to use .com when operating in international markets.

Third, what about cost? The CA Domain Registrar doesn't currently charge a registration or maintenance fee, while the Internic and Network Solutions Inc. do. Once a domain is registered the name holder controls all aspects of the name, including anything to the left of the name, providing it's followed by a period. For example, if a company's registered domain name is zoo.net, it may use www.zoo.net without additional registration or cost. It's only a matter of reprogramming the computer that responds to zoo.net to be aware of the new address, and to direct the information to the www.zoo.net computer.

With the domain name registered and an Internet connection in place, a business can determine its desired cyberspace uses. Allowing employees to "surf" the Net is one. E-mail use and the creation of Web pages are others.

Almost all cyberspace dwellers use e-mail, which can be arranged quite easily by contacting a local ISP. But what does a company do with a Web site? General information about a company's products, personnel, and finances is only one application. Many others are emerging as the technology develops and as penetration rates increase.

The Internet also permits cheap customer support services. General enquiries, previously fielded by telephone attendants, may now be automated using Internet modes such as the Web. A Web site with a comprehensive database of frequently asked questions is relatively inex-

General enquiries, previously fielded by telephone attendants, may now be automated using Internet modes such as the Web.

pensive to build and maintain. Forms or text boxes allowing customers to enter free text questions ("How often should I clean my machine?") may yield quick answers at great savings. Companies dealing in such technological products as computer hardware or software currently employ these services with great success. Less technologically oriented companies will soon follow.

For specific or complex customer support, e-mail provides an excellent way for a customer or subscriber to submit product-related questions. The system's effectiveness will depend on how quickly the customer receives a response. Unlike the telephone, e-mail conversations are immediately documented and traceable; customers do much of the work. Problems are often more carefully thought through when one writes them out. There are no busy signals when e-mailing, and this alone may provide some relief to customers who feel that their enquiry has been sent, received, and is being investigated. Finally, problems solved through e-mail correspondence are easily transferred to a frequently asked questions database system. In this way similar future enquiries can be answered without further labour.

The American company Cisco uses an automated client problem tracking system with remarkable effectiveness. Cisco, which sells telecommunications hardware and software, estimates that a majority of its customer enquiries are handled using a frequently asked questions database system. The resulting cost savings have enabled Cisco to connect the remaining enquiries directly to the engineers responsible for the product in question. Cisco has become the dominant player in the telecommunications router industry.

The stock brokerage industry provides another example of effective Internet use. Although there are still security concerns with order systems that allow customers to buy and sell securities over the Internet, the industry has successfully off-loaded many other enquiries. The most striking example is stock quotations. Anyone with Web access may, without charge, ascertain a stock's price, volume, and high/low and bid/ask prices with a maximum ten-minute delay. For a small fee even that delay may be removed. While professional investors may prefer more expensive systems capable of providing data and a statistical analysis in real time, the Internet deflects many consumer-level enquiries. Mutual fund companies provide another good example. Canadians are intensive mutual fund participants, investing billions of dollars each year. They're also obsessed with checking fund quotations daily. Fund companies such as Altamira Inc. use the Internet to satisfy their clientele's appetites for information. The company saves on human telephone operators, since fund information and end-of-day unit pricing are available on its Web site.

Software companies have also recently found that the Internet provides a cost-effective way to distribute software products and upgrades. The *shareware* explosion is directly related to Internet growth. Shareware refers to a software product that can be freely downloaded and distributed ("shared") by users. (Users may have to pay a licence fee if they want to keep using the product beyond a certain free period.) Software companies will sometimes allow unlimited use of the product, hoping that users will buy the product's more robust versions. This is known as *freeware*. The Internet also provides a good software testing ground. Many software companies now provide trial releases of their product to

Internet users in order to obtain user feedback that they may incorporate into the final commercial release.

Electronic Data Interchange

Another emerging use of open network systems such as the Internet is for "just in time" order systems and other computerized inter-business linkages known as *electronic data interchange (EDI)*. Formerly available at high costs, they're now being developed more cheaply for smaller-size businesses. Wide EDI deployment, however, has yet to occur. EDI involves the "electronic preparation, communication, and processing of business transactions in a predefined structured format, using computers and telecommunications." It enables one company's computer system to carry out business transactions with another's. Fully functional EDI systems avoid all human intervention. Rather, human beings set up the system, implement a comprehensive EDI agreement, and press the button. Computers take over.

EDI cost savings are many. With a "just in time" order system a manufacturer that processes various ingredients into a product can reduce expensive on-hand inventory. Consider parts used in an automobile manufacturing plant. If the plant could limit parts on hand to three or four hours' worth of production, and be assured that new parts will arrive as needed, the space and personnel savings would be considerable. Or how about retailers such as Sears, who pay for expensive retail floor space. If Sears could reduce its sofa stock at a given store to two rather than six it would reduce inventory costs. With a computerized ordering system connected to both the sales system at Sears and the sofa supplier (whether Sears' warehouse or a third party), when two sofas are sold a new pair would quickly appear. Retail computerization permits data entry at the point of sale terminal. It's then transmitted to inventory control and processed. When new inventory is needed the request is transmitted electronically to the supplier's computer system. A delivery order is created, and inventory is shipped immediately.

While savings are easily apparent, costs are not. EDI previously required a closed network system, i.e. one with dedicated telecommunication lines between buyer and seller. This was expensive, and worthwhile only for large accounts. As well as the physical costs of telecommunications and computer hardware, systems implementation required substantial coordination and business expertise, producing fortunes for systems analysts and EDI consultants over the past two decades. Note too the EDI equation's legal side. Recall that information transmitted from one company's computer system could trigger an event, e.g. the shipping of a product, at another company's. The legal implications, though hidden, are large. What price will be paid? What are the other terms of the agreement? Who bears the responsibility of a computer breakdown? These are all important questions for parties to these agreements. EDI contracts establish the parties' legal relationship and attribute risks to various "mishaps." They're complex, detailed documents; a niche practice in EDI contracting has developed among lawyers. Legal advice and a sound legal infrastructure are significant costs to be factored into any EDI project assessment.

Open Network EDI and Intranets

With the broad and low-cost availability of open network architecture such as the Internet, EDI is becoming increasingly attractive to smaller organizations. Recall three EDI project costs: physical hardware and connections, systems analysis and activity coordination, and crafting the parties' legal relationship. The developing cyberspace reduces each.

Many companies, large and small, have internal local area computer networks (LANs). LANs are simply computer networks physically located in the same area. An office where computers are "networked" constitutes a LAN. Some companies have further connections into the Internet. Thus, many firms currently operate on the same virtual network. We're also seeing the rise of Intranets, which were originally defined as internal company networks operating on the same communication standards as the Internet, or small Internets. The Intranet definition, like the technology driving it, is ever evolving. Intranets can, with appropriate security devices, operate using Internet facilities. This technique of "piggybacking" — closed network systems on open networks — is rapidly growing. Use of the existing wiring infrastructure can result in enormous telecommunications savings, especially where a firm's offices are geographically dispersed. Open network EDI systems further extend Intranet technology. Piggybacking on open networks produces dramatic decreases in the costs of telecommunications technologies through routers and servers, and enhances EDI advantages.

While technology comes online quickly, creating industry-wide standards and finding people who can coordinate EDI projects is a slower process. Companies such as Microsoft and Netscape are battling to refine Intranet software. Security infrastructure to protect confidential information on open networks vulnerable to hacker attacks and corporate espionage is urgently needed. As with many commercial activities that involve cash or confidential information on open networks, these Intranet systems will emerge on a grand scale only when encryption and security technology become generally available and business develops confidence. A relatively conservative prediction estimates wide deployment of open network EDI systems by the year 2000.

The third factor required for network-wide commerce is a sound legal framework for digital transactions. Commercial transaction law dates back centuries, and much of it directly applies to cyber-transacting. But some questions arise that are unique to the digital environment and require the reform of existing laws. Issues of contracting, property ownership, liability, privacy, enforcement, and conflicting legal jurisdictions are all central to doing business efficiently on the information highway.

Conclusion

At various places in this book we deal with issues of convergence. One of the buzz words of the information age, the term has several meanings. It refers to the coming together of technologies, businesses, and regulatory structures. It also refers to the move toward a uniform digital information structure, which is fuelling great progress in content delivery. As Nicholas Negroponte has pointed out, cyberspace is about being digital. (The generation of useful content, however, is a different challenge. As Pamela Samuelson notes, we're constructing roadways before we have the cars to fill them!) Examples of new digital services to watch for in Canada include: personal communications service (PCS), a digital cellular service that exploits its digital nature by providing fax, pager, e-mail, and storage services to subscribers; direct to home satellite (DTH) that currently offers users a universe of some 150 channels; and digital radio transmitted through cable television wiring, which offers crisp digital quality and specialized programming. Furthermore the Internet, which continues to expand daily, is offering many new services. These include personal computer television (PCTV) and digital Internet-based radio, which offer traditional services through the digital medium and through new devices such as a computer; and even long distance digital telephone and video conferencing services, which can be accessed at virtually no cost using the Internet (although current quality is poor).

3 Businesses in Transition

Teaching an Old Dog New Tricks

Seventeen years ago Chrysler was saved from bankruptcy by a massive bailout by the U.S. government. In 1996 *Forbes Magazine* chose Chrysler as its "company of the year." Chrysler's spectacular turnaround provides us with a window upon the extraordinary transformations in business processes over the last two decades. It's sweet irony that a car manufacturer — "old technology" — opens our discussion of the effects of new technology on both business processes and their legal framework.

According to *Forbes*, Chrysler outperformed GM and Ford by a substantial margin in 1996 with a 6 percent return on net sales, compared with GM's 4 percent and Ford's 3 percent. Chrysler increased its market share in 1996 from one in seven to one in six vehicles sold in America. In financial strength, Chrysler is similarly solid: $7.5 billion in the bank, $1 billion a year in dividends, and $2 billion set aside for stock buybacks in 1996. Jerry Flint of *Forbes* cites Chrysler head Robert Lutz: "We've moved beyond 'never again'; we've moved on to 'why not?'"

What's different about the "new" Chrysler Corporation? Flint writes that "the spirit around the place these days is more Silicon Valley than Rust Belt." Flint is referring to Chrysler management's audacity, but the turn of phrase is revealing. There's a decidedly "digital age" aspect to the winning management style. The keys to success, according to *Forbes*?

- the new Chrysler platform team: engineers, designers, suppliers, and factory men work together around each vehicle platform
- the platform team means speed and reduced costs: the new Durango sport-utility vehicle, coming next fall, took only 24 months to design and manufacture
- the supplier relationship involves bringing them in early with the platform team: one of the reasons why Chrysler's product development costs are so low (2.7 percent of revenues, half that of the competition's) is that the suppliers do much of the work
- the use of high-tech computer design software
- Chrysler isn't as vertically integrated as GM and Ford, so it can outsource more easily.

Notice the language: teamwork; high technology that speeds, improves, and integrates the design, manufacture, and distribution processes; networked relationships with suppliers; heightened responsiveness to rapidly changing consumer demands; outsourcing; and, implicitly, globalization. It's all there. These are the key elements of the new economy from a business process perspective. How are they related? They're all facilitated by new technology and a mindset in sync with the demands of a knowledge economy. How are they treated legislatively? By a legal system still struggling to get in sync with the last paradigm shift in business processes.

In this chapter we examine the corporate metamorphosis at three levels. First we study the inter-enterprise (business-to-business) implications of electronic commerce. How are typical business transactions evolving? Second, we discuss its intra-enterprise significance. How is the workplace transforming? Third, we consider the information revolution's impact on the marketplace and the relationship between business and the consumer. We conclude with a discussion of how these changes are creating tension in the legal framework that structures these business relationships. How can the law evolve to become more responsive to a digital economy?

Electronic Commerce and Inter-Enterprise Transacting

Electronic Commerce

Lawrence Livermore coined the expression "electronic commerce" (EC) in 1989. It's the consolidation of technology, material, people, and processes on an electronic network for commercial transactions. According to the Society of Management Accountants of Canada, EC at its most basic level is "an infrastructure for companies to communicate with their suppliers and customers over an electronic network."[1] At its broadest level, electronic commerce facilitates the adoption and implementation of new business processes. EC involves doing business electronically across the spectrum of the inter-enterprise relationships. It brings the entire supply chain — suppliers, customers, and vendors — online via an electronic infrastructure.

Strictly speaking, it's not the *electronic* part of EC that makes it so revolutionary. Rather, it's the *digital* aspect of the technology used as the backbone of EC that gives it its versatility and efficiency. This is because once information — text, sound, or images — is in digital form, it can

Wiring for the Competitive Advantage

Worldwide competitiveness and productivity require businesses to employ and embrace electronic commerce tools such as EDI and e-mail. Several North American retail giants, including Price Club, Wal-Mart, and Provigo, as well as automotive manufacturers such as Ford and General Motors, grasped this early on. Wal-Mart's entire operation, for instance, is "wired." When one buys a pair of socks the purchase information and product data is sent to a centralized Wal-Mart information hub as well as Wal-Mart's sock supplier. The sale is acknowledged not only so that the company can track its income and disbursements, but also so that it can determine — instantly, digitally — when to place a new order for socks. This process avoids delays, ensures the maintenance of appropriate levels of stock, renders warehousing largely unnecessary, and ultimately drives down prices. According to the May 1996 issue of *Harper's Magazine*, Wal-Mart has worldwide sales that outrank the GNP of 161 countries.

be copied, altered, revised, transformed, and transmitted in myriad ways. The fax machine, despite its ubiquitous use in the business context, is "old technology" in this sense. It still relies on making imperfect copies of symbols on paper, rather than perfect copies of bits and bytes.

Using a broad range of technologies, EC supports the buying, selling, and distribution of goods and services. Moreover, EC enables companies to exploit information technology to enhance efficiency and to create new business opportunities. EC links software and telecommunications technology within a global communications infrastructure. It builds an electronic bridge between an organization's internal and external processes.

A Paperless Economy

We're in the midst of a "paradigm shift" from a paper-based economy to a digitized, electronically based economy. This doesn't mean that we're using any less paper. In fact, we're using ever more! It does mean that, from an economic perspective, the location of legitimacy, meaning, and value lies in electrons, not pulp. Just as in the past when paper currency replaced gold and the "bill of lading" replaced the contents of a cargo ship, we're now finding that paper-based, negotiable instruments are being replaced by electronic ones.

We're moving from "paper" currency to electronic currency; from paper securities to electronic securities; from paper contracts and invoices to electronic ones. The result is a huge increase in efficiency coupled with a reduction in costs. The circulation of invoices — duplicated, transcribed, and filed (not to mention "damaged" or "lost") — accounts for roughly 7 percent of most business transaction costs. These costs can be virtually eliminated when companies introduce electronic invoicing and automated contracting systems such as EDI. The efficiency and cost reduction stems not merely from getting rid of paper. Once in a digitized form, information can be copied instantly, sent instantaneously over great distances, reformatted, charted, or otherwise rendered useful.

Secondly, the "paperless" economy has had a huge impact on design. From fashion to architecture, from engineering to publishing, computer software has unleashed enormous potential for the exploitation of creative energy and the reduction of costs. Think of Boeing's new 777 or Chrysler's Durango sport-utility vehicle. Virtually no expensive models or mock-ups. Simultaneous input from engineers, mechanics, and potential customers. Increased precision. Less waste. Consider desktop publishing: sophisticated multimedia in the hands of the individual. Imagine architectural software that allows the user to see what the building will look like in three dimensions. Virtual home buyers walk into a virtual kitchen to assess its layout or the amount of direct sunlight in the pantry — even before the house is built. The effect of the software isn't merely to reduce costs; it makes possible the formerly impossible. It inspires new ways of thinking and working together.

Outsourcing

More and more businesses "outsource" worldwide, i.e., rather than using their own employees, companies are increasingly subcontracting aspects of their production and marketing. Outsourcing has three principal advantages for business. First, it alleviates the necessity of investing capital and developing expertise in the whole range of technologies and manufacturing processes. Second, and related to the first, it provides companies with a greater degree of flexibility in rapidly evolving markets. When technology changes a company can simply change suppliers, rather than working to overhaul a department. Third, outsourcing is used as a means of reducing labour costs. The wages of highly educated workers in India or Southeast Asia are as little as one-tenth those in North America. This last point explains why corporate plans to outsource have met with increasing resistance by the labour movement in North America and Europe. The leading issue in the October 1996 strike by General Motors Canada's employees wasn't wages, but outsourcing. Similarly, the main resistance to privatization and deregulation of telecommunication utilities around the world comes from the unionized workers who fear job loss.

Globalization

The evolution toward knowledge- and innovation-based manufacturing, combined with the shrinking costs of communications and transportation (the result not only of deregulation, but also of efficiency gains culled from new technology), have resulted in globalization: the erosion of nation-state borders. Globalization has increased dramatically, moreover, as legal trade barriers fall and economic cooperation intensifies (think of FTA, NAFTA, EU, APEC, for instance) in an increasingly international marketplace and workforce.

Globalization occurs at all levels of industry: production, marketing, sales, trade, and investment. Businesses coordinate production internationally, manufacture products in lower-wage countries, and ship them on demand as needed. This reduces reliance on both local markets and local labour pools. Businesses target a wider spectrum of consumers worldwide.

Convergence

In a digital economy all information is converted into a single form: a string of 1's and 0's. Whether it's a text, an image, or a sound, it can be digitized. This simple fact has profound consequences. Perhaps first among them, from a business perspective, is a blurring of the lines between once distinct realms of commercial activity. Encyclopaedia Britannica is forced to compete with Microsoft, for instance, because encyclopedias are now sold on CD-ROM, in multimedia form. Cable television companies battle with the telephone industry over who will control access to the Internet. Sony and Toshiba are making a splashy entrance into the PC market. The entire photography industry — camera manufacturers, filmmakers, film developing outlets — is wondering if the technology that sustains it is already obsolete. Digital cameras and video recorders have arrived, and they're here to stay.

Convergence brings with it exciting new commercial possibilities: new alliances formed, such as Microsoft's alliance with NBC; new products to launch, such as PCTV, Web TV, and digital telephones; new means of serving customers, such as virtual showrooms, Internet customer service, and customer data collection facilitation. But convergence also brings with it new challenges. Competition may come from unlikely sources, for instance a once entirely distinct domain.

What does this mean from a business process perspective? It means, once again, that the digital economy is an accelerated economy. The pace of technological change is increasing unabated. The result? Flexibility is key to successful corporate structure and product development.

WORKPLACE TRANSFORMATION

Three aspects of the digital economy stand out as affecting the workplace and, in general, the internal functioning of the corporation. The digital economy is a *knowledge*, a *global*, and an *automated* economy. We examine these aspects in turn. But first consider the business processes that are being replaced by this transformation.

"Taylorism" Rejected

Business processes adopted in the workplace say a good deal about how workers are perceived by their managers. Corporations with elaborate modes of employee monitoring and control, for example, implicitly suggest that their employees are untrustworthy. Manifold levels of management, organized in a pyramidal, hierarchical structure, suggest that there are significant differences in human capacities: that our differences are more important than our similarities.

In the latter half of the nineteenth century and the first half of the twentieth the dominant business process paradigm invoked these very assumptions. Innovations in manufacturing technology, combined with Darwinistic employer ideology, offered an ideal culture for the development of a hierarchical, authority-centred personnel management structure. This workplace ideology was often explicitly premised on managerial elitism. The business process model that developed under such premises — "scientific" standardization of tasks, high degrees of employee monitoring, and hierarchical layering of management — became associated, rightly or wrongly, with the philosophy of Frederick W. Taylor.

Although "Taylorist" processes have been strikingly tenacious, they are also undoubtedly on the wane. In the 1970s, new business processes — variously known as "quality of work life" (QWL) or "employment involvement" (EI) — began to emerge in order to address feelings of alienation among workers (the "blue collar blues"). More recently,

TAYLORISM IN A NUTSHELL

According to Professor Marleen O'Conner:

- "Taylorism" seeks to maximize productivity by developing a high degree of specialization among workers.
- In general, this system separates "thinking" work from "doing" work to develop technical expertise.
- The production process is segmented into independent work assignments involving simple, repetitive motions that minimize judgment required from workers.
- Decision-making takes place through a centralized managerial planning department.
- Ultimate managerial authority rests at the top of a pyramid-shaped hierarchy. At lower levels, managerial discretion is constrained by rigid work rules.
- This hierarchical system stresses managerial preservation of control over the production process by reducing the firm's dependence upon labor cooperation.
- To ensure control, Taylorism employs extensive monitoring, assuming that workers will shirk their duties when given the opportunity.
- In addition, jobs are defined narrowly so that workers are prevented from understanding the production process so that they cannot reduce the pace of work and the amount of production.
- To minimize the risk that workers will limit production, Taylorism seeks to inhibit worker solidarity by using discrete job assignments that reduce the need for communication between employees.
- For these reasons, Taylorism tends to produce an adversarial atmosphere that leads to a low level of employee commitment.[2]

however, such programs are implemented for their productive value, quite apart from their effect on employee morale.

In a digital economy Taylorist business processes are manifestly counter-productive. Bureaucracies lack the requisite flexibility to adapt to the accelerated pace of technological change and to ever more individualized, global, and sophisticated consumer demands. Moreover, bureaucracies "lock in" all the information, knowledge, and accumulated wisdom of those who know the products best: employees.

Taylorism's rejection has given birth to a new perception of employees' capacities and their important role in the corporation. Labour is increasingly seen as a resource, rather than a cost. The employee has

The Democratization of the Workplace

Under the influence of new technology, corporations are converting from traditional hierarchical structures to flatter, networked structures. Far greater numbers of people can participate in decision-making. Consider these two recent examples cited by John Byrne:

> J.M. Smucker Co., the Ohio-based maker of jams and jellies, more recently enlisted a team of 140 employees — 7% of its workforce — who devoted nearly 50% of their time to a major strategy exercise for more than six months. "Instead of having just 12 minds working it, we really used the team of 140 as ambassadors to solicit input from all 2,000 employees," says President Richard K. Smucker. "It gave us a broader perspective, and it brought to the surface a lot of people with special talents." The company, which has struggled to grow in a mature market, now has a dozen viable initiatives that could double its $635 million revenues over the next five years. One of them is a just-announced alliance with Brach & Brock Confections Inc. to make Smucker's jellybeans, the first of several co-branded products to be developed under the pact. The idea came from a team that included staffers who ordinarily would never have had a role in strategy formulation.
>
> Unlike slow-growing Smucker's, Finland's Nokia Group had been exploding at a rate of 70% a year in the booming telecommunications business when it chose to involve 250 employees in a strategic review early last year. "By engaging more people, the ability to implement strategy becomes more viable," says Chris Jackson, head of strategy development at Nokia. "We won a high degree of commitment by the process, and we ended up with lots of options we hadn't looked at in the past."[3]

potential, and is to be consulted, tapped, and rewarded rather than monitored, confined, and controlled. Whether adopted reluctantly or embraced wholeheartedly, the new business processes place greater responsibility in the worker's hands.

The Digital Economy as a "Knowledge Economy"

Don Tapscott writes of the digital economy:

> In an economy based on brain rather than brawn, there is a shift toward knowledge work. In the new economy the key assets are intellectual assets, and they focus on the knowledge worker. This is causing companies around the world to develop new ways of measuring and managing their intellectual capital. For Peter Drucker, knowledge is not simply another resource along with the traditional factors of production such as labor, capital, and land; for him, it is the only meaningful resource today. Consequently, the knowledge worker is any organization's greatest single asset.[4]

But what are the implications of a knowledge economy for business process transformation? Here we explore a few of the most dominant themes.

"Lifelong Learning"

If workers are seen not as an expense but as a resource in a knowledge economy then they must be cultivated, rather than stunted or uprooted. Don Tapscott writes that because the digital economy is based on knowledge work and innovation, there's a convergence between work and learning: "In the old economy, life was divided into the period when you learned and the period when you worked. One went to school to develop a trade or competency, then one simply kept up to date with developments in that field. In the new economy, one must expect to 'reinvent' one's knowledge on a continual basis." The Information Highway Advisory Council of Canada (IHAC) emphasized this point by adopting the principle that "lifelong learning should be a key design element in building the Information Highway."[5]

Why? First, the speed at which new knowledge must be acquired has increased dramatically. The shelf life of new products is increasingly diminishing. They must be replaced, retooled, and reinvented. Employees are similarly expected to update their skills regularly. They must familiarize themselves with new technology, new business processes, and broadened fields of inquiry. Ford's Louis Ross muses: "In your career, knowledge is like milk. It has a shelf life stamped right on the carton. The shelf life of a degree in engineering is about three years. If you are not replacing everything you know by then, your career is going to turn sour fast." Learning has thus become a continuous, lifelong process.

Second, most workers no longer expect to remain with the same company during their entire working life. Because their career paths are increasingly likely to shift over time, workers need to develop skills that are transferable or that transport them outside their particular domains of specialization. What's lost in job security and stability is gained, at least in part, in flexibility, manoeuvrability, and increased potential for self-actualization.

Stan Davis and Jim Botkin argue effectively in *The Monster Under the Bed* that education — once the purview of the church, then of government — is increasingly falling to business. Business must train knowledge workers: witness Hamburger U., which trains more than 10 000 McDonald's employees a year; Motorola U.; Hewlett-Packard U.; and Sun Microsystems' Sun U. Davis and Botkin present data to show that in 1992 the growth in formal budgeted employee education grew by 126 million hours in the United States. This represents the equivalent of almost a quarter of a million additional full-time college students. According to the authors, employee education is growing 100 times faster than academia (partly because North American firms did so little employee training to start with). This new emphasis on worker training marks a radical shift from the general perception of the "over-educated" worker.

Control over the Means of Production

In the digital economy control over the means of production is increasingly shifting toward the individual. The old "economies of scale" existed because individuals and small companies couldn't afford the capital investment required to purchase the most efficient, sophisticated tools of the trade, nor the number of employees required to run them. Consider the publishing industry. Only 100 years ago it could be easily controlled by press barons and governments because printing presses were enormous, expensive, unwieldy machines, available to only the few. Now anyone can publish professional-looking documents and distribute them anywhere in the world as fast and as efficiently as the largest corporations.

This is true of virtually all knowledge products. Internet software giant Netscape, a multi-billion dollar company, didn't even exist three years ago. A few people from the MIT computer lab set it up with minimal assets. Victor Keegan of the *Guardian* writes: "It is the first company in history to be worth $5-billion by giving away its product." Netscape can make infinite copies of its products and distribute them anywhere in the world virtually for free. Purchasers and users travel through virtual space to "download" their products. No warehouses, no distributors, no sales clerks. Although few, if anyone, will create the next Microsoft or Netscape, the basic tools are available to average citizens.

Among other things, this means that large businesses face competition from unlikely quarters. For IBM, Microsoft sprang out of nowhere. Now Microsoft is locked in mortal battle with upstart Netscape. It also means that large, unwieldy companies have a tendency to break themselves up: witness the make-overs at Big Blue and AT&T. Joseph Schumpeter's "destructive capitalism" is alive and well as the new millennium approaches. Again, flexibility, responsiveness to change, the release of creative energies through the devolution of decision-making powers, and the broadening of sources of input are all resulting themes of business process transformation.

Access to Information: Knowledge as Power

The digital economy has brought with it an enormous "declassification" of information. Where knowledge was once "proprietary," stored in filing cabinets, books, and even vaults, it's now increasingly entering the public domain. The Internet has greatly facilitated this process. The Department of Justice has placed the full text of all federal statutes on the Net. Corporations are increasingly adopting "open" rather than closed or proprietary computer operating systems. Tens of thousands of Web sites are exploding onto the Web each year, with information on just about any subject imaginable. Encyclopedias that once cost over $2000 in their printed, "hard copy" form are now available on CD-ROM, or over the Net, for a fraction of that amount. Communication among employees, between offices, and across time zones is simple, and available to anyone with an Internet connection. Collaboration on work-related projects is greatly facilitated. Employees can participate in the decision-making process more easily. It's simple to attain access to relevant information, and to transmit that information to the party or parties concerned.

But this access to information can come with a bite, as Tapscott points out. In October 1994, Intel's Pentium computer chip was selling briskly: rave reviews, strong profit. By the end of the month, however, the milk began to turn sour. A university professor posted a message on the Internet reporting that the chip was flawed. The message circulated through cyberspace to thousands, and a massive consumer protest ensued within days. Intel downplayed the problem, using traditional public relations ploys. The CEO's explanations, however, produced an uproar. A Web server with Pentium jokes appeared. IBM announced a shipment halt. By December, Intel conceded its error and agreed to a general recall. As James and Theodore Barr note, in a digital economy "time is collapsed, facts are quickly checked, loss of credibility can be instantaneous, second chances are rare and harder to effect, grandstand plays had better be perfect, and the playing of one audience against another is far easier to detect."[6]

The Digital Economy as a "Global Economy"

We've already seen the effect of globalization on inter-enterprise business processes. But what about the workplace? Ubiquitous and inexpensive access to personal computing and global communications networks linking businesses and nations opens the doors to "virtual workplaces" and "virtual employees." These virtual workers are linked via corporate communication networks. Consequently, corporations can hire workers from other lower wage countries. University or high school graduates from various Asian countries are available for perhaps one-tenth the cost of their North American equivalents.

In cyberspace, time and space become irrelevant. Workers in Seattle can collaborate over the Internet with employees living in Bangalore, just as easily as they can collaborate with those working across town.

BANGALORE, INDIA

Jeremy Rifkin, in *The End of Work*, writes:

> Nowhere is the contrast between the high-tech future and the low-tech past more apparent than in Bangalore, India, a city of 4.2 million that is fast becoming known as that country's Silicon Valley. Global companies like IBM, Hewlett-Packard, Motorola and Texas Instruments are flocking to this city located atop a 3,000 foot plateau some 200 miles west of Madras . . . In a country teeming with poverty and social unrest, Bangalore "is an island of relative affluence and social stability." Touting some of the best-trained scientists and engineers in the world, this Indian city has become a high-tech mecca for global electronic and computer firms eager to set up shop close to burgeoning new markets.[7]

The Digital Economy as an "Automated Economy"

Digital technology has brought with it enormous efficiency gains for corporations. The paper trail can be replaced with an electronic one. Data collection, storage, and analysis are greatly facilitated. Computers and robots replace human beings in a multitude of mundane, repetitive tasks. Information technology — think of the exponential growth of Intranet implementation — allows employees, managers, and directors to communicate with each other far more easily and far less expensively than previously possible. Why fly a bunch of directors in for a board meeting when they can meet without moving by using video conferencing?

But the efficiency gains of globalization and automation have a much-discussed flip side. The two overriding issues? Job loss and high-tech stress.

Job Loss

Automation replaces human labour with machine labour. Almost inevitably, it means job loss. According to Jeremy Rifkin, more than 75 percent of the labour force in most industrial nations engage in work that's little more than simple repetitive tasks. Automated machinery, robots, and increasingly sophisticated computers can perform many if not most of these jobs. We say "almost inevitably" because at least three alternatives to job loss due to automation currently exist: a reduced work week, increased productivity with the same employees, and alternative use of employee capacities through retraining.

On the Turbulent Energies of the New Capitalism

The following exchange, printed in *Harper's Magazine* in May 1996, neatly captures a range of stakes in play in the ongoing "downsizing" debate:

> ALBERT DUNLAP: The responsibility of the CEO is to deliver shareholder value. Period. It's the shareholders who own the corporation. They take all the risk. And how does the CEO maximize value? He does that by focusing on profit. But how does he get profit? By making the best products, by building the best facilities, by having the best workforce, by globalizing his company. And, yes, sometimes you have to get rid of people . . .
>
> ROBERT REICH: AT&T — a highly profitable company — announced on the first business day of 1996 that it would be laying off 40,000 people. Now, quite apart from the question of whether that was wise or good for AT&T's own business strategy, let us acknowledge two things. Number one, there are social costs in doing that. There are communities in New Jersey that are now different than they were before. Property values may now be lower, people are less secure. But number two, there are consequences extending beyond AT&T. Every time a large company announces a major layoff, a chill is sent through the living rooms and kitchens of millions of American homes . . .
>
> GEORGE GILDER: The fact is that layoffs are a good thing. I remember back in the early Seventies in Seattle, Boeing laid off about half its workforce. It was widely prophesied that this was the end of the line for Seattle, that Seattle was going to be the basket case of the future. Since then, Seattle has become the richest and most prosperous city in the country. Pittsburgh was, at the time of the collapse of Big Steel, regarded as a hopeless case. What was the result in Pittsburgh? Thousands of new machine shops and small businesses emerged.

In North Carolina, tobacco companies laid off scores of thousands of people. It was supposed to be a catastrophe. The people there have prospered.

The fact is, layoffs are crucial to growth. The more layoffs in a particular area, the more business starts and the more long-term economic growth . . . Systems of credentialism get entrenched, and opportunities close. And I think an economy with less credentialism and more opportunities is desirable. It takes courage, guts, to lay people off, but it unleashes new powers.

RONALD BLACKWELL: When you say that layoffs are good, George, all you are telling me is that you have never had a plant gate slammed in your face. You've never gotten a pink slip. You've never experienced anything like that or you couldn't say things like that.

The point of restructuring a company is not to put people out of work — or, at least, it shouldn't be. It's to gain some flexibility to respond to the environment in which the company exists. Al [Dunlap], when you take over a company, it's usually in bad shape. You've got to gain some flexibility in order to turn it around. Now you seem to think that the only way to gain flexibility is through layoffs. I don't think that's true. . . . [Xerox] invented xerography, lost half its market share in the late Seventies, and then regained much of that market share in the Eighties with a competitive strategy that defined what the "high road" means. People's jobs weren't slashed. Management didn't think they had to start by cleaning house in order to realize hidden share value. What they came to understand was that they had an enormous untapped competitive resource in their business, and that was the knowledge workers have about what they do, which management not only does not but cannot get except from those workers. People won't contribute to the success of your organization unless they're secure in their livelihood . . .

PAUL TOUGH: If there's a high road and a low road that a company can take, and the high road works, why would a company take the low road?

RONALD BLACKWELL: Well, the low road is a lot easier to follow. You don't have to change the way you do business, you don't have to do anything except find some cheap workers somewhere. The only problem with the low road is that it's downhill. If not for the company, then for society.[8]

Dunlap and Gilder sing the crusading theme of the "Business Process Reengineering" (BPR) movement, which has resulted in hundreds of thousands of layoffs in North America and Europe since the late 1980s.[9] Their stance is becoming increasingly questioned, however, even in business circles. According to a 1996 American Management Association survey, of the major firms that downsized between 1989 and 1994, 34 percent increased their productivity, 36 percent remained the same, and 34 percent actually saw productivity decline. One of the main reasons for the failure of BPR is employee resistance and resentment. The survey found that in 86 percent of all instances of downsizing employee morale decreased. The new business processes were resisted, or used without enthusiasm. Resentment over the loss of colleagues lingered. Moreover, these companies are left with far fewer of their essential sources of knowledge and growth: their employees. This fact highlights a theme that's emerging through the implementation of new business processes: the importance of trust. "Teamwork" only works if employees trust that their employers won't use the efficiency gains that result from greater employee input to lay off or further exploit those same employees. Recent reports show that downsizing in the context of BPR is on the wane.[10]

High-Tech Stress

As Jeremy Rifkin notes, up until the modern industrial era bodily rhythms and economic rhythms were largely compatible. Craft production was conditioned by the speed of the human hand and body and constrained by the power that could be generated by harnessing animals, wind, and water. By contrast, today's computer culture operates at a breathtaking pace. The accelerated lifestyle has its price. The workplace's increased rhythm has augmented workers' impatience, resulting in unprecedented levels of stress. One study found that a computer response time exceeding 1.5 seconds was likely to trigger user impatience and stress. Computer monitoring of employee performance means that workers are reluctant to take the time to speak with customers, as this slows down the number of items a cashier can scan across an electronic grid, for instance, or the number of callers a customer service representative can respond to daily. According to a 1986 All

Toyota Union survey, more than 124 000 of the company's 200 000 member workers suffered from chronic fatigue. These are some of the reasons why the International Labour Organization (ILO) has called stress the twentieth century disease.

Establishing a New Relationship with Customers in the Digital Age

How are businesses altering their customer relations in the digital economy? We consider here four principal themes: a movement toward "mass specialization," consumer participation in the production process, improved customer service and, once again, globalization.

Mass Customization

Information technology permits businesses to synthesize the "custom made" aspect of the pre-industrial economy with the "mass production" of the Industrial Revolution. The result is "mass customization." To use an analogy taken from the familiar context of word processing, information technology allows for the merger of individualized "fields" with mass "documents." Consider two examples.

Agents

One of the more recently developed Internet tools with multiple potential applications for business and personal use is the "agent." This is a software tool that roams through cyberspace to find information personalized according to the user's interests. The agent then assembles the collected information into an attractive, readable form. A company called Pointcast offers an agent that searches a set of reputable online sources for international and local news, stock market information, sports, weather, entertainment, and intelligence on a number of specific industries. The information is culled and sorted, and the result is a graphically impressive, personalized electronic newspaper. Turning the notion of "broadcasting" — i.e. sending precisely the same information to everyone — on its head, "pointcasting" selects from a broad field of information, reducing it to what the customer will find relevant, useful, or interesting. The software, which is free, has obvious applications for businesses that make a point of tracking media coverage of their industry.

Direct Marketing

The Canadian direct marketing industry is now an $11-billion business. The U.S. market is several times larger. Direct marketers' success is largely due to the effective use of information technology, which serves the industry in three fundamental ways. First, it facilitates the collection of consumer data: addresses, purchases, and service use. Second, it enables raw data cross-referencing. This helps direct marketers establish "consumer profiles." Third, it enables direct to home marketing in a "mass customized" fashion: "Congratulations, Sunny Handa of Montreal, you've just won the opportunity . . ."

Consumer Participation in Production

Concomitant with mass specialization is consumer participation in the production process. Here we revisit two familiar situations.

Boeing

When Boeing began planning its new 777 it brought its customers in right from the start. Rather than build a plane from scratch and only subsequently find a market for it, Boeing asked potential clients what they were looking for. With the help of computer graphics, the company was able to demonstrate to their customers exactly what various design features would look like *in advance* of production. Costs were reduced, as was time to production; and customers obtained the satisfaction of getting what they wanted.

Levi's

Recall the custom-fit jeans offered over the Internet discussed at the beginning of this book. The service ensures that the customer gets *exactly* what she's looking for. But there's more. Because the customer, not a sales representative, completes the order form — which is sent electronically to all parties concerned — there's an efficiency gain. It results from customer participation in the production process: the time spent by the customer, on her own, establishing her own needs, is time that Levi's *doesn't* spend, either inquiring into those needs or guessing them.

Improved Customer Service

Cyberspace business opportunities are enormous: e-shopping, billing, banking, and product distribution. There is, at least on the surface, powerful potential: improved customer service, reduced operating costs, smaller inventory, fewer errors and enhanced accountability, access to more information, and continuous rather than periodic data collection and updates. Customers purchase items at retailers; the information goes immediately and directly to suppliers. Consider several examples of how information technology enhances customer service.

Call Centres

In Canada, corporations large and small, engaged in industries as diverse as aerospace, manufacturing, natural resources, couriers, and financial institutions, have created call centres. Many of these are located in New Brunswick, an emerging IT (Information Technology) haven. Call centres enhance operational productivity, improve the quality of customer/client service, and increase potential sales by offering access to a wider, international market. Emerging innovative computer and telecommunications technologies enable companies to set up business operations at long distances from their head offices.

Teleshopping

The computer, and soon interactive television, create new commercial opportunities such as shopping, banking, and other financial transactions. One need never leave home (except for more pleasant excursions!). Teleshopping's benefits are numerous: user friendliness, accessibility, reduced costs for business and consumer, and access to a vast array of merchandise, from groceries to real estate, at the touch of a button. Businesses can deliver their services across existing networks. They can increase sales by penetrating a wider market, or by targeting market niche groups that would never exist in sufficient concentration in a single location.

Teleshopping's limits are those inherent to the medium: the consumer can only view products, and not feel their texture, smell them, or try them on. These are the limitations of catalogue shopping in general. Secondly, there are initial user costs: purchases are made through personal computers running telecommunications applications and sophisticated software. High quality video resolution, increasingly the norm, is essential.

Internet Shopping

A multitude of influences heighten global consumer expectations. Enterprises must compete fiercely to attract and maintain business. Without the traditional marketplace's geographical and physical constraints, comparison shopping has acquired new and broader dimensions. In fact, software exists to conduct electronic comparison shopping. Consider, for example, ten book retailers advertising their wares in the electronic marketplace. Each uses the slogan "Best book bargains." Consumers browse the Net, search for a book (product) by its name

Enterprises must compete fiercely to attract and maintain business. Without the traditional marketplace's geographical and physical constraints, comparison shopping has acquired new and broader dimensions.

(author, title), and conduct an almost instantaneous price comparison. Guess what? The consumer discovers that all these competitors offer the same "unbeatable deal." Suddenly time and space barriers, which previously allowed businesses to separately claim the best prices, collapse.

Not surprisingly, companies must do more to distinguish themselves by product, service, or price in order to compete in the electronic marketplace. Flashy graphics and hype alone won't secure long-term profitability for Internet retailers. One Seattle-based virtual bookstore, Amazon.com Inc., understood this. Amazon offers services beyond those of traditional bookstores or print and electronic retail catalogues. It features a database containing over 1.1 million book titles — five times the largest bookstore's physical inventory. When a browser selects a book, the program will provide other related books that might interest him. Amazon supplies up-to-date information, such as a book's paperback release, and makes recommendations to the consumer. In short, the Internet offers customer services to a mass consumer base unthinkable in the non-virtual sphere.

Globalized Customer Service

A final dimension of globalization's effects on business processes relates to how businesses interact with their customers. In general, we're witnessing a globalization of goods markets. The possibility of worldwide price comparison and competition, substantially increased as a result of the Internet's dramatic spread, heightens consumer demands and product variation.

Electronic merchants aren't restricted by geography, size, or industry. Trade agreements have lowered traditional barriers to international or inter-jurisdictional markets. Naturally, this has expanded business

Companies are* forced *to compete globally and to expand their operations beyond national borders simply in order to survive.

opportunities. At the same time, however, this has meant that many companies are *forced* to compete globally and to expand their operations beyond national borders simply in order to survive. Thus, many corporations have turned to the telephone, and now the Internet, as a cost-effective way to attract and serve an international client/customer base.

The Internet unveils a "whole world" of business opportunities and potential niche markets. Accordingly, small and medium-sized enterprises (SMEs) with specialized or knowledge-based products — or those that position themselves as attractive centres for outsourcing — can greatly benefit from participation in the digital world. With a call centre in place, even SMEs are only a telephone call away from their clients, *wherever* they may be.

Tensions in the Governing Legal Paradigm

The existing legal framework is still largely based on assumptions and corporate models from the Taylorist era. Unsurprisingly, therefore, both corporate and labour law are experiencing tension as business processes undergo radical change. Here we explore the principal issues facing corporate and labour law resulting from or affecting business process transformation. We suggest plausible avenues of evolution.

"Teamwork"

In the 1930s — an era with aspects of extreme distrust, and even violence, between labour and their employers — many corporations sought to undermine the labour movement by establishing their own "unions." The U.S. Congress, convinced that these company unions posed a problem, amended the *National Labor Relations Act (NLRA)*. Congress made it unlawful for an employer to dominate or interfere with such an organization, and prohibited employers from contributing money or other financial support to a labour organization.[11] In Canada, such company unions are similarly considered to be "unfair labour practices." The *NLRA* amendments were justified by the adversarial context of Taylorist working conditions. They're awkward, however, in an era of efforts to break down barriers to workplace cooperation.

In two instances, *Electromation* (1992) and *Dupont* (1993), the National Labor Relations Board (NLRB) held that "employee involvement groups" or "work teams," as established in these two companies, violated the *NLRA* prohibitions against company unions. The rulings have widespread significance, since teams exist in more than 30 000 workplaces in the United States.[12] Digital age workplace innovation will continue to face a substantial legal barrier unless the *NLRA* is amended, or these two court decisions overturned.

In 1995, the U.S. Congress attempted the former approach by introducing the *Team Act*.[13] The purpose of the Act was to loosen *NLRA* restrictions on work teams in the aftermath of these two NLRB cases. The Act met with resistance from many union leaders fearful of a return to corporate co-optation. It appears that the fear was largely unfounded, however. In the context of the controversial bill, Michael Leroy undertook one of the few detailed surveys yet in order to see how these "teams" actually function. He concluded that there's no evidence to suggest that these teams are anything like the company unions of the 1930s. Leroy writes:

> It is part of a management philosophy that transcends the matter of union representation. Instead, its purpose is to reduce layers of management, to appropriate employees' knowledge of how work is actually performed and how it can be improved, and to improve product or service quality by making employees more accountable for their own performance.[14]

Canada hasn't faced the same controversies related to "teamwork" as have Americans, in part because Canadian labour relations boards are set up to defuse antagonisms between labour and management through mediation and labour-management representation on the boards.

In this section we've discussed how U.S. labour law suffers from its failure to evolve beyond its Taylorist assumptions. The *NLRA* assumes that the only possible relationship between employers and employees is an antagonistic one. We'll look to the European model of the works councils and to an American study of "teamwork" in action, both of which demonstrate that such assumptions are unfounded. In the next section, however, we'll examine the same problem from the perspective of corporate law in order to show a similar lag in the tenacious and pervasive assumptions of lawyers and business leaders.

Stakeholder Expansion

Al Dunlap's claim presented earlier ("the responsibility of the CEO is to deliver shareholder value. Period") finds support in doctrine such as

Richard Posner's *Economic Analysis of Law*, and in classic, albeit somewhat dated court decisions such as *Dodge v. Ford Motor Company* and *Parke v. Daily News Ltd.* In the former, American decision, the Court found that Henry Ford's stated ambition — "to employ still more men to spread the benefits of this industrial system to the greatest possible number, to help them build up their lives and their homes. To do this, we are putting the greatest share of our profits back in the business [rather than paying out dividends to the shareholders]" — was illegal. The Court held: "A business corporation is organized and carried out primarily for the profit of its stockholders. The powers of the directors are to be employed for that end." The latter, English case involved a newspaper that had been the subject of a merger. The Court found that the board of directors' decision to ensure that their present staff and pensioners benefited fully from the proceeds of sale was similarly illegal. "The directors of the defendant company are proposing that a very large part of its funds should be given to its former employees in order to benefit those employees rather than the company, and that is an application of the company's funds which the law . . . will not allow."

The position, though defensible, is no longer good law. In the United States and England courts have recognized the validity of charitable donations by corporations, for instance. In the leading Canadian case on the subject, *Teck,* Justice Berger states:

> A classical theory that once was unchallengeable must yield to the facts of modern life. In fact, of course, it has. If today the directors of a company were to consider the interests of its employees no one would argue that in doing so they were not acting *bona fide* in the interests of the company itself. Similarly, if the directors were to consider the consequences to the community of any policy that the company intended to pursue, and were deflected in their commitment to that policy as a result, it could not be said that they had not considered *bona fide* the interests of the shareholders.[15]

Marleen O'Conner examines movements away from the "shareholder supremacy" legal corporate model. She finds that a reconception of corporate law is necessary — and concomitant to changes taking place in labour law — given the altered circumstances of our digital economy. The problem is that while there's a growing consensus as to the value of greater employee participation in the firm's decision-making process, a "prisoner's dilemma" occurs. That is, if employees feel that the efficiency gains that result from their increased participation in the production process simply result in layoffs, then the employees lose their incentive to make the new scheme work. Similarly, if employers feel that employees are shirking their responsibilities, then the employers will likely reject the participatory scheme in favour of more traditional methods of monitored production. For these reasons trust/distrust is becoming a recurring theme in "team work" schemes.

O'Conner suggests two means of overcoming the prisoner's dilemma. They both involve different modes of increasing stakeholder participation in corporate governance, since the key is to recognize employees' actual stake in the firm. The first proposal is to establish a director's fiduciary duty to employees. In layperson's terms, a fiduciary duty involves heightened responsibility; it's a legal duty to treat another person's interest above your own. Such a duty is generally imposed when one is in a position of power over another who is without the means to protect fully his own interests. (The classic example is the duty of a trustee to serve the interests of the beneficiary of a trust fund.) O'Conner's second proposal is to set a specific legal standard governing the director's obligation to protect employees from opportunistic conduct. She writes:

> Many American directors currently view their role as balancing the interests of employees and shareholders, but not as neutral arbiters. When shareholders' and employees' interests directly conflict in situations like plant closings and layoffs, studies indicate that directors refrain from expressing their moral sentiments about employees due to their belief that they have a legal obligation to maximize shareholder wealth. By absolving directors from their responsibility to act as moral agents, the current legal regime promotes an end-game problem that threatens collaboration in the employment relationship.[16]

There's room in corporate law for the accommodation of such ideas. Under the *Canadian Business Corporation Act (CBCA)*, for instance, directors have a fiduciary duty to the "corporation."[17] Canadian courts have already used this provision to establish that directors have a fiduciary duty to minority shareholders. There's no inherent need for this provision to equate the corporation with its shareholders, any more or less than with its employees. Courts could develop a director's fiduciary duty to both employees and shareholders on an equal footing.

As business practices undergo transformation in the digital economy it will become increasingly important to avoid legal chauvinism or dogmatism. The new economy requires flexibility, creativity, and an openness to new legislative solutions.

Works Councils

Where else can we look for guidance in assessing the merits of teamwork? Are there other legislative models available to us?

Europeans have far greater experience with the teamwork approach to business operations. "Works councils" are commonplace in Europe, though rare to non-existent in the U.S. and the U.K. In Canada, they exist only in the context of occupational health and safety. The purpose of works councils — sometimes referred to as "employee councils" or "second channel institutions" — is to give workers a voice in shop floor and firm governance. They also facilitate communication and cooperation between management and labour on production-related matters, more or less free of direct distributive conflicts over wages. They thus have a status and functions distinct from, though not necessarily in competition with, those of unions.

Rogers and Streek's assessment of works councils, based on the U.S. National Board of Economic Research (NBER) research, is extremely positive. While employees and their employers may not share common goals, the councils tend to serve the interests of both. "Workers are interested in representation and expanded democracy, while firms look for gains in efficiency and performance."[18] The authors break down the councils' virtues into three aspects: contributions to efficiency, democracy, and regulation. The first, efficiency, is of particular interest here:

- *Trust*: Trust is essential for success in the new economy. "For firms to decentralize production decisions, managers must trust workers not to misuse their increased discretion. For workers to contribute to efficiency, they must trust management not to exclude them from the benefits of their effort. The formal institutionalization of worker participation rights contributes to the growth of trust . . . While trust is an intangible resource that cannot be legislated, legislation can ensure against the self-interested short-term actions that destroy trust and can foreclose options . . . This is what strong council legislation does."

- *Information Flow*: "Recognizing that information exists at many levels of an organization leads to the understanding that it is inefficient for management to make key decisions without mobilizing information held by others and investigating the validity of divergent information in collective deliberation." Increasing information flows from management to labour can lead to worker concessions in difficult economic times, saving troubled enterprises; increasing information flows from workers to management helps both sides devise new solutions to problems. Councils provide an incentive for truthful exchange, and a disincentive to underinform.

- *Diffusion of "Best Practice"*: "Councils serve liaison functions with the environment outside the firm, often helping the firm perceive and import good practice." Councils in several countries can call in expert advice, and in Germany, council members can attend training courses, thus helping to diffuse innovative practices and technical information.

- *Industrial Upgrading*: "Councils can pressure managers to consider productivity enhancement as opposed to other competitive strategies." Employers learn about workers and the conditions under which they work in order to consider training and management methods that correspond to employee interests. "These pressures, diffused throughout the economy, exert a cumulative force for restructuring along the path of upgrading labor."

Employee Training

The 1994 NBER study of training strategies in countries with advanced economies showed that the only country with a lower incidence of training than the U.S. is Canada! Such neglect of worker training is short-sighted, and adversely affects the interests of both employee and employer. The study concludes that the benefits of increased training would be enhanced by the following:

- Greater employer participation in training to increase the probability that skills will be related to demand. Firm-based systems seem to work better than school-, individual-, and government-based systems of training.
- Employee representation in determining the content of training includes more general skills as well as firm-specific skills. Absent such training participation, training would be too narrow.
- Certification of skills through a nationally recognized process. This would increase general training as well as workers' willingness to accept lower wages during training. Certification would also provide an alternative route to formal higher education for establishing technical skills, and would allow workers to obtain the benefits of their skills in other workplaces, in a society in which job-switching is frequent.

In a digital economy, a skilled, flexible workforce is the key to prosperity. Companies, and legislators, will be increasingly forced to explore new ways of facilitating ongoing employee training.

Altered Work Week Facilitation

The digital economy manifests the following paradox: although automation has significantly increased productivity such that the same amount of goods can be created in far less time, a concomitant reduction in the number of working hours hasn't taken place. The dramatic productivity gains of the first stage of the Industrial Revolution in the nineteenth century were followed by a reduction of the work week from 80 hours

A Flexible Work Week?

Experiments in Europe have demonstrated that flexibility can be effective:

- In 1993 Volkswagen announced its intention to adopt a four day work week to save 31 000 jobs that might otherwise have been lost to a combination of stiffening global competition and new work technologies and methods that had boosted productivity by 23 percent.
- At Hewlett-Packard's Grenoble plant, management adopted a four day week, but kept the plant running twenty-four hours a day, seven days a week. The three shifts are varied in length, such that those who work the night shift work fewer hours than either the morning or afternoon shift. The employees are paid the same wages as they previously received, despite working, on average, six fewer hours a week. The extra compensation is viewed by management as a tradeoff for the worker's willingness to operate under a flexible hours arrangement. Production has tripled, largely because the plant is never idle.
- Digital Equipment offered its workers the option of a four day week with a 7 percent pay cut. 530 of the company's 4000 employees accepted the offer, thus saving 90 jobs that would have been lost through re-engineering.
- The Commission of the European Union and the European Parliament have both gone on record in favour of shortening the work week to address the issue of unemployment. A Commission memorandum warned that it was "important to avoid the hardening of two distinct groups in society — those with stable employment and those without — a development which would have disruptive social consequences and would endanger the very foundations of all democratic societies in the longer run."[20]

to 60. And as industrial economies made the transition from steam to oil and electric technologies, the productivity increases led to a further decrease in the work week from 60 hours to 40. Some economists suggest that, given our current efficiency gains, we'll inevitably move from a 40- to a 30- or even 20-hour work week. Yet, despite the fact that overall productivity in America, for instance, has doubled since 1948, Americans are working longer hours now than they were at the onset of the information-technological revolution.[19]

Conclusion

The digital economy is substantially altering business processes. The dominant themes of the new economy are networking, globalization, convergence, workplace democracy, knowledge, and flexibility. Successful businesses are responding to these changes, developing new ways of interacting with other companies, facilitating new forms of cooperation with and among their employees, and uncovering new ways to service increasingly demanding customers. True to its conservative nature, the law has lagged in its response to these changes. By focusing on the flashpoints of current tension we've attempted here to anticipate the sorts of changes that will likely occur in corporate and labour law.

4 Electronic Privacy

Free-Flowing Information

The uninhibited flow of financial information makes our credit economy possible. In the global village, our neighbours are electronic. The exchange of personal information enables creditors to trust consumers, about whom they have no first-hand knowledge. Accurate credit-history information allows creditors to charge lower interest rates to reliable debtors, thus encouraging debtors to keep their promises. By turning consumers into repeat players information networks blunt the temptation to cheat creditors.[1] Accordingly, both individuals and businesses benefit from the information economy's efficiency.

But there's another side to the story.

In the digital economy privacy issues claim first order concern. U.S. and Canadian public opinion surveys consistently reveal high anxiety levels over privacy generally, and the erosion of privacy brought on by new information technology specifically. Louis Harris' U.S. surveys show a progressive increase in concern, up from 67 percent in 1978 to 84 percent in 1994. Ekos Research's 1993 Canadian survey showed high consumer wariness: 92 percent expressed concern about their personal privacy, and 52 percent reported "extreme concern." A 1994 Gallup Canada survey for Andersen Consulting revealed that over 80 percent of the Canadians polled expressed concern about their personal information collected by companies through cyberspace.

Why has privacy become such a pressing issue?

First, a digital economy is a *networked* economy. Private, government, and corporate computer systems are linked together over the information highway. Once private information enters the public stream — as a result of inadvertence, deliberate posting, or hacking — there's no way to control or prevent its circulation. This has of course always been the case, but it's far easier now to copy and circulate information once it's in digital form. Moreover, digital networking permits prying without physical presence: a temptation too difficult for some to resist.

Second, the information economy is an *accelerated* economy. As a September 1996 *Globe and Mail* editorial quipped, when information goes faster, it changes form and function. The editorial cited a simple phone book as an example. It's a mundane collection of basic personal data: names and numbers. But in digital form — on CD-ROM, for instance — it's possible to access every U.S. and Canadian telephone directory. By typing someone's name you can obtain their street address and telephone number. The digital directory also works in reverse: type in a telephone number and you'll get the name of the person to whom it belongs, as well as their address. There's more. The CD-ROM tells you the names and numbers of a person's next-door neighbours, or of everyone with a given postal code. Now, cross-reference this information with another database, say that of consumer purchase habits or medical information, and you get the picture.

Third, we're witnessing a general blurring of the lines between the public and private sectors. The trend toward government downsizing and increased contracting out of government functions to the private sector means the release of personal information held by the public sector. More matching of public and private sector information — such as the linking of data on welfare recipients with bank or financial information in order to ascertain their eligibility — narrows the gap. Detailed personal information is increasingly held up, at least potentially, for public scrutiny.

Fourth, surveillance capabilities that would make James Bond proud have moved from the military to the marketplace. Consider these examples discussed at the September 1995 Advanced Surveillance Technologies Conference in Copenhagen. A staggering 90 percent of British towns have or are in the process of implementing closed circuit television monitoring systems (CCTV) in public spaces. British Telecom (BT) is exporting a technology that permits switching on a phone line from a central location in order to overhear what's happening in the vicinity of a selected telephone. Many countries around the world are developing "Intelligent Transportation Systems": computer and communications systems that monitor and manage road traffic. Some car rental companies have installed global positioning systems in their cars. Satellite technology can be similarly used. Local cellular systems and other new personal communications systems can track phone locations using conventional radio and microwave technology. Olivetti's "Active Badge" marks a person's location in a building and records when and where she was last observed. Bellcore's "Cruiser" and Xerox EuroParc's "Rave" include audio-visual features. Finally, Steve Wright predicts that "biometric systems," which measure such organic features as retina configuration, will structure the next wave of surveillance methods.

What does all this mean for businesses? First, they need to protect their own data from leaks, hacking, or illegal search and seizure. Second, they need to think about the privacy concerns of their employees, and how workplace surveillance will affect overall production. Third, companies need to respond to their customers' fears about how personal information is being used and abused. In this chapter we treat each of these themes before presenting the legislative framework for privacy protection in Canada and the U.S.

What's All the Fuss About?

Here we present concrete examples of privacy issues on the use of new information technology in a business context. We treat two broad categories of concern: workplace and consumer privacy. Issues related to the security of electronic information as it's transferred through cyberspace are treated separately in the next chapter.

Workplace Privacy

What privacy concerns really arise in the workplace? Our focus here is on the potential for privacy abuse, not "typical" employee experiences.

Electronic Mail Systems (E-Mail)

E-mail has found its way into the everyday life of North American business. E-mail systems now incorporate information in a variety of forms, including typed memos, spreadsheets, photographs, video clips, and bar codes. Inexpensive and efficient, many of its virtues take on a more sinister aspect when examined from the worker privacy perspective. As mentioned in Chapter 2, unless it's protected by encryption and elaborate password systems an e-mail message has the same security level as a postcard. That is, anyone who happens upon electronic mail may read it. Moreover, by following the electronic trail that e-mail creates employers may monitor individual employees' correspondence, even after such mail has been "deleted."

A survey of U.S. managers indicated that the searching of e-mail files is one of the most frequently used forms of employee monitoring. In February 1996, the Society for Human Resources Management (SHRM) reported that 36 percent of U.S. organizations with e-mail access their employee e-mail records for business necessity or security reasons; 7.7 percent do random reviews of employee e-mail; and 70 percent said that an employer should retain the right to read anything contained in a company-owned electronic communication system. The Epson and Pillsbury cases (discussed in the "Recent Case Law" box on page 77) were litigated in this context.

Voice Mail Systems

Voice mail is an electronic telephone messaging service that allows for non-simultaneous voice communication between two or more individuals. Most public organizations now use it. Though its advantages are many and well-known, insecure systems or improper implementation can lead to privacy breaches similar to those related to e-mail. A 1995 *New York Times* study found that over 27 percent of managers regularly scan employees' voice mail. The technique has led to U.S. litigation. For example, a former McDonald's restaurant employee filed a $1-million lawsuit against his employer. Voice mail messages indicating that the married employee was having an affair were accessed by his employer, who played them back to the employee's wife and others. And Ontario privacy commissioner Tom Wright provides this amusing anecdote: when a Manitoba lawyer attempted to call a government employee, he overheard a passionate voice mail message from the employee's lover instead!

Computer Networks and the Internet

Most network software packages contain features that allow system administrators to monitor such things as how many pages you've printed, what files you've copied, and when you logged on. Some packages, such as Novell's NetWare, even let administrators remotely access files on your computer — without you knowing about it. Others monitor employees' keystroke rate. Moreover, sophisticated software makes it simple to monitor the basic content of employees' files, including e-mail, by gleaning such key words as "résumé" or "sex." Similarly, programs such as Net Access Manager, WebTrack, and Internet WatchDog enable employers to secretly monitor what their employees are doing online — including the Web sites they visit, how much time they spend there, and the types of files they download. As we'll see later in the chapter, many of these techniques may be illegal under the U.S. *Electronic Communications Privacy Act* (*ECPA*) and analogous Canadian legislation.

Consumer Privacy

Modern North American mobile lifestyles bring us into contact with people who may not know us personally, except through the personal information we provide about ourselves. The collection of and trade in personal information has become commonplace and lucrative. Here we discuss briefly the privacy concerns that many consumers share, largely resulting from the use of new information technology.

Credit Reporting

Credit reporting is hardly a new phenomenon; what is new is that computer technology permits the collection and transfer of data at a hitherto unheard-of scale. Recent surveys show that U.S. credit bureaus hold more than five billion records.[2] On average, they trade information on each American citizen five times daily. They contain data on consumers' credit cards, loans, payment histories, bankruptcy liens and judgments, past addresses, years of birth, and social security numbers. Moreover, they routinely sell this information, as mailing lists, to direct marketers. This alone troubles many consumers, but it becomes more frightening when one realizes that such information may well be inaccurate. One New York credit bureau, Consolidated Information Service, found errors in 43 percent of their files: reason enough for businesses to avoid using disreputable credit bureaus.

In Canada, the largest credit reporting agencies — e.g. Equifax and the Canadian Banker's Association (CBA) — have adopted voluntary privacy codes that address consumers' most pressing concerns. These agencies have served as a model for many businesses in gaining their customers' trust and assuaging fears related to privacy matters.

Transactional Data and Personal Profiling

The staggering expansion of computer data storage capacity, the linking of businesses by electronic payment systems, and the integration of sales and ordering databases have revolutionized manufacturing and marketing processes. With EDI, producers manufacture and ship goods to warehouses, suppliers, and even retailers in direct response to their clients' sales. Linking an individual to a particular purchase is merely one segment of the chain, and facilitates direct marketing and market analysis. The Industry Canada publication *Privacy and the Canadian Information Highway* notes that "in the new networked environment, every business — large or small, reliable or not — will have the capacity to generate information files on its customers or to purchase customer databases from other sources." The information highway holds enormous potential to compile profiles of individuals' needs, lifestyle habits, and purchase choices. Provision of such new services as video on demand, electronic magazines, and catalogue services permits the collection of an ever wider range of information about a person's interests. It's already possible to track the e-mail addresses, home addresses, and newsgroups

The information highway holds enormous potential to compile profiles of individuals' needs, lifestyle habits, and purchase choices.

in which an individual participates, as well as the Web sites that have information related to that individual. According to some reports, over 10 000 U.S. lists of data about people are now available for rent.[3] The message for business using these lists is that it's always prudent to first investigate their accuracy and their origins.

Caller Identification

Caller ID displays incoming telephone numbers on certain types of telephones. It even displays unlisted telephone numbers. And when combined with telephone directory database systems it provides the caller's home address, leading the way to junk mail and telemarketing. Finally, when linked to record retrieval technology, caller ID can signal a computer to retrieve automated records associated with the displayed number at the moment an employee picks up the telephone. This kind of technology is troubling for many consumers, since the automated record retrieval systems may call forth personal information not necessary to the consumer's call.

Smart Cards

New "smart card" technologies that use embedded computer chips are replacing the magnetic strips currently used on credit cards and pass keys. Detailed information, a photo, or even data linked to a biometric identifier such as a thumbprint or retinal scan can be encoded on a person's card. More and more financial institutions are considering the use of "cash" smart cards. These electronically store the value of cash authorized by a bank ATM machine. Although they're promoted as being privacy-friendly, anonymous, and cash-like by companies such as Mondex, privacy expert Simon Davis charges that the card's computer chip contains a full audit trail of all transactions, potentially available not only to the consumer but also to retailers and financial institutions. As an Industry Canada publication comments, "With the current rates of fraud in card-based authorization systems — be they credit, phone, or medical benefits cards — there is a growing pressure to move to a more reliable system of identification. Privacy advocates, however, fear the potential of such cards to facilitate unacceptable levels of data matching."[4] Unauthorized access to and use of the information stored on such cards entails the leaching of enormous quantities of personal information.

Single Identifier Numbers

In 1990 Lotus Corporation announced plans to use credit-bureau files to create a personal computer database containing the names, addresses, demographic information, and purchasing habits of 120 million consumers. The product was abandoned after the company received 30 000 letters of complaint. But the service's allure appears too great to pass up. Lexis-Nexis, a well-established research firm used by corporations and individuals nationwide, advised its subscribers in June 1996 of a new product — P-TRAK Person Locator file — that "puts 300 million names right at your fingertips." It's "a quick, convenient search [that] provides up to three addresses, as well as aliases, maiden names, and Social Security numbers."[5]

The use of such single identifier numbers as the social insurance or social security number (SIN and SSN) allows for great precision in linking various database resources. This permits, among other things, the establishment of detailed personal profiles. Although legislation prevents government institutions from publicly disseminating information gathered in association with one's SIN and SSN, this isn't the case in the private sector.

Intrusion

Finally, disturbances or intrusions by telemarketers or targeted advertising mail is a privacy nuisance that concerns many Canadians. For instance, Canadians deemed automatic dialling-announcing devices (ADADs), used for commercial solicitation, sufficiently invasive and annoying that the CRTC banned their use in Canada. Still, "junk e-mail" has now joined the ubiquitous "junk mail" and "junk fax." The Canadian Direct Marketing Association (CDMA) estimates that direct-response marketing currently generates $11 billion in sales in Canada. Erik Larson, author of *The Naked Consumer*, discovered that 63.7 billion pieces of junk mail were sent from the companies he studied — making America the most "junk-filled" country on the planet!

The privacy issue is ultimately one of balance: to be able to exploit the efficiency gains of the information economy on the one hand while respecting cherished individual privacy on the other. We next discuss why respecting public privacy concerns makes good business sense.

The Benefits of Respecting Public Privacy Concerns

Consumer Confidence

Business must reassure consumers that the information they send over the Internet to vendors while browsing, inquiring about, and purchasing products will be securely transmitted, received, and stored — and that such information won't then be used to violate their privacy. The CDMA has recognized the importance of consumer confidence in the commercial use of personal information. It was the first industry group to recommend national legislation protecting personal information. Its May 1996 communiqué said:

> Every Canadian is entitled to fundamental protection of their personal information. And the CDMA believes legislation is the most effective means of ensuring all private sector organizations adhere to the same basic set of rules in handling this information. . . .
>
> Consumer confidence is essential to the success of Canadian business. That's why we see this kind of legislation very much in everyone's interest.

More recently, the CDMA has recommended the protection of consumer privacy concerns in cyberspace as well.

Improved Customer Service

Identifying and meeting customers' needs and expectations is a central imperative of today's business environment. Without accurate information about their customers businesses can't effectively focus their efforts, time, or resources. Failure is costly and inefficient. The adoption of privacy protection practices can assist businesses to concentrate resources and improve the quality of their customer services. Pierrot Paladeau, a Quebec privacy advocate, lawyer, and business consultant, reports that companies he's worked with have saved hundreds of thousands of dollars by introducing privacy-protective measures.[6] These companies had spent thousands of hours each year collecting, compiling, storing, and reading information that was unneeded and never used.

Moreover, as Tom Wright notes, the most reliable source of information about the customer is the customer. Privacy protection practices emphasize the involvement of customers in the compilation and management of their information. Customers indicate their own preferences, thereby allowing businesses to respond effectively and efficiently to their needs. By recognizing the customer as a valuable source of information to be respected and protected, businesses can market their products or services only to those who've indicated receptiveness to such information. This focuses resources and improves the quality of customer service, since it avoids alienating customers who don't want to participate in direct marketing schemes. In this sense, two of the leading privacy principles — accuracy and consent — serve business interests effectively, even as they protect the public.

Employee Satisfaction

Why should businesses care about employee privacy concerns? First is the issue of trust discussed in Chapter 3. New business processes emphasize teamwork, whose potential can only be realized if employees are willing to contribute fully to corporate productivity. Capable, motivated, and loyal employees are crucial to business success. In *Workplace Privacy*, Tom Wright observes that "when invasions of privacy occur, employees often feel that self-worth, morale, and the over-all quality of working life are eroded. The ensuing negative impact of invasions of privacy on work quality and productivity is hidden human and real costs (e.g. absenteeism and employees' compensation claims), not often calculated by employers."[7]

Moreover, many technological means of monitoring employee productivity pose problems related to accuracy and efficacy. Counting keystrokes will uncover little or nothing about the *quality* of the employee's work, for instance.

An overwhelming number of techniques are deployed to watch, quantify, and assess employees' work. Businesses must ask whether these techniques really improve services, productivity, and employee loyalty. Businesses can help avoid unnecessary employee resentment and mishap by establishing, in conjunction with employees, clear policies for the appropriate use of e-mail, voice mail, and Internet capabilities.

Avoiding Legal Sanctions

The worst case scenario is this. A corporation violates privacy rights and is sued. Litigation, even when successful, is costly. In Canada such actions are rare to date, but as we've seen they're increasingly frequent in the U.S. Virtually all Canadian privacy litigation heralds from Quebec, the only province with private sector privacy legislation.

Despite the relative paucity of Canadian litigation, the boy scout motto "Be prepared" nonetheless applies. Privacy concerns are on the rise. More and more, companies will have to account for how they've protected information. As Toronto lawyer Duncan Card wrote in 1995, this means checking internal protocol regarding employees' levels of access to other employees' files (especially medical or social security records), addressing e-mail privacy concerns, and educating employees to sensitize them to security issues. While businesses must know about and comply with all existing privacy laws, they should also anticipate how the law is evolving. To these two points we now turn.

The Current Legal Framework

Here we address the current regulatory and legislative climate for privacy in the U.S. and Canada.

Constitutional Privacy Protection

The Canadian *Charter of Rights and Freedoms* — like the U.S. *Bill of Rights* — doesn't guarantee the right to privacy, except indirectly through such provisions as the protection from unwarranted search and seizure. Two other judicially determined constitutional rights warrant mention here. First, the right to conduct some forms of speech activity anonymously has been upheld by the U.S. Supreme Court in *Talley v. California*. This decision is significant for cyberspace, since a high percentage of Internet communications take place anonymously or through pseudonyms.

Recent Case Law

Consider the following sampling from recent U.S. case law of businesses battling privacy issues in court:

In 1990 the U.S. Secret Service thought they had finally tracked down a notorious group of computer hackers. They were mistaken. They raided the offices of an Austin, Texas, role-playing games publisher called Steve Jackson Games. The Secret Service seized several computers, including those operating "Illuminati," the company's BBS. Hundreds of users had been actively posting materials on Illuminati when it was shut down. During the course of the investigation, a secret service official individually opened and deleted all the electronic mail stored on the system.

What protection did Steve Jackson and his clients have against this improper seizure? What compensation could they claim for this privacy breach? Was it a breach of privacy? Was the electronic mail *private*? To what legislation could they turn? These issues came to trial in 1993.

The plaintiffs — Jackson, his company, and three of his clients — claimed that by seizing the Illuminati BBS and opening the electronic mail stored on its hard drive, the Secret Service violated both the *Electronic Communications Privacy Act (ECPA)* and the *Privacy Protection Act (PPA)*, notably the former Act's prohibition against the interception and disclosure of private electronic communications. The trial judge decided for the plaintiffs. The Secret Service had violated both laws. They had improperly seized and disclosed private electronic communication. Jackson's company was awarded over $50,000 for lost sales under the *PPA*. Moreover, Judge Sparks found that each plaintiff was entitled to $1000 in damages under the *ECPA*, though he rejected the contention that the electronic mail had been "intercepted."

Jackson appealed this last point, insisting that the e-mail had been "intercepted" according to the *ECPA*. The Court of Appeal disagreed. They found that e-mail stored on a computer was like a conversation stored on a cassette tape. Accordingly, they affirmed the trial judge's decision on this point, concluding that Congress did not intend for "intercept" to apply to "electronic communications" when those communications are in "electronic storage."

Now two examples of workplace privacy litigation. In 1989 Epson employee Alana Shoars found printouts of two months worth of electronic mail messages sent to or from her office. She claimed that the company had inappropriately monitored her private communications, and filed a class action suit for her and her colleagues. Was the e-mail on the company computer system "private correspondence"? Was the interception and printing of the electronic mail analogous to wiretapping? The state court thought not. It ruled that e-mail wasn't covered by California's wiretapping statute and that the California Constitution's right to privacy provision didn't cover business information.

Second, in early 1996, executives at Pillsbury fired a manager after finding a printout of an e-mail message in which the manager criticized several of his supervisors. He called them "back-stabbing bastards!" The Pennsylvania District Court, in *Michael A. Smyth v. The Pillsbury Company*, upheld the company's right to read all the manager's other e-mail, despite the fact that Pillsbury had assured its employees that their e-mail was confidential.

Finally, a case of consumer-led privacy litigation. In 1996, a Virginia resident, Ram Avrahami, filed a suit in state court against *US News & World Report*. He challenged the right of the magazine to sell or rent his name to another publication without his express written consent. Mr. Avrahami claimed that the magazine benefited commercially from his name, thus violating the Virginia Code which protects every person from having his or her name used for commercial purpose without consent. Avrahami lost at trial, but the case is on appeal. American privacy advocates are using the matter as a test case, and are helping to cover Avrahami's legal expenses. The case raises a critical question for the future of the privacy debate: who has the right to control personal information?

Second, in *Gibson v. FLIC*, the U.S. Supreme Court upheld the right of the NAACP to protect its membership list from government scrutiny on the basis of the constitutional right of association. Cavazos and Morin argue that this decision might provide constitutional protection against government seizure of mailing lists and bulletin board user lists. Note, however, that constitutional protection doesn't apply to communication between private individuals; rather, it protects us from the abuse of government powers.

Canadian Legislation

In Canada, only Quebec has comprehensive privacy legislation. The Quebec Charter of Rights and Freedoms protects individual privacy,[8] and is backed by the provisions of the Civil Code, which protect privacy in general (even the privacy of companies), as well as two specific privacy laws that treat individual privacy concerns in the private and public sectors respectively. In 1994, Quebec's *Act Respecting the Protection of Personal Information in the Private Sector*[9] came into effect. Unique in North America, the law offers a comprehensive data protection scheme for the private sphere, thus complementing and completing the public sector privacy act, an *Act Respecting Access to Documents Held By Public Bodies and the Protection of Personal Information*,[10] which came into effect in 1982. The new legislation applies to any private enterprises conducting business in Quebec involving the gathering, use, and communication of personal information. It's loosely based on the OECD principles discussed below. Strongly resisted by the business community, the law was significantly modified before adoption so as to acknowledge common commercial practices. Although not without its detractors, it's been received with general approval.[11]

To date, complaints heard by the Commission de l'acces a l'information, the agency that oversees the application of both public and private sector legislation in Quebec, have focused on two main areas: overzealous requests for personal information by small businesses such as video stores and landlords, and the use by financial institutions of standard form contracts that include "consent" provisions authorizing extensive investigations of credit reliability. Although the law permits fines of up to $20 000 for infractions, the Commission has thus far taken an educational stance regarding infractions of the new law. Commission president Paul-André Comeau reports that commercial enterprises have been very cooperative in implementing the new legislation. Multinational corporations and financial institutions, for instance, quickly developed measures to comply.

The rest of Canada treats privacy in a piecemeal fashion. The federal government and four common law provinces — Ontario, Saskatchewan, Alberta, and British Columbia — have privacy legislation covering the public sector; none have specific private sector protection. Instead, federal legislation treats privacy issues on a sectoral basis: the *Telecommunications Act* has provisions to protect the privacy of individuals, including the regulation of unsolicited communications; amendments to the *Criminal Code* make it a criminal offence to intercept private communications and to cause "mischief" to electronic data; the *Radiocommunication Act* now forbids the divulgence of intercepted radio-based telephone communications; and the new *Bank Act*, *Insurance Companies Act*, and *Trust and Loan Companies Act* permit regulations governing the use of information provided by customers. In addition, all English-speaking provinces except New Brunswick and Alberta have some form of legislation protecting consumer credit.

U.S. Legislation

The *Electronic Communications Privacy Act (ECPA)* is the most important American statute dealing with privacy as it relates to electronic commerce. Originally the Act focused on wiretaps, but in 1986 it was broadened to include digital communications. In general, the *ECPA* makes it illegal to intercept or disclose private communications. It provides victims of such conduct a right to sue anyone violating its mandate. Any government agent, business, or individual violates the law if he:

- does or tries to intentionally intercept any electronic communication; or
- intentionally uses or discloses the contents of any electronic commu-

nication, knowing or having reason to know that the information was obtained through the interception of an electronic communication in violation of the ECPA.[12]

The strength of this provision will depend in large measure on how courts interpret the word "interception." The statute itself defines it broadly as meaning "the aural or other acquisition of the contents of any wire, electronic, or oral communication through the use of any electronic, mechanical, or other device." As some commentators have noted, however, courts have already narrowed the application of the provision.[13] For instance, one court held that the act of interception must occur at the moment of the transmission of the communication. Thus in *Jackson Games,* discussed above, the Court decided that the U.S. Secret Service hadn't "intercepted" the e-mail stored on the seized computers.

The *ECPA* treats *stored* electronic communications; its main target is hackers. Thus, it's illegal to:

- intentionally access without authorization a facility through which an electronic communication service is provided; or
- intentionally exceed an authorization to access a facility; and thereby obtain, alter, or prevent authorized access to an electronic communication while it is in electronic storage in such a system.[14]

Cavazos and Morin succinctly summarize the sorts of violations that are likely covered by the Act:[15]

EPCA prohibitions	Examples of violations
Interception of electronic communication	• keystroke monitoriing • tapping a data line • rerouting an electronic communication to provide contemporaneous acquisition
Unauthorized access to electronic communication service	• obtaining an account through "hacking" • using inadvertently granted authority to read or alter other people's e-mail

	• using a bug or other system flaw to read other user's private messages • preventing others from accessing their stored private messages
Disclosure of electronic communications	• divulging the contents of e-mail to which you were not a party

Secondly, the *Privacy Protection Act (PPA)* forces government agents to obtain a subpoena, rather than a simple search warrant, before they can search for or seize documents that are related to the dissemination of information to the public. The subpoena allows the publisher to cooperate in an investigation, to avoid unnecessary disruption of publication, and to challenge the request for documents *before* they're taken. The *PPA* evidently applies to electronic publishing, since the trial judge based the bulk of his award to the plaintiffs in *Jackson Games* on the Secret Service's violation of this law.

Common Law Actions

William Prosser identified four grounds of legal action for breaches of privacy in a classic 1960 U.S. article: intrusion into one's private affairs, public disclosure of private facts, appropriation of one's personality, and publicity that places the plaintiff in a false light in the public eye. Because analogous common law on privacy concerns is underdeveloped in Canada, and because the established legal tests for such torts are demanding, the common law is unlikely to provide reliable recourse for Canadians who believe that businesses have used new information technology to abuse their privacy rights. We treat plausible developments in Canadian privacy common law in *Getting Canada Online*.

European Privacy Protection

While the North American approach to privacy protection typically leaves private sector data protection to market forces, Europeans have enacted legislation requiring both private and public sector organizations to abide by the same data protection principles. The first attempt at harmonizing European data protection laws was the Organization for

Economic Co-operation and Development's (OECD) 1980 *Guidelines on the Protection of Privacy and Trans-border Flows of Personal Data.* Canada and the U.S. are signatories. The OECD Guidelines establish ten basic principles for privacy protection. They undergird the vast majority of privacy protection schemes throughout the world, including the Quebec private sector privacy law, the CDMA and Canadian Businesses Association (CBA) codes, and the Canadian Standards Association (CSA) Model Code. The Guidelines are voluntary, and carry no force of law. Consequently they've been applied with varying degrees of assiduousness.

A number of industry associations and businesses have instituted voluntary privacy codes, also loosely based on the OECD Guidelines. The CDMA, the CBA, and Stentor have each issued privacy codes for their members. The independent Canadian Cable Television Standards Council administers privacy principles as part of the cable industry's general standards. Such codes are purely voluntary and carry no legal force.

The Future of the Framework

As most major corporate players realise, now is the time to address privacy issues and not when forced by litigation or government regulation. New information technology is revolutionizing the way North Americans do business. If privacy policies aren't integrated into employee training and the manner in which such technology is used at the planning and design stage, the results will assuredly be costly down the road.

Given the public concern over privacy issues and the rapid evolution of the information economy, business should prepare now for comprehensive privacy legislation in Canada. Both the CDMA and Canadian privacy commissioner Bruce Phillips propose that such legislation is necessary. Why? Here we use the Canadian situation as a case study for the likely evolution of North American privacy legislation generally.

Voluntary Codes Deemed Inadequate

As mentioned above, a number of companies have voluntarily developed their own privacy codes. Privacy advocates argue, however, that these codes fail to protect consumer interests adequately. A Public Interest Advocacy Centre study of voluntary codes in Canada, for instance, found that such codes suffered from the following problems: a conflict of

If privacy policies aren't integrated into employee training and the manner in which such technology is used at the planning and design stage, the results will assuredly be costly down the road.

interest in under-inclusion of consumers in the code development and code administration process; inadequate code coverage; low consumer awareness of issues and of code provisions; lack of adequate sanctions; general lack of systematic procedures to measure or monitor compliance; and evidence of low levels of compliance with the code.

Tom Wright, the Ontario Information and Privacy Commissioner, suggests that a legislative model based on self-regulation through sectoral codes of practice in conjunction with an independent oversight agency is a viable model. This viewpoint is echoed in the 1995 final report of IHAC: "While voluntary standards are useful for engaging business in the protection of personal information, there remains the need for effective, independent oversight and for all parties to have the same rules."

Call for a Level Playing Field

In response to its report "Privacy and the Canadian Information Highway," Industry Canada found across-the-board concern about the current patchwork of federal/provincial legislation and regulations on privacy. This led to an almost unanimous call for a "level playing field" wherein data protection exigencies are standardized and consistently enforced in Canada. The problem with the current situation is that it creates inconsistent burdens on business and unequal privacy protection from jurisdiction to jurisdiction. Moreover, some business organizations may achieve discriminatory and unfair marketing advantages. For instance, a failure to create a level playing field could lead to the creation of "data havens," whereby the most lenient jurisdictions may attract businesses that seek to evade privacy protection measures. Also, artificial legal distinctions must be made about where data is "located" when it travels the information highway.

National and International Legal Developments

National and international legal developments are also creating incentives for Canadian businesses to address privacy issues. In Canada there's a "pull" from two sources. First, the Quebec experiment with private sector privacy legislation, with the odd caveat, has been successful. Second, in a collaborative effort involving members of government, consumer and privacy organizations, and business leaders, the CSA developed a Model Code for privacy, finalized in March 1996 and discussed below, that has met with almost unanimous approval.

Moreover, recent international developments provide new privacy legislation "push." In response to the perceived inadequacies of the OECD Guidelines and subsequent attempts at giving bite and uniformity to the application of basic privacy protection principles, in July 1995 the European Union formally adopted a *Directive on the Protection of Personal Data and on the Free Movement of Such Data.*[16] It prohibits the trans-border flow of personal information to countries without adequate protection. The initial draft of the Directive, when circulated, increased pressure to strengthen private sector data protection throughout North America.

How Business Can Address Privacy Concerns

Businesses must address privacy concerns now, at the nascent stage of the implementation of new information technology in their commercial practices. We suggest that businesses conduct a "privacy audit" of their operations and then act upon perceived deficiencies. What personal information is being collected about customers and employees? By what means? With what level of consent? With what assurances of accuracy and secure storage? Accessible to whom? Is this information necessary?

Is the manner in which it's collected respectful of employee and consumer privacy concerns?

To help businesses address such concerns, we summarize the ten privacy principles developed in the CSA *Model Code for the Protection of Personal Information* (see below).[17] The principles recall those developed by the OECD in 1980, the basis for virtually all subsequent privacy legislation. The CSA Model Code will, in turn, influence new privacy legislation in English Canada. For instance, the IHAC report recommended that "the federal government should act to ensure privacy protection on the Information Highway. This protection shall embody all principles contained in the CSA draft [now final] *Model Code for the Protection of Personal Information*."[18] By becoming aware of and responding to these principles now, business will go a long way toward addressing the privacy concerns that stem from the commercial use of new information technology.

CSA *Model Code for the Protection of Personal Information*

1. **Accountability**
   An organization is responsible for personal information under its control and shall designate an individual or individuals who are accountable for the organization's compliance with the following principles.
2. **Identifying Purposes**
   The purposes for which personal information is collected shall be identified by the organization at or before the time the information is collected.
3. **Consent**
   The knowledge and consent of the individual are required for the collection, use, or disclosure of personal information, except where inappropriate.
4. **Limiting Collection**
   The collection of personal information shall be limited to that which is necessary for the purposes identified by the organization. Information shall be collected by fair and lawful means.
5. **Limiting, Use, Disclosure, and Retention**
   Personal information shall be limited to that which is necessary for the purposes identified by the organization. Information shall be collected by fair and lawful means.

6. **Accuracy**
   Personal information shall be as accurate, complete, and up-to-date as is necessary for the purpose for which it is used.
7. **Safeguards**
   Personal information shall be protected by security safeguards appropriate to the sensitivity of the information.
8. **Openness**
   An organization shall make readily available to individuals specific information about its policies and practices relating to the management of personal information.
9. **Individual Access**
   Upon request, an individual shall be informed of the existence, use, and disclosure of his or her personal information and shall be given access to that information. An individual shall be able to challenge the accuracy and completeness of the information and have it amended as appropriate.
10. **Challenging Compliance**
   An individual shall be able to address a challenge concerning compliance with the above principles to the designated individual or individuals accountable for the organization's compliance.

Conclusion

Personal information about consumers and employees is an essential and lucrative commodity. It's one that must not be abused, however. Businesses must move quickly to recognize and embrace their obligations to respect individual privacy. They must start to see privacy protection as an integral and necessary part of doing business, just as twenty years ago business began seeing environmental protection as integral to its concerns. Finally, businesses should recognize their customers and employees as owners of their personal information, to be consulted in the development of policies or practices that could potentially impact on customer privacy.

5 SECURITY

INTRODUCTION

No one feels fully secure in cyberspace. Public awareness of computer crime has been heightened, for better or worse, by movies, television, and books glamorizing high technology. The potential for fraud is perceived to be great in a computerized environment, and it is this fear, rational or not, that chills cyberspace commerce.

Computer crime is a broad term, applying to many forms of computer abuse that constitute recognized criminal offences. A non-exhaustive list includes:

- unauthorized access or use of a computer, service, or data
- unauthorized reproduction of a computer program or data
- manipulation or alteration of data, programs, or a computer system's hardware
- spreading a computer virus
- misappropriation of information via a computer or telecommunications system.

While "cyberspace security" covers a wide range of activities from hacking to cryptography, here we limit ourselves to a discussion of

> **CREDIT CARD FRAUD**
> The U.S. National Research Council estimates that credit card fraud averages $20 per card each year. It's feared that this number will rise dramatically should these transactions gain wide use in cyberspace. Credit card companies are currently reluctant to authorize merchants to accept cyber-transactions.[1]

commercial transaction security. Other forms of computer crime do affect business, e.g. hacking into a business' computerized accounting system. But it's the topic of commercial transaction security with which the public is least familiar — and the most exposed.

What business chiefly needs to flourish in cyberspace are secure, efficient, and effective methods to conduct commercial transactions. Only when technology allows for secure transactions will business shift confidently into cyberspace. Yet while technological solutions will go some distance toward solving these problems, they must be underpinned by laws. Seismic technological shifts have caught legislators, judges, and lawyers by surprise. We live in an information age, yet an examination of existing laws yields a different version of reality.

While law may lag, business advances. Indeed, it's business that frequently drives technological innovation and gives impetus to legislation.

Because of cyberspace's global, multi-jurisdictional structure, national legislation by itself will not achieve the desired results. Business must adapt to cyberspace, rather than vice-versa.

But business is a relative newcomer to cyberspace, whose standards and conventions have evolved independently of commercial concerns. Because of cyberspace's global, multi-jurisdictional structure, national legislation by itself will not achieve the desired results. Business must adapt to cyberspace, rather than vice-versa.

We identify three principles as being crucial to the successful adaptation of electronic commerce to the Internet. Information must be communicable:

- without fear of third-party alteration ("alteration")
- in such a manner that it can't be read by third parties ("interception")
- so that the recipient is assured of the sender's identity ("authentication").

We use these three principles as the framework to discuss issues of security, and the technological and legal responses to them. We'll examine public key infrastructure (PKI), a system for the publication and distribution of cryptographic keys. In our opinion, this new technological-legal proposal is currently the best hope for promoting and securing a favourable climate for business transactions in cyberspace.

E-MAIL TIP

The February 19, 1997 *Globe and Mail* published the following tip: "Oxford University has developed a widely emulated Code of Practice for its E-mail messages. Among the guidelines: 'Create E-mail messages with the same care you do formal and informal written business correspondence. Remember, your E-mail message can end up in the hands of people other than the intended recipient.'"

PREVENTING ALTERATION

To alter a message in cyberspace is relatively simple. It may be done purposely, or it may "just happen" due to equipment failure or carriageway "noise." The Internet's "complex neurology" and its packet-based communication system render messages particularly susceptible to alteration. For a message to travel on the Internet it must be broken down into packets, or small chunks. These travel from computer to computer until they reach the intended destination, where they're reassembled into the original message. Alteration of the message can occur at each computer responsible for forwarding a packet. And if there are damages to or electromagnetic interference on the transmission lines, some of the 0's and 1's constituting the message may also be altered, resulting in a garbled final reconstruction.

Technological prevention of message alteration involves some mathematical wizardry. One technique currently employed is called *hashing*. A hash is a mathematical result, i.e. a number, that's calculated using each message's contents. Often represented as a long set of numbers, the hash is unique to each set of information, e.g. a typed document, and is communicated with the message. If, upon receipt, the recipient computer applying the same mathematical hashing algorithm fails to achieve the same mathematical result, then the message has been altered. The mathematical litmus test of truth has failed.

Canada

Preventing alteration doesn't lie solely within technology's domain; existing legal controls also constrain this behaviour. The computer and telecommunication crime sections in the Canadian *Criminal Code* are relatively new (1985), and target specific behaviour. Section 430(1.1) creates the offence of willful mischief in relation to computer data and computer programs. It specifically proscribes:

- the destruction or alteration of data
- rendering data meaningless, useless, or ineffective

THE CROWN'S CALL

In Canada, the federal Parliament has the power to create and classify offences in the *Criminal Code*. Prosecution is left up to the provincial Attorneys General. Criminal offences are categorized as summary or indictable (corresponding American terms are misdemeanor and felony, respectively). The choice of proceedings has a number of effects, including the trial and appeal procedures, the level of trial court, and the maximum penalties available at law. Some offences are known as "hybrid," meaning that the Crown prosecutor has an unfettered discretion to proceed either by way of indictment or on summary conviction.[2]

The *Code*'s Section 342.1 prohibits the unauthorized and fraudulent use of a computer system or computer service. Both provisions are hybrid offences, i.e. they can be prosecuted either by indictment or summarily. Both carry ten years maximum imprisonment for indictable offences or six months for summary convictions. To date, however, most offenders have received only fines, occasionally combined with community service and probation.

- the obstruction, interference, or interruption of data or programs; or
- of the persons using the data.

The U.S.

The U.S. has similar legislation enacted by both federal and state level governments. The federal *Computer Fraud and Abuse Act (CFAA)* is best known. It proscribes hacking-type offences. Based on the federal government's jurisdiction over interstate commerce, it's an offence to access, without authorization, government computers or those with financial information, or to traffic in passwords if it may lead to the former offence.

Another key piece of U.S. federal legislation is the *Electronic Communications Privacy Act (ECPA)* discussed in the previous chapter. That Act, although primarily concerned with privacy protection, makes it an offence to intercept or re-route electronic communications, to hack or use a computer or account without authorization, to access computerized information without authority, and to divulge electronic communications to which one was not a party. While the *ECPA* gives government agencies broad powers, it also provides for private rights of action against offending parties. Private persons may sue under the Act for damages, including punitive damages.

Other U.S. laws, such as the federal *Wire Fraud Act*, have also been used in prosecuting commercially related computer crime. In order to claim jurisdiction these federal statutes require some form of interstate activity. Meeting this test isn't as difficult as one might imagine. If the crime directly or indirectly causes an effect beyond a single state, then the law applies. Take stolen credit cards, for example. Where a purchase is made and the credit card issuer is contacted to approve the sale, if that call goes out of state then the federal statute (here the *Wire Fraud Act*) applies. This is especially relevant in cyberspace, where information may be routed out of state before it even crosses the street. Whether information transmission in cyberspace qualifies as interstate is unpredictable in any given case, but the U.S. federal government potentially has great powers in this environment. Recall too that in many states local legislation applies in much the same way as does federal legislation.

Given the technological and legislative protection available, electronic message alteration is of less concern than other security issues, such as interception.

Interception: Deterrence by Encryption

Cryptography protects information while it's stored or in transit. Derived from the Greek terms *krypto* (secret) and *graphos* (writing), cryptography is the science of rendering communications indecipherable by all but authorized parties. Its oldest form is a private key-based system, also known as symmetric cryptography. Here a mathematical algorithm — a series of number steps — is used in conjunction with a secret key that's known only to the people performing the encryption and decryption. The secret key operates as a variable in concert with the encryption algorithm, and is different for each set of users. The data comprising the

Secret Keys

Secret keys usually reside in encrypted form on a computer. Generally a pass phrase or password, known only to the key holder, is used to access them. Other access technologies are beginning to emerge, including hardware tokens, e.g. smart cards, and biometric tokens, e.g. retinal scans or thumbprints. These new devices may be used on their own or in combination.

information to be encrypted is then mathematically altered using the algorithm and key. The resulting data is useless to third parties, since it may be transmitted or stored without fear of others seeing or using it. To decrypt the data one simply applies the algorithm in reverse, using the secret key.

Developed in the 1970s, *asymmetric* cryptography is crucial to the operation of a PKI and cyber-commerce. Here the encrypting and decrypting keys are different, so that once the message is encrypted the encrypting key won't be able to decrypt the message. That's left to the other key, and vice versa. This mathematical trickery has spawned a system of public and secret key pairs, whereby a person can widely distribute his or her public key and keep its counterpart secret.

Someone sending encrypted information simply uses the public key (in conjunction with a computer program that supports the requisite encryption algorithm) to encrypt the message. The public key holder may then transmit or store the message for retrieval by the secret key holder, who decrypts the message with his or her secret key. The mathematical explanation for this operation is highly technical, and beyond this discussion.

The unauthorized interception of data is also proscribed by the following three criminal law measures:

Telecommunications Theft

The *Criminal Code*'s Section 326 targets theft of a telecommunications' service and unauthorized use of a telecommunications' facility. It defines "telecommunication" as:

> any transmission, emission or reception of signs, signals, writing, images, sounds or intelligence of any nature by radio, visual, electronic or other electromagnetic system.

This is sufficiently broad to cover theft of cable, telephone (wired and cellular), satellite, radio, and facsimile services. As with many high technology crimes, this is a hybrid offence. Where the value of what's stolen exceeds $1000, theft is an indictable offence; for lesser amounts, it may be prosecuted summarily or by way of indictment, at the prosecutor's discretion.

In *R. v. McLaughlin* the Supreme Court of Canada ruled in 1984 that a local area network couldn't be considered a telecommunications facility; rather it's a "computer service." This presumably applies to other computer networks such as the Internet. In response, Parliament amended the *Criminal Code* in 1985 to prohibit theft of computer services.

Electronic Communication Interception

The *Criminal Code* prohibits interception of a private communication,[3] which is defined as:

> any oral communication, or any telecommunication . . . and includes any radio-based telephone communication that is treated electronically or otherwise for the purpose of preventing intelligible reception by any person other than the person intended by the originator to receive it.

Note that the "inclusion" ensures that encrypted ("unintelligible") messages are protected by the prohibition. In addition to preventing surreptitious (i.e. without legal authorization, such as through a judge's warrant) wire tapping by government agencies, these laws also apply as between individuals. The maximum penalty is five years imprisonment.[4]

In the U.S. similar laws, including the *ECPA* and *CFAA* as well as state laws, protect persons from unauthorized interception of electronic communications.

Export/Import Control

Another set of U.S. laws pertinent to cryptography technology are import and export of arms regulations. Under the U.S. *International Traffic in Arms Regulations (ITAR)* and *Arms Export Controls Act (AECA)*, cryptography products are "munitions" and "defense articles." Accordingly, the U.S. State Department tightly controls their export. It justifies these restrictions as being necessary to ensure that encryption isn't used by terrorists, child pornographers, drug dealers, and spies. Other countries, e.g. France and China, limit the import and use of cryptographic products. Only the U.S. actively restricts their export.

Certain "exempted" encryption products, primarily software, may be exported, especially if their primary purpose is to ensure data integrity and not data encryption. Encryption formulae are rated secure according to the length of the key used. Exports of symmetric encryption products that employ 40-bit keys or less are permitted (five 12-bit keys for asymmetric encryption products). In August 1995 this was increased to 64-bit keys, providing that the newly allowed 24 bits of these keys are left in escrow with the U.S. government. And in certain cases the export of these products may fall under the control of the Commerce Department, which takes a more relaxed approach. Nevertheless, even this form of control has proven to be quite onerous and hotly debated.

Restricting the export of these products has severely hampered the U.S. cryptography industry and technology enhancement — and has crippled cyber-commerce development. So in March 1996 Congress was presented with a bill entitled the *Encryption Privacy Telecom Act*. It proposes a relaxation of many *ITAR* and *AECA* restrictions and encourages the development of a strong cryptography industry:

> The . . . Act . . . would enhance the global competitiveness of our high-technology industries, protect the high-paying good jobs in those industries and maximize the choices in encryption technology available for businesses and individuals to protect the privacy, confidentiality and security of their computer, telephone, and other wire and electronic communications.
>
> The guiding principle for this bill can be summed up in one sentence: Encryption is good for American business and good business for Americans.[5]

But this quote ignores the Bill's most far-reaching effect: to bring America and the world on board with cyber-commerce.

Authentication: Certification and Digital Signatures

Our final concern with securing electronic transactions is authentication: assuring the identity of the transaction's participants.[6] In cyberspace how do we know with whom we're dealing? Recall our custom-fit Levi's jeans example at the outset of the book. It's risky to simply accept purchase orders without knowing whether the senders are who they say they are. This difficulty already exists for conventional credit cards and cheques. Using signatures to verify the identity of the card holder and cheque writer is the most common way of assuring identity, as is the examination of other identity papers such as a driver's licence or passport. Similarly, cyberspace has adopted the "digital signatures" technique.

The purpose of a traditional handwritten signature is to associate a person with a signed document. Signatures provide evidence of this association. They also provide a sense of formality or ceremony, signifying the transaction's importance and the signer's approval. Signing a document also connotes a sense of finality: the signer intends to be bound without further changes to the document. Typically the law requires that a signature be a mark, with certain intended effects, made by a person. Signatures may or may not be required on paper; they may be electronic marks.

We should distinguish between "digital signatures" and simple "electronic signatures," for lack of a better term. Contrary to popular belief, "digital signatures" aren't electronic renderings (or bitmap, i.e. digital picture, representations) of written human signatures or human-made marks. The latter are "electronic signatures," and have proven to be of limited value in formalizing commercial activity in cyberspace. A faxed signature is an example of an electronic signature.

Digital signatures aren't singularly associated with the signer, as are electronic signatures. Rather, a digital signature varies both with the signer *and* with each document that's signed. A digital signature on document A signed by a user will be different from the digital signature on document B signed by the same user. We briefly set out below the procedure of digitally signing a document and verifying the signatory. It combines the techniques of hashing and public key cryptography previously discussed:

TABLE 1: CREATING A DIGITAL SIGNATURE

1. Begin with an electronic message.
2. Hash the message.
3. Take the resulting bytes (the result of the hash) and encrypt it with one's secret key.
4. The result is the signature.

TABLE 2: VERIFYING THE DIGITAL SIGNATURE

1. One must have the following information:
    - the signed document
    - the public key of the signatory
    - the algorithm used in hashing the document
    - the algorithm used in the asymmetric encryption of the key.
2. Decrypt the digital signature using the public key of the signatory.
3. This will provide the original hash result.
4. Rehash the document.
5. Compare the two hash values.
6. If the values are the same one knows that the document was signed by the person claiming to be the signatory.

But even with a digitally signed document uncertainty still exists as to who the sender was. Note that within step 1 of Table 2 the signatory's public key is required. *The method by which this public key is obtained is crucial to the transaction's security*. A's receipt of B's electronically sent public key followed by a signed document verifies only that a document was sent by someone. It gives no assurance as to B's identity.

To overcome this problem we need a system to certify the public key holder's identity. This requires a public key infrastructure (PKI). There are several secure ways of obtaining a public key while being assured of the identity of the person to whom it's attached: e.g. visiting a company's office and having a company representative provide the key in person, or seeing the key of a large well-known organization printed in a reputable newspaper. Both examples provide good assurance as to the key holder's identity. Of course this method of verification is generally impractical, especially where key verification is sought on a transaction basis. Since there's often little personal assurance as to the public key holder's identity, PKIs are needed on a global level.

The most common solution to the "identity problem" is to use a trusted third party, known as a certification authority (CA), to authenticate the key holders' identities. CAs are computerized databases that issue digital certificates, and may be run by government or the private sector. A *digital certificate* is nothing more than a computer record sent via a computer network, such as the Internet, to a requesting party. It contains, at the minimum, the certification authority's name, the name of the person being certified, and that person's public key. Each database may differ in the extent of information about its clientele that it chooses to hold. It might include such attributes as profession, age, colour of hair, etc. CAs employ various schemes to ensure their clientele's identity. For example, the U.S. company Verisign Inc. issues four classes of certificates according to the extent of its client identity assurance. Depending on the desired level of certification, this assurance may require mailing to Verisign copies of such identity documents as birth certificates, or even making a personal visit to the company.

This system of trusted third parties raises puzzling legal and technological questions. The legal issues are many. They include risk allocation in contractual disputes, reliance on digitally signed documents in tortious actions, and use of digitally signed documents as evidence in judicial proceedings. Technological issues involve such decisions as the structure of the hierarchy of trust (who can certify whom), the method of distributing certificates, the frequency of certificate updates, and the systems of revoking compromised keys.

An overarching concern is the certifier's trustworthiness. Why trust the CA? The answer has both legal and technological implications for the PKI system structure. At one extreme is the X.509 solution, whose standard to date has employed a relatively rigid hierarchical structure with certification flowing down a certification hierarchy or tree. Government is a likely top candidate for this system. At the other extreme is the grassroots Pretty Good Privacy (PGP) method, which is astructural. Its topology is flat; each person is trusted to certify him- or herself.

We'll examine the benefits and drawbacks of each of these methods. The choice of PKI will reflect the future structure of network commercial transactions — so policy should be made with caution.

Current PKI Approaches

This section contains highly technical and complex descriptions of existing PKI proposals. We set these out for those who are interested in these technologies. You may, however, comfortably skip to the next section, Legislative Proposals.

Although public key cryptography was invented in the mid-1970s the need for a PKI was only considered a decade later. Given the technology's novelty only a handful of PKI solutions have emerged — and even fewer have been implemented. In 1988 the International Telecommunications Union (ITU) described the first functional framework, known as the X.509 standard. In recent years, a public-key cryptography computer program known as Pretty Good Privacy (PGP) has gained widespread use. PGP and its PKI have nothing in common with any X.509 implementation. One is the antithesis of the other. Within the last year several other PKI approaches have been proposed, most notably the Simple Distributed Security Infrastructure (SDSI), the Simple Public Key Infrastructure (SPKI), and the X.509-based Public Key Infrastructure (PKIX).

Pretty Good Privacy (PGP)

PGP uses the simplest form of PKI, and was conceived as a simple way to encrypt and/or digitally sign electronic mail. PGP users maintain a list of all the keys of people with whom they correspond. They can use those keys to encrypt information for, and receive encrypted information from, those correspondents. Because the user maintains the list of keys, she has complete control over which keys she trusts. PGP also has a mechanism that lets the user delegate her trust to other keys, in effect saying "I trust the person associated with this key enough to let that person tell me if another's key is trustworthy."

In this way PGP defines a "web of trust" PKI. For example, if Alice trusts Bob and Bob trusts Carl, then Alice implicitly trusts Carl also. It's estimated that for a PGP web of trust to reach everyone in the world, these trust chains will be, on average, six to seven levels deep.[7] PGP's trust model requires no central trust authority, which makes it a popular Internet grassroots-level tool. But several shortcomings exist with this form of PKI, precluding it from widespread adoption as a standard for conducting electronic commerce.

First is the lack of any coherent mechanism for revoking PGP certificates. Since PGP eschews any central authority, there's no direct, automatic way of determining a certificate's current validity. This restricts PGP to a few hundred users before it becomes impractical and unmanageable.

Second is the simple nature of PGP certificates. A PGP certificate merely relates a public key to an e-mail address. No claims are made regarding the person behind the e-mail address. Nor are there any provisions for carrying further information, such as a key expiration date or credentials.

Third, PGP's popular trust model also has its limitations. Though Alice may trust Bob, when Bob trusts Carl he may define his trust differently than does Alice. So any keys that Alice receives from Carl (through Bob) may turn out to be unacceptable to Alice, even though Bob may find them perfectly suitable. This forces Alice to no longer trust Bob, not because Bob's unreliable but simply because they define their trust differently. Under this scenario, PGP's mechanism for delegating trust is ineffective. Its advantages are lost.

X.509

An X.509 PKI proceeds differently from that of a PGP. PGP's certificates are simple; X.509's are complex. PGP uses a flat model where each entity is its own ultimate authority; X.509 thrives in a rigid, hierarchical environment. X.509 has a workable, if imperfect, certificate revocation mechanism; PGP's is haphazard at best.

Digital White Pages

An X.500 directory can be thought of as a computerized White Pages, wherein every person, organization, and company has an entry describing public information about itself, e.g. phone numbers and addresses. Worldwide adoption of X.500 directories is hampered by the standard's complexity and by the readily available, although less sophisticated, Internet system of e-mail addresses and domain names.

In the 1980s the ITU proposed a worldwide computerized directory standard known as X.500. The X.509 standard was defined to allow X.500 directories to distribute public-key certificates. Early experience with X.509 revealed several shortcomings, now resolved. The current version 3 (or X.509v3) sets out a relatively more flexible PKI framework. There are no implementations yet using X.509v3.

Most PKI applications available today are based on the X.509 version 1 (V1) or version 2 (V2) standards. Netscape's famous Navigator Web browser uses X.509 (V1). Visa and MasterCard have recently proposed (but not yet implemented) the X.509v3-based Secure Electronic Transaction (SET) specification for Internet-based credit card transactions.

X.509 emphasizes the link between a public key and the identity of the person or entity who controls the corresponding secret key. Technologically, the responsibility for ensuring that the subject of a certificate is properly identified lies solely with the X.509 Certification Authority (CA). This linkage has legal implications notwithstanding the absence of legislation defining a PKI structure. By holding itself out as an identity certifier, a CA may be liable in contract and/or tort for the information it publishes in its certificates. Assume that a CA^1 has published a certificate relating a public key K to person X employed by company A. When person Y verifies that a received document (e.g. a purchase order) was digitally signed using the private counterpart of key K, then assuming that Y trusts CA^1, Y will rely upon the certificate's claim that the document was signed by X *and* that X works for A. If any of the information in the certificate is false, then Y may have recourse against CA^1. We discuss this further in the section below entitled "Certification Authorities (CAs) and the Law."

Multiple CAs and Certification Paths

Unfortunately the story doesn't end here. Its complexity multiplies in a widespread PKI involving multiple CAs. In general, Y won't directly trust the CA that signed X's certificate but will most likely trust another CA

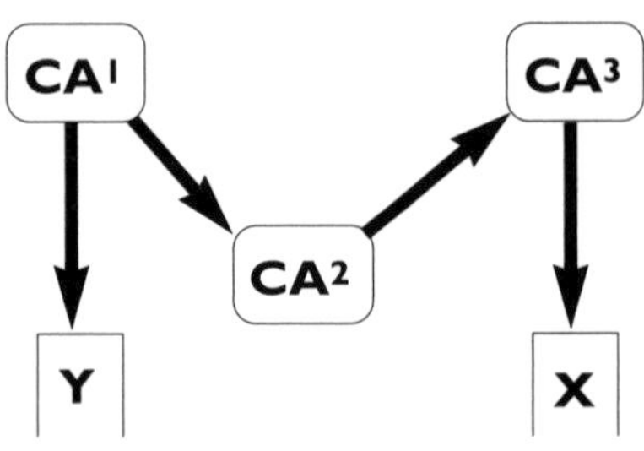

Figure1: CA relationship

altogether. To ascertain that X signed a document, Y will have to construct and verify a *certification path* from Y's trusted CA to X's CA.

A certification path is a chain of certificates, each signed by a different CA. Each CA asserts that it trusts another CA's certificates. Expand the previous example to the more general case involving certification paths. Assume that Y's CA is named CA^{1} and X's CA is named CA^{3}, and a third CA called CA^{2}. Neither X nor Y have dealt directly with CA^{2}. However, Y's CA, CA^{1}, has issued a certificate stating that it trusts CA^{2}'s certificates. CA^{2} issued a certificate stating that it trusts CA^{3}'s certificates. The chain is illustrated in Figure 1. The heavy arrows indicate an issued certificate.

When Y wishes to verify that X signed a document, Y must verify the path from CA^{1} to X. That is, Y must verify: (i) that CA^{1} has signed a certificate stating its trust of CA^{2}, (ii) CA^{2}'s trust certificate for CA^{3}, and (iii) CA^{3}'s certificate for X. There will be an arbitrary number of CAs between Y's and X's CA.

Certification paths resemble the structures in PGP's web of trust. However, X.509 recognizes the limitations of a trust web, and provides mechanisms to make certification paths more useful. Much of X.509's complexity stems from the need to limit a CA's liability when constructing certification paths. Since Y is trusting CA^{1} for so much, CA^{1} has to be prudent when it decides to trust another CA. In fact, X.509 allows CA^{1} to refine how it trusts other CAs. One CA can decide to trust another only with respect to certain policies, such as for keys that are used to sign casual e-mail. Trust can also be restricted to specific domains. For example, in the above situation, CA^{2} can state that it only trusts CA^{3} when CA^{3}makes statements about company A, e.g. perhaps CA^{3} is company A's principal CA. In addition to these built-in trust controls, X.509 benefits by moving trust management out of the hands of regular users and placing it in the CAs. The CAs are better suited to assume the burden and liability of trust management, and it's assumed that they'll pay much greater attention to managing their trust relationships.

But even with X.509's trust refinement capabilities, liability isn't always easily assigned. Recent legislation has focused on defining liability within an X.509 PKI. But many consider this work to be confusing and overly complex because of the unrefined way that X.509 identifies its entities.

Due to its X.500 roots, an X.509 identity carries considerable information. People are identified not only by their names, but also, for example, by one or more phone numbers, where they live and work, and even what role they play in their company. The problem is that X.509 expects the CA to validate all this information before it creates a certificate, even though the data may originate from disparate sources external to the CA. The CA will be forced to use elaborate identification schemes that are costly and frequently unreliable. This places the CA in an awkward position should liability attach where its information is incorrect. This wouldn't be the case if a PKI had more flexible definitions of a person's identity.

X.509 also manifests its X.500 origins in other ways. The X.500 directory is a rigid, hierarchical, tree-like structure. Consequently, X.509 works best when it's used in an environment where such a structure already exists or can be imposed. Ideal are large corporations, where authority chains are clearly demarcated and each person has one or more superiors and subordinates, all of whom have well-defined roles and responsibilities.

While X.509 may competently represent the workings within an organization, it functions poorly as a surrogate for an inter-organizational framework. There's no convenient, global structure for X.509 to mimic. People and organizations, let alone nations, are reluctant to subordinate their electronic identities to others. What if an organization like Bank of America were forced to position itself on a certification rung below its competitor Citibank, or vice-versa? X.509 works best when there's a single, trusted source of authority — but the real world rejects such elegant simplicity.

When X.509 was first conceived the Internet wasn't the fast-growing phenomenon we know today. At that time most computers *weren't* connected to the Internet; X.509 was designed for an "off-line" world. Today this manifests itself most clearly in the way X.509 revokes certificates.

Returning to Figure 1, suppose that Y has obtained a valid chain of certificates from the PKI and has accepted X's purchase order. A week later, X returns to Y with yet another order. If X's original certificate hasn't expired, there's no need to repeat the verification. If, however, there's been some change, e.g. X has lost his job and lacks the authority to issue purchase orders, then Y should have this information.

Ideally Y should check with the certification authority each time she initiates an online contact with X. When X.509 was initially proposed it was assumed that generally computers would be intermittently connected and that direct contact with a certificate's source would be infrequent. Yet it was also recognized that certificates would be useless unless their validity could be updated.

To solve this problem, X.509 uses a Certificate Revocation List (CRL). This requires that a certification authority periodically list all outstanding certificates revoked for whatever reason. By accessing the latest list, the certificate user could validate the certificate without contacting the CA.

Unfortunately, this solution begets other problems. First, there's a lag between the time that a certificate becomes invalid and the next CRL is issued — a window during which a relying party may accept what it falsely believes to be a valid certificate. To solve this problem, X.509 proposes that CAs dealing with more "sensitive" information issue their CRLs more frequently. This lowers the window for false validation, but doesn't close it.

Second, CRL lists may quickly grow to impractically frequent transmission. To reduce download frequency and file size, which consume time and resources, X.509 uses the "delta-CRL." This simply lists changes made to a full CRL. With delta-CRLs a certification authority need only issue full CRLs infrequently. In between they can issue CRL updates using delta-CRLs.

Notwithstanding these solutions, X.509 CRLs still falter badly as compared with online approaches where one validates a certificate by querying the authority directly. There's no lag time between certificate revocation and the propagation of that fact; one immediately knows the certificate's status. The online approach eliminates the need for users to download lists of irrelevant certificate revocations and to store and manage these lists on their own systems. Note that one may use X.509

with an online revocation system. However no such system exists today, nor has one been proposed.

PGP and X.509 have one thing in common: their certificates are known as *identity certificates*. An identity certificate joins a person to a public key, identifying who owns which keys. Concerns have recently been raised about the certificate's lack of anonymity. When MasterCard and Visa designed their Secure Electronic Transaction (SET) specification, they took elaborate steps to ensure that a merchant need never know a purchaser's identity, not even his card number.

These and other concerns have led to approaches that define *attribute certificates*. These don't identify the party behind a public key; rather they specify a capability, credential, or permission. For example, an attribute certificate states that the person represented by a given public key is allowed to access a particular server, or make a purchase up to a specific value.

For business to widely adopt any PKI system it must be seamless. It must engage and complete the authentication process "behind the scenes" without troubling the user, and it must occur instantaneously. Without this it's unlikely that PKI technology — and high volumes of electronic commerce — will take hold in cyberspace. Additionally, any technological deployment must be accompanied by sound legislation governing use and liabilities in electronic commerce. Only when both law and technology are in place will business feel at ease venturing into cyberspace.

Legislative Proposals

Although various legislative proposals are in draft stages, only Utah has enacted measures for widespread certification and digital signatures. California has enacted public sector legislation, anticipating that as a model user the state government will catalyze the private sector. The Canadian federal government is studying proposals, and will likely follow California by enacting public sector legislation prior to considering widespread legislation. In a longer-term vision, the September 1995 Canadian report recommended: "[t]he Department of Justice and other departments should review and suggest changes to federal legislation and statutes to provide greater certainty to the areas of digital signature and public key infrastructure services." Nothing concrete has yet emerged. At both the federal and provincial levels, Canada is regrettably taking a wait-and-see approach to the U.S. initiatives.

The Utah law[8] embraces the PKI, digital signature approach. It primarily concerns certification parameter setting and risk allocation. It's not mandatory that a certification authority follow the Act's parameters, but where it does the law provides a safe harbour for the CA and for persons relying on the digital signature. In this way the Act prescribes an optional set of guidelines for certification authorities. If the CA in question "opts in" it must comply with the Act's requirements. The legal effect of compliance is to reverse the burden of proving that the digital signature was forged. Thus, if Y attempts to purchase goods from X and uses a legally compliant CA, X may rely on the certificate, knowing that if it's been forged it will be to Y's detriment. The Act shifts the risk of loss away from retailers and suppliers, and imposes the burden on the secret key holder. If the secret key holder Y should lose or divulge his key he must inform the CA of the compromised key as soon as possible; until he does so he'll remain potentially liable for all transactions where his certificate is relied upon. Under existing law, the party who relies on a non-digital signature typically bears the onus of proving its authenticity. Utah reverses this onus.

Another legislative solution gaining increasing support is the UNCITRAL Model Law on Electronic Commerce. One part deals with communication of data messages and electronic contracting. It sets out rules governing formation and validity of contracts, recognition of data messages, and their attribution and receipt. For PKI attribution, a key holder is deemed to be the message's originator if:

> in order to ascertain whether the data message was that of the originator, the addressee properly applied a procedure previously agreed to by the originator for that purpose; or the data message as received by the addressee resulted from the actions of a person whose relationship with the originator or with any agent of the

originator enabled that person to gain access to a method used by the originator to identify data messages as its own.[9]

The UNCITRAL model code is more technologically neutral than the Utah legislation, and provides an alternative to policy makers. As a model it doesn't have legal force, but provides another example of how a digital signature law might work.

Whether or not the Utah Act is effective, it alerts us to the panoply of issues surrounding CAs. In jurisdictions that lack updated legislation for electronic transactions, existing law will apply. This will create uncertainty for electronic commerce. While no law is required for a CA to begin its operations, the potential for liability deters industry from developing CAs. Others who use and rely on digital signatures are uncertain as to who's responsible if something goes awry. Potential problems include reliance on a certificate or signature that:

- is no longer valid
- is sent by an unauthorized third party engaging in fraud
- wrongly represents characteristics of the party it is certifying
- is sent by mistake; or
- is mistakenly believed to represent some other party.

In each case, the law should provide a clear and consistent answer as to who — the sender of the information, the recipient, or the CA — bears the risk of loss. Existing law does address these situations in a conventional setting. However, superimposing a third party who brokers "trust" is a complicating factor. Analyzing the many possible relationships between the parties, contractual and otherwise, and the applicable law is complicated and beyond our scope. Answers vary from jurisdiction to jurisdiction.

Certification Authorities (CAs) and the Law

We discuss contracts and torts at length later, but it's useful to consider CAs' contractual and tort liability here. CAs occupy a new place in the world of commerce, and overlaying their input on a commercial transaction will affect the legal risks involved.

Contractual Liability

A CA may have a contractual relationship with one or both parties to the transaction. They'll pay the CA for the certainty desired in transacting with one another. In order to impose contractual liability on a CA one

---

CAs occupy a new place in the world of commerce, and overlaying their input on a commercial transaction will affect the legal risks involved.

---

must characterize the certification product. Is it a good or a service? Answering this is key for Canadian and U.S. sale of goods and consumer transaction laws.

Many other contractual issues remain as well. For instance, should the *Statute of Frauds*, which requires certain contracts to be made in writing, apply to digital commerce? Should it be adapted or scrapped?[10] In the U.S. there is great pressure to amend the *Statute of Frauds* provision of the *Uniform Commercial Code*[11] to reflect electronic contracting. The present case law is unclear as to what constitutes "signed and in writing." The result? Great uncertainty and some reticence in contracting electronically.

Goods

Generally, the sale of a good carries certain implied warranties, including a warranty of merchantability and fitness for purpose. Merchantability is the broader of the two standards. It requires that the good, in this case the digital certificate, be of a marketable standard according to industry practice. The implied warranty for fitness of purpose is only of use where the buyer of the good has informed the seller, here the CA, of the nature of his or her need. If so, and the good wasn't fit for the buyer's purpose, then the risk of loss passes to the seller. A CA, advised of a client's certification needs, must be diligent in providing the requisite level of certificate security. A breakdown in the CA's identity verification may result in liability under this head. Of course, express contractual terms between seller and buyer will prevail. In the case of a commercial retailer dealing with a CA, it's likely that attention will be paid to such terms at the outset of the relationship. In certain jurisdictions, consumer protection legislation exists which mandates terms that can't be avoided by contract. In such cases, the CA must be made aware of this potential liability.

Services

If one characterizes a CA product as a service, a different set of rules apply. Services lack the implied warranties of goods. In services, the law recognizes contractual liability for negligent misrepresentation in certain cases. These require that a "special relationship" exist between the parties such that it's reasonable for a person to expect that the information given will be acted upon. This principle raises the question as to where one draws the line between reasonable and unreasonable reliance and special and non-special relationships. Without direction, these choices are left to the courts, and to date they have scarce experience with digital commerce and electronic certification systems. Uncertainty is exacerbated by the law's complexity concerning contractual misrepresentation, and whether the misrepresentation was a term of the contract. Remedies available to the aggrieved party vary with this answer.

In addition to sale of goods claims and contractual liability for negligent misstatement, in situations where one or neither party has a contractual relationship with the CA there may be a claim in tort for misrepresentation and possibly product liability.

Tortious Liability

Negligent Misrepresentation

Under negligent misstatement law, anyone who has suffered damage as a result of relying on the digital signature may bring a claim. Typically, the defendant will be the one with the deepest pockets, likely the CA. For example, assume a CA certifies to the public, i.e. non-paying members of its service, that a given member has a currently valid public key, with perhaps other characteristics such as the ability to act as a purchasing agent for his employer. Some CAs will offer these advanced services. If the key has been revoked, or some other information is relied on by a member of the public to his or her detriment and it's false, there may be an action for negligent misrepresentation.

The Supreme Court of Canada ruled in *Haig v. Bamford* that liability will attach where the defendant had actual knowledge of a limited class of persons who would use and rely on the statement, here the certification.[12] In *Queen v. Cognos Inc.* the Supreme Court identified five general requirements for a successful claim:

- a duty of care based on a "special relationship";
- a false representation;
- a misrepresentation negligently made;
- a claimant reasonably relying upon the representation; and
- damage to the claimant caused by the reliance.

Finally, in *Canadian National Railway Co. v. Norsk Pacific Steamship Co.* the Supreme Court added proximity — the closeness of the relationship between the parties — to the list of five factors, holding it to be the controlling factor.

These three Canadian cases illustrate that negligent misrepresentation is still not settled in tort law. The issue of proximity will likely be the battleground upon which the first CA tort contests will be waged. It's unclear whether a CA is sufficiently proximate to Internet users who access its lists. What constitutes a special relationship in cyberspace? Is a cyber-visit by a third party to the CA's computer server to retrieve a certificate sufficient? What if the CA e-mails the certificate? As with many cyberspace issues, settling the misrepresentation issue, through legislation or judicial determination, will impact on the cyber-commerce community and its willingness to rely upon PKIs.

Product Liability

Product liability law applied to information providers is relatively new and underdeveloped. As with contract law, the characterization of information as a good or service is crucial. Here liability requires that the injury be caused in relation to a good and not a service. If the certification of a digital signature is labelled a product, it's possible that any inaccuracies may be actionable should any harm arise from its use.

Two mid-1980s U.S. cases considered product liability where information was the alleged product in aircraft instrument approach charts prepared from Federal Aviation Administration (FAA) information. In *Aetna Causalty and Surety v. Jeppesen*, Jeppesen drew aircraft landing approach charts using scales departing from industry practice. A pilot flying into Las Vegas crashed while relying on these charts. In *Brocklesby v. Jeppesen*, it was claimed that another plane crash resulted from Jeppesen's defective aviation charts. The Court found:

> Jeppesen approach charts depict graphically the instrument approach procedure for the particular airport [and] . . . includes . . . all pertinent aspects of the approach such as directional heading, distances, minimum altitudes, turns, radio frequencies and procedures to be followed if an approach is missed. The specifications prescribed are set forth by the FAA in tabular form. Jeppesen acquires this FAA form and portrays the information therein on a graphic approach chart. This is Jeppesen's "product."[13]

In both cases the Court concluded that the charts constituted a product. Thus strict liability applied. The Court ruled that even though the FAA information was inaccurate, and the defendant couldn't legally deviate from it in its preparation of the charts, strict liability demanded that the defendant be held responsible for selling a defective and unsafe product. The Court was concerned with the fact that the charts were mass-marketed, and furthermore that "the charts were not a service rendered for a specific circumstance."[14]

It's been argued that the charts in these cases are similar to the information and the work of database providers, in that both "commonly represent data in a format different from the one in which it was initially required."[15] As well, both are mass-marketed and neither are considered to be a service rendered for a specific circumstance — two factors instrumental to the Court's findings. It seems that, without further legislative guidance, CA liability is likely where certificate "manufacture" is done negligently. This result is to some extent anticipated by the Utah law, which seeks to create a safe harbour only if the CA satisfies certain standards.

Conclusion

Public key infrastructures are a rapidly evolving technology that will potentially provide a feasible solution to the problems of conducting cyberspace commerce. However, new standards for more effective PKIs continue to emerge. The final national or even global PKI will likely be very different from current technology. A future PKI will emphasize online operation, where digital certificates are verified instantaneously by their sources. It will operate within both hierarchical and non-hierarchical models, and will use a more refined model of trust through authorization certificates that minimize reliance on third parties (CAs).[16]

Lawmakers must keep abreast of technological developments if they wish to craft law appropriate to cyber-commerce. Legislating now requires a degree of crystal ball gazing and should be undertaken with caution. Nevertheless, early familiarity with the technology is essential to a dialogue between lawmakers and the PKI industry in order that solutions will reflect both parties' concerns. Moreover, legislation should remain as technologically neutral as possible. Rapid technological obsolescence will wreak havoc on a developing system of cyber-commerce that relies on a consistent and secure PKI.

The Utah law provides a good first step in that it provides PKI users with a choice of legal regime. Without such specific legislation, existing legislation and case law will apply. Traditional contract and tort rules are likely to yield arbitrary results, producing the uncertainty so loathed by business.

CA legislation such as the Utah Act raises interesting policy issues. Currently the mathematical possibility of successfully forging a digital signature is infinitesimal, but this may change rapidly as new processing technologies are developed. However, the Act assumes both the current state of technology and that the key holder is the weakest link for key compromise. This is consistent with economic contract law theory (discussed in Chapter 8), which places the risk on the best risk bearer.

The Utah law isn't problem-free. Critics argue that it places the risk upon those least able to bear the loss. Since there will always be losses due to business forgery, business factors these into the price that's equally distributed and borne by all. To reverse the burden of loss should result in a lowering of price by an equal amount. Is this desirable? Will this reversal create a new private digital signature insurance industry, which through added transaction costs will reduce overall wealth? We must answer these questions and choose the best PKI model to create an efficient system.

Critics also contend that while the law professes technological neutrality, accepting that public keys and digital certificates are essential to electronic commerce involves some technologically laden choice. They argue that by legislating at this early stage Utah has chosen a PKI solution that may not be ideal; leaving such electronic commerce decisions to the marketplace may be more prudent now. These criticisms have some merit, but fail to recognize that stability in cyberspace requires a cooperation between law and technology. The marketplace is uncomfortable with the uncertainty generated by a transjurisdictional global network without controls. It's more accustomed to legal controls that are effective and enforceable and that generally promote efficiency. That said, the Utah law doesn't represent the ultimate in commercial cyber legislation. Nor should it. Its allocation of risk to the secret key holder involves a policy choice that may not accurately reflect the most prudent, workable, or socially desirable choice. Both legislation and technology must evolve to suit the needs of society and the marketplace. Thus, give Utah full marks for starting the ball rolling.

Before high-volume, transaction-based cyber-commerce becomes a way of life business will require the deployment of a seamless PKI system accompanied by legislative support. Business is now pushing for the development of suitable technologies. The banks and credit card companies are especially active, allying themselves with Internet giants such as Netscape, Verisign, and Microsoft. This is sensible, since these organizations have the resources to carry off a large information infrastructure project. We're likely to see several technologies emerge, followed by a period of reconciliation where standards coalesce. Once this occurs legislators should be prepared to act quickly to support the prevailing technology. We anticipate a minimum of five years before this structure begins to appear.

6 THE REGULATORS

INTRODUCTION

Should electronic commerce in cyberspace be regulated? Can it? Who are the referees of communications law? Can they enforce their regulations? What changes is electronic commerce forcing on regulation? And

> **IRAQ VERSUS THE INTERNET**
>
> The February 14, 1997 *Globe and Mail* carried this story:
>
> The Iraqi Government has declared war on the Internet. The government newspaper *Al-Jumhuriya* recently called the Internet "the end of civilizations, cultures, interests and ethics." The paper also contends that the computer network "is one of the American means to enter every house in the world. They want to become the only source for controlling human beings in the new electronic village." There is no access to the Internet in Iraq.

what changes in regulation does it need to function more effectively and efficiently and for maximum public good? Can regulation be technologically neutral? Is the nation state as regulator irrelevant in the information age's global village?

This chapter is a tale of two approaches to the law — top down and bottom up. The first is "heavy" conventional law, with its administrative machinery, enforcement through penalties, and licences with conditions that include regulated rates. Deploying top-down command and control, conventional law possesses the virtues of certainty and predictability and the defects of inflexibility, cost, and getting chronically "out of touch." The second approach is readily adaptable rule and forbearance from rule. These comprise new public standards or their absence, and a rapidly changing mix of formal and informal law. The approach is bottom up, market driven, decentralized, and chaotic. It has the virtue of flexibility and adaptability, yet bears the burden of uncertainty and lack of reach or unenforceability.

Although neither approach is dominant, we're currently moving from the first to the second, from top down to bottom up. But the devolution is far from complete, and not entirely predictable. One thing seems certain, however: the rate of change in the information age requires flexibility. While some describe law as the "restraints that make one

FORGET TOP-DOWN?

The U.S. Federal Communications Commission (FCC) spent nine years developing and attempting to impose a standard (top down) for high definition digital television (HDTV). It took Bill Gates and his PC industry colleagues several weeks to convince the FCC that the standard was irrelevant due to changes in technology. *Fortune*, December 23, 1996, bills this story as: "The End of TV As We Know It. Forget HDTV. Forget interactive television. Forget the 500-channel universe. Instead start thinking of PCTV." It quotes the president of Sony: "Maybe we should redefine convergence as collision."

free," the new "law," conversely, speaks more to the freedom from legal restraints altogether.

Why is any law necessary for electronic commerce? The answer lies in the metaphor of the information highway: human beings in motion require rules for the road.

We begin the first half of the tale by briefly reviewing the traditional regulatory apparatus for communications law in Canada. We glance at the 1996 U.S. *Telecommunications Act*, the main American framework legislation. We've chosen this focus on traditional regulatory machinery for the sake of simplicity. While it affects only the backbone of electronic commerce and not its entire mind, body, limbs, and nerve endings, it nonetheless illustrates the central dichotomy between regulation and freedom in the digital age. We also look briefly at criminal law sanctions, with particular reference to obscenity in cyberspace. Why obscenity? Commercial traffic in obscene material is one of the fastest growing areas of cyberspace and the roughest to regulate. It raises some of the most difficult issues for the rule of law, in particular the classic balance between freedom of speech and public order. It also illustrates many of the tensions that volatile new business and technology present for geographically and culturally specific rules and regulatory systems.

Then we consider the second half of the tale — alternate forms of regulation or forbearance from regulation that are forced or engineered by electronic commerce. We end with some questions on which of these tales better describes the information age, and whether and how we can find an optimum blend or a delicate and dynamic balance between the two.

Throughout this discussion we begin to perceive the Internet as an intruder: it doesn't fit well into traditional regulatory regimes, and requires adjustments at a quicker pace than the traditional regulatory machinery allows.

Canadian Regulation

Three principal statutes govern the Canadian information highway:

- The *Telecommunications Act*
- The *Broadcasting Act*
- The *Radiocommunications Act*.

Each of these Acts has undergone substantial reform in the last decade, signifying a commendable response by government to the challenges of new technology and changing business. But is it enough? Can national governments keep up with electronic commerce and find the right balance of constraint where necessary, but not necessarily constraint?

We consider each Act in turn. We then examine some of the conflicts and problems they pose for electronic commerce, and responses to them.

The Telecommunications Act[1]

This Act, which is the responsibility of the Minister of Industry, was completely revised in 1993. It governs telecommunications carriers within federal jurisdiction, i.e. those engaged in inter-provincial and international communications. As recently as 1989 the Supreme Court

> The Canadian *Telecommunications Act* has a strong socio-economic orientation, with seven broad objectives:
>
> - orderly development of a Canadian telecommunications system that serves to strengthen the social and economic fabric of Canada and its regions
> - access to affordable and reliable services in both urban and rural areas in all regions, and responsiveness to users' needs
> - enhanced efficiency and competitiveness of Canadian industry
> - Canadian ownership and use of the infrastructure
> - increased reliance on market forces and efficient, effective regulation where required
> - stimulating R&D and encouraging innovation
> - protection of privacy.

of Canada resolved the federal-provincial jurisdictional conflict over who regulates telecommunication carriers largely in federal favour.[2] It left local telecommunication carriers essentially alone, subject to provincial authority.[3] The U.S. revolution hasn't been as clear and complete. State authorities still have substantial presence as referees, with resulting regulatory duplication.

To make it work, legislation often requires complex administration and enforcement, and the *Telecommunications Act* is no exception. It assigns the major responsibility to the Canadian Radio-Television and

Telecommunications Commission (CRTC), an administrative tribunal at arm's length from government. It licenses carriers and fixes their terms and conditions. Until recently, highly detailed "line by line" regulation of charges for telecommunications services occupied much of the CRTC's time. But the 1993 Act's introduction of the competition objective will enhance reliance on market forces to establish optimum levels of accountability, cost, and quality of service — and begin a trend toward deregulation.

This Act must function in the context of other legislation, laws, and international agreements. For example, while it has its own penal provisions and sanctions for contraventions it also relies on other statutes to accomplish its objectives. One is the *Criminal Code of Canada*[4], which we'll briefly explore later.

Another is the *Competition Act*[5], which promotes competition and deters anti-competitive behaviour. How does it square with a *Telecommunications Act*, which grants a monopoly franchise over a specific geographic area and fixes the rates the carrier must charge with no flexibility for consumer demand? The legal answer is the "regulated conduct defence." The public interest is protected through regulation of the carriers' conduct by an overseeing public tribunal, here the CRTC. Thus, while the Competition Bureau frequently intervenes in CRTC hearings to apply its general expertise to this industry, it yields to the specific expertise and governance of the CRTC and presumes that the public interest is best served in this instance by otherwise anti-competitive behaviour. As the scope of competition increases with multiple carriers and rival services, we anticipate substantial reduction in the CRTC's micro-supervision and greater reliance on the Competition Bureau's after-the-fact supervision.

The Broadcasting Act[6]

This Act was substantially revised in 1991, following an earlier update in 1968. It governs three broadcasting activities: programming, distribution, and networks. It's the responsibility of the Minister of Heritage Canada, and the CRTC is its principal administrating agency.

The Act's cornerstone is the definition of broadcasting: "any transmission of programs, whether or not encrypted, by radio waves or other means of telecommunication for reception by the pubic by means of broadcasting receiving apparatus, but does not include any such reception of programs that is made solely for performance or display in a

> The Canadian *Broadcasting Act*'s clear cultural orientation is illustrated by this excerpt from its objectives[7]:
>
> > The Canadian broadcasting system should encourage the development of Canadian expression by providing a wide range of programming that reflects Canadian attitudes, opinions, ideals, values and artistic creativity, by displaying Canadian talent in entertainment programming and by offering information and analysis concerning Canada and other countries from a Canadian point of view . . . the programming originated by broadcasting undertakings should be of high standard.

public place." If an activity is caught by this definition then the licensing and other comprehensive conditions of the Act apply. These include prescribed levels of Canadian ownership, Canadian-content "air" time and channel quotas, Canadian-content access, foreign access restriction, mandatory contributions to Canadian content development funds, and special tax incentives and grants for Canadian content. All of these are intended to protect and promote Canadian identity and content, with particular consciousness of the fact that the Canada-U.S. border is one of the most open in the world, and that U.S. content in Canada is pervasive.

But as the multimedia universe unfolds the distinction between carriers and content providers blurs. Consider convergence in business. Disney, Time Warner, Turner, ABC-Capital Cities, McCaw, and MCI are now merged into one business empire in the U.S. In Canada, Rogers-Maclean Hunter have combined into one Canadian business conglomerate of cable television, satellite broadcasting, long distance, local and cellular telephony, newspapers, and magazines. The definition of broadcasting will become increasingly unclear as technology develops, satellite and other wireless communications conquer national borders, and public-private distinctions melt.

Several advisory bodies have thus recommended that the CRTC undertake public hearings to revise the definition of broadcasting,[8] but this has yet to occur. The problem is exacerbated by competing federal administerial responsibilities and philosophies. The Ministry of Industry is focused on economic growth and productivity and consumer choice, and favours a narrower definition of broadcasting. The Ministry of Heritage Canada is focused on cultural identity, Canadian content, and citizen education and favours a more all-encompassing definition of broadcasting in order to bring new multimedia activities under the cultural protection and promotion provisions of the *Broadcasting Act*. However these opposing philosophies are reconciled, the redefinition of broadcasting — when it inevitably occurs — will substantially shape the information highway map.

This duality of purpose is duplicated in the *Telecommunications Act* and the *Broadcasting Act*. One is primarily economic; the other primarily cultural. Up to now one regulated carriers; the other regulated content providers. And while business and technology have merged carriers and content providers into one, the two regulatory philosophies have yet to conceive how they'll do the same.

Is It Broadcasting or Telecommunications?

Consider this example: Is video on demand broadcasting? VOD is like traditional television in that it's "broadcast" from a central transmitting facility available to the public in general. It's unlike traditional television in that each member of the public may choose to accept the offer of services and strike an individual contract to view a movie in his or her private home. As a chosen service it impacts only on the contracting party. Is this a broadcasting activity governed by the *Broadcasting Act* administered by the CRTC and Heritage Canada? Or is it a telecommunications activity governed by the *Telecommunications Act* and the Ministry of Industry? Near VOD — a movie available over cable or direct to home (DTH) satellite television at a fixed time, e.g. 7 p.m. and 9 p.m. — raises a similar question. However it's a little closer to traditional television, in that it may only be seen at a scheduled time by the general public rather than the precise time determined by a contracting individual.

Competition will introduce other multimedia activities using "radiowaves or other means of telecommunication," which will extend this debate.

The Radiocommunications Act[9]

This Act was substantially revised in 1989. It governs the allocation, authorization, and technical regulation of all public and private radio, from telecom carriers to radio stations to radio communications with police cruisers, ambulances, and taxis. It's the responsibility of the Minister of Industry; the CRTC isn't directly involved. This regulation is increasingly carried out in coordination with such international agencies as the International Telecommunications Union (ITU). In accordance with national borders extended skyward, the Act allocates jurisdictions, or areas in space, for satellite placement and terrestrial "footprints." It also allocates space, or ranges, on the radio spectrum as measured by the hertz cycle. This ensures that standards for earth-hugging radio spectrum signals are coordinated so as to avoid interference and provide for maximum use of available capacity.

This Act was designed so that national governments could ration out the scarce commodity of the radio spectrum (or more precisely, spots on

Wiretapping in the Information Age?

Consider the following new criminal offence. Madame X has deciphered the encryption code that disguises the signals for a U.S.-based satellite television distributor with Canadian subscribers. She's done this through a computer-based "cracking" of the code. Each subscriber has a black box on the television set with a decoding chip to decrypt the signals. Madame X sells to a subscriber a refashioned black box with the "cracked" chip. This cracked chip enables the subscriber to pirate the signals and no longer pay the prescribed black box and subscription fee.

Madame X was charged under the *Radiocommunications Act* for "tampering with radiocommunications signals." Conviction carries fines of up to $5000, with a maximum jail sentence of 12 months. For corporations the maximum fine is $25 000. She was tried in Hull, Quebec, for her third such offence, and fined $3000.

The economic significance of this crime is substantial. First, subscribers can avoid the $25 to $100 monthly subscription fee for the service. Second, subscribers avoid the $500 to $1000 cost of buying the regular black box. Third, Canadian firms pay large sums for the Canadian distribution rights to U.S. programs. The value of that investment is substantially eroded if the U.S. signal can be intercepted directly.

that spectrum) in order to permit radio communication in space. These governments have used different calculations of the public interest in making these decisions and awarding franchises. But compressing technology is making the space less scarce — and the broader range of signals is making the reach of national governments less secure.

Changes and Tensions

Perhaps the most useful way of discerning the interplay of these Acts and new legal and public policy challenges is to chronicle some of the major Canadian regulatory changes in the past decade:

1. 1984: licensing of competitive telephone cellular services
2. 1989: Supreme Court of Canada decision upholding federal jurisdiction over all major telecommunications carriers
3. 1989: Canada-U.S. Free Trade Agreement opening the Canadian market for competition in enhanced telecommunication services, followed in 1992 by the North American Free Trade Agreement (NAFTA) extending the market to Mexico
4. 1989: the privatization of Teleglobe (providing overseas telecommunications); 1991: privatization of the government holdings in Telesat (providing satellite communication) and opening Teleglobe's monopoly to competition by 1998
5. 1992: licensing of competitive public cordless telephone services
6. 1992: CRTC decision opening facilities-based competition in long-distance voice telecommunications
7. 1994: CRTC "framework" decision, which:
    - split the telephone rate base into regulated (local telephones) and competitive (long-distance)
    - proposed price caps (carriers are allowed to set their own rates up to a specified maximum in place of rate of return, where carriers' "profit" is set by the CRTC as a specified percentage return or yield on the carriers' investment)
    - removed earnings regulation altogether from the competitive segment; proposed a carrier access tariff to encourage interconnection by rival suppliers

- proposed rate rebalancing to reduce the cross-subsidy from profitable long-distance to losing local services
- proposed competition in local phone service, allowing telephone companies to penetrate the broadband video market through a video dial tone, which for example permits movies on demand. Most of these changes are now the subject of detailed CRTC hearings, which should be completed by 1998.

8. May 1995: CRTC's Convergence Report giving more detail to allow telephone companies into the cable and related businesses and vice versa, and identifying a number of barriers to be eliminated before each would be allowed into the other's domain in order to ensure fair and sustainable competition. In August 1996 the Ministers of Industry and Heritage Canada issued their Convergence Policy statement, clarifying the policy framework for competition between telcos and cable, expected to commence fully in January 1998.

What do these changes over a decade represent? First, there's a relentless drive towards deregulation, with the traditional top-down monolithic control yielding to more flexible and market-sensitive supervision. Second, the move to deregulation does not, at least immediately, eliminate regulation. Governments can't simply vacate the field, given that previous regulation accords the established players a built-in advantage over newcomers. Further regulation seems necessary to level the playing field for new and old players.

Third, new technology and business forms are dramatically changing what the services are, what they contain, and who delivers them. For example, the traditional wired telephone companies face wireless and cordless technology, as well as content providers, cable carriers, and satellite distributors. And to this list we have yet to add a sleeping giant: the regulated monopoly public utilities that provide electricity through a cable to each home. What role, if any, will these large entities play on the information highway as they emerge from traditional regulation? And will smaller, nimbler entrepreneurs conceive and craft new services to scurry past the giants?

Business and technology, as well as carriage and content, have merged or converged — and Marshall McLuhan's phrase "the medium is the message" has descended with a vengeance. Business seeking predictability, fairness, enforcement, speed, and cheapness from the law is swimming in a swirling sea, with few if any of those moderating measures.

We've reviewed eight regulatory events of the last decade. Consider now several other recent "epic" entrepreneurial events that demonstrate how new ways of delivering information highway services present novel legal and policy changes.

International Trade Negotiations

With the Uruguay Round in 1994 the General Agreement on Trade and Tariffs (GATT) negotiations completed a major exercise to liberate international trading in goods and services. Negotiations on communications infrastructure and services were postponed for the next round convened by the World Trade Organization (WTO). These were commenced, but further postponed in the fall of 1996 with a February 15, 1997 deadline for conclusion. In the U.S. delegation's view insufficient liberalizing proposals had been tabled. Meanwhile, the European Union is committed to introducing competition in telecommunication infrastructure and services as of January 1998.

In the last hours of February 15, 1997 an agreement was reached among the WTO nations that will open domestic markets significantly to foreign-based telecommunications providers. This will diminish the ability of nation states to establish a new regulatory equilibrium by focusing only on its domestic providers and local environment. Moreover, it will reinforce the perspective of the information highway as a global market and not a series of discrete national ones.

Direct to Home Satellite Telecommunications

DTH now operates in the U.S., with some services providing over 100 television channels (and with projections for 500). The U.S. services aren't licensed for broadcasting in Canada, since they don't meet Canadian ownership or content requirements as determined by the CRTC. Nevertheless, an estimated 250 000 to 300 000 Canadian homes have subscribed to these "grey market" services using U.S. billing addresses.

In September 1994, the Expressvu consortium — grouping several large, Canadian cable operators, Bell Telephone, and Tel-Com, a satellite communications supplier — was exempted from licensing under the forbearance policies of the CRTC. Services were to start by September 1995, but this deadline was missed due to equipment and satellite capacity failures. Now the consortium has begun to erode.

Meanwhile, a federal government-appointed advisory panel recommended a reversal of the exemption to Expressvu (which subsequently obtained a licence). The panel also recommended more relaxed conditions to permit some competition in DTH services, including greater participation from U.S. partners in Canadian consortia provided Canadian ownership and content agreements were respected. As of February 1997 further DTH licences have been sought. But there's no certainty that a Canadian service will be offered, successfully launched, and sustained against U.S. competitors.

The U.S. grey market competitive services continue to penetrate Canada, presenting a difficult law enforcement problem for Canadian authorities. Does one prosecute the manufacturer or vendor of satellite dishes that may or may not be located in Canada, the distributors of the signal located in the U.S., the agency collecting the monthly subscription fee (which may be a U.S.-located creditor being paid by the Canadian subscriber's credit card with a U.S. billing address), or the Canadian consumer? And when 250 000 homes have already entered the grey market does government risk a Boston tea party if prosecution is vigorously undertaken?[10]

Three Canadian-based enterprises have now launched DTH services. First is Star Choice Television of Fredericton, N.B., with a March 1997 start-up offering 11 television channels plus music at a cost of $900 for the black box hardware and $20 for a monthly subscription fee. An additional 22 video and audio channels in the East, and 11 in the West, are now available. Shaw Communications of Calgary launched in Spring 1997[11] and in March 1997 bought Star to accelerate its own launch date and provide coast-to-coast service. Expressvu of Toronto with Bell as its major partner will offer its DTH service in September 1997.

What lessons can we draw from this brief glimpse at a new technology/

business development? First, it's been a nightmare of regulation. (One senior regulator described it as "the dossier sent from hell.") Second, the effort to preserve a Canadian presence — either exclusive or shared with U.S. providers — has been sorely tested, partly through the pervasiveness of the new technology from the U.S. and partly because, like many new technologies, DTH hasn't fulfilled its promise of faultless, on time, and within budget delivery. Third, the growing grey market tests the rule of law — and the reluctance of federal authorities to enforce the law in the absence of an up-and-ready Canadian service is telling.

Personal Communication Services (PCS)

These services use wireless technologies on the radio spectrum through mobile or portable terminals. With compression of signals a much smaller portion of the radio spectrum supports a much larger amount of data, allowing new value-added services from pagers to remote sensing. Four licences have been issued: two to Bell Mobile and Rogers Cantel, which already hold cellular phone licences; and two to newcomer competitive firms.

So what? First, because these new services provide a new platform for delivery they'll add to the competitive array with better quality and range of capability and, one hopes, lower cost. Second, although these are competitive services, they're not wholly deregulated. The federal Ministry of Industry's Spectrum Division — the largest revenue collector after the Ministry of National Revenue — allocates the scarce spectrum space. Third, the government didn't simply auction the space to the highest bidder and to one monopolist; rather it allocated not one, but four licences. Two were brand-new competitors that were treated as members of an "infant industry" to add to the range of players. As well as guarding two spaces for new entrants, the four licences were awarded on the basis of a sophisticated point-scoring criteria, which included not simply cost and quality but accessibility to less serviced areas, R&D investments, jobs created, Canadian content, speed of roll-out, and promise of export. Hardly Adam Smith's invisible hand alone at work.

Local Multipoint Communication Services (LMCS)

This service uses a combination of wired and wireless communication to provide two-way multimedia services at the community level, with Canada divided into 57 geographical "communities" for licences. Seventeen firms applied to the Ministry of Industry, for licences ranging from coverage across the entire 57 regions to several regions only. Four licences were granted in autumn 1996, adding to the competition in both telecommunications and broadcasting.

The observations for advent of LMCS service are similar to those for PCS, except that LMCS is now more comprehensive than PCS, connecting video plus audio into the home and creating another competitive platform to the radio, television, and data communication services already discussed. Again, new technology arrangements and new business formations are dramatically altering previously regulated functions. The old rule of law is challenged.

THE POWER OF INFORMATION

Government's role isn't limited to regulation; it's also expected to promote electronic commerce and to operate as a model user. A good example is Industry Canada's Strategis (http://strategis.ic.gc.ca) — Canada's largest online business information site. It has 50 information collections, three gigabytes of trade data, listings of 27 000 companies willing to do business, and several hundred hot links to domestic and international organizations. It's organized under eight headings:

- Company Information: 175 000 federally incorporated companies
- International Business Opportunities, Trade, and Investment Information
- Business Information by Sector
- Micro-Economic Research and Statistical Analysis
- Technology, Innovation, and Investing
- Business Support and Services
- Consumers and the Marketplace: Service, Laws, and Regulation
- Human Resources and Training.

The 1996 U.S. Telecommunications Act

In Canada the federal government has almost complete responsibility for telecommunications, whereas in the U.S. it's a shared federal-state responsibility.

It's useful to take a quick glance at developments in the U.S., the leading engine of the changes we've discussed throughout the book. The U.S. *Telecommunications Act* was signed into law by President Clinton in February 1996 after long and bitter struggles in Congress. A complete overhaul of the 1934 *Communication Act*, its objective is "to provide for a pro-competitive deregulatory national policy framework designed to accelerate rapidly private sector deployment of advanced telecommunications and information technologies."

The new U.S. Act strengthens the federal hand by giving a prescriptive authority to the Federal Communication Commission (FCC) over the states.

The Act doesn't contain any measures to reduce or eliminate foreign ownership restrictions, since these are dealt with through bilateral (e.g. Canada-U.S. Free Trade Agreement, later trilateral with Mexico to form

> The U.S. *Telecommunications Act*'s major provisions:
>
> - Allow competition in the provision of local service and lift the monopoly of local carriers.
> - Many states allow local competition. The new Act will harmonize and expand this.
> - Open new lines of business to the local carriers through their entry into long distance service and equipment manufacturing.
> - Allow telephone companies to offer video programming.
> - Provide measures to promote and protect universal service. The Act creates a new support system administered by a joint federal-state board to ensure access to advanced services at affordable rates.

NAFTA) and multilateral trade negotiations (e.g. the WTO negotiations, which reached a successful conclusion on liberalized telecommunications facilities and services). At the Brussels G7 Information Society Conference in the spring of 1995, Vice President Gore surprised the delegates by proposing to reduce or eliminate foreign ownership restrictions on a reciprocal basis with any other nation that offered similar treatment to U.S. nationals. We should expect more of these trade liberalization initiatives, particularly from the U.S. as it uses its superiority in technology and content to build a global information infrastructure.

Measures to control obscenity and violence on television and computer networks were introduced in Title V of the Act, called "The Communications Decency Act" (CDA). Its constitutionality was immediately challenged[12] as offending the first amendment freedom of speech guarantees. It was struck down at the trial court level and has just been ruled unconstitutional by the U.S. Supreme Court.[13] The Act's prohibition of obscene content was so sweeping and the U.S. first amendment freedom of speech protection is especially strong. The Supreme Court's guidance judgement provides some guidance on a middle ground. Congress will probably reintroduce a less restrictive and more balanced control on indecent communication to overcome the Court's ban.

Given that the re-elected Democratic President and the majority Republican Congress both pledged to limit obscene communication in the 1996 presidential and congressional elections, this will be an interesting test of the durability of election rhetoric. Moreover, this political exercise illustrates the difficulty of classic legal questions in the information age. Should and can governments control what goes on the information highway? These questions provide a useful introduction to our next discussion of criminal law.

Criminal Law

Space permits only the most cursory examination of criminal law regulation of electronic commerce. Sanctions are usually needed in many areas of law to ensure that people obey it. This is as true in electronic commerce as in most areas of human endeavour, especially where greed rears its ugly head. Copyright infringement, software piracy, fraudulent contracts, and breaches of security are examples of potential criminal issues in cyberspace. Here we focus briefly on obscenity, an area where criminal law efforts to govern cyberspace are particularly fragile. (As we've noted, the efforts to regulate telecommunication obscenity in the 1996 U.S. *Telecommunications Act* led to that portion of the legislation being struck down as unconstitutional.) Moreover, obscenity provides substantial commercial activity in cyberspace.

The Regulators

The three levels of national government — federal, provincial, and municipal — have distinct regulatory roles. The federal government is responsible for enacting and (with the exception of the *Criminal Code*) administering federal legislation, and for negotiating conventions with other national governments. The federal statutes of greatest interest for us are the *Criminal Code*, *Broadcasting Act*, *Telecommunications Act*, *Canadian Human Rights Act*, *Customs Act and Excise Tax Act*. Under the Canadian Constitution, provincial governments have authority over property and civil rights. Thus provincial power relates to the control of obscenity in two ways: (1) consumer protection legislation covers such things as labelling and display requirements; (2) film and video review boards may limit content and dissemination. As well, provinces enforce the *Criminal Code* and therefore are largely responsible for criminal law regulation. Finally, by delegation of provincial authority municipal governments may regulate and enforce zoning and licensing bylaws, controlling such matters as the location and distribution of "adult entertainment." This raises the question of whether a municipal authority will be able to control virtual space.

Obscenity

The Canadian *Criminal Code*[14] makes it an offence to "make, print, publish, circulate or possess for these purposes obscene materials."[15] The focus is on the communication, not the possession of obscene materials. The Code's intent is to restrict traffic in obscenity, not possession of obscenity for personal use. Moreover, trafficking for commercial gain will be most likely to attract the police. A more specific provision of the Code deems obscene "any publication a dominant characteristic of which is the undue exploitation of sex, or of sex and any one or more of the following subjects, crime, horror, cruelty and violence."[16]

Estimates of cyber-pornography vary widely and engender much debate. Consider the following comment from the *Internet Handbook for Canadian Lawyers*:

The Debunking of the *Cyberporn* Story

When *Time* magazine published the cover story *Cyberporn: Exclusive* in July 1995, Internet users reacted like any community under attack: they fought back. Within days, the Net was overflowing with material criticizing the story and deconstructing the underlying study on online pornography. The response included the paper *A Detailed Analysis of the Conceptual, Logical, and Methodological Flaws in the Article 'Marketing Pornography on the Information Superhighway,'* prepared by Vanderbilt University professors Donna Hoffman and Thomas Novak. They concluded that *Time* misinterpreted the study's findings, and moreover that the study's methodology was seriously flawed. *Time* reported that the study found 83.5 percent of the images on Usenet to be pornographic. In fact what the study's author actually wrote was "among the pornographic newsgroups, 4,206 images posts were counted, or 83.5 percent of the total posts." The true percentage of images on Usenet that were pornographic was *3 percent.* Which amounted to less than half of 1 percent of all Net traffic.

Worse, said Hoffman and Novak, *Time* presented the study as "an exhaustive study on online porn," and left readers with the impression the study's focus was the Internet. In fact, the study's emphasis was not the Net at all, but privately run adult-oriented Bulletin Board Systems. As if all that wasn't convincing enough, Hoffman and Novak proceeded to take apart the study line by line, revealing a "vast array of conceptual, logical, and methodological flaws."

The debunking of the study was complete when it was revealed that its author, 30-year-old Carnegie Mellon University undergraduate Martin Rimm, had in fact planned to use the study data for a book to be called *The Pornographer's Handbook: How to Exploit Women, Dupe Men and Make Lots of Money*, offering marketing tips to operators of adult BBSes.

Canadian courts rely on a two-part test to ascertain whether or not the material in question is obscene:

- Does the material involve the "undue exploitation of sex"?
- If so, is it the dominant theme of the material, or is it essential to a wider artistic, literary or other purpose?

The test for "undue exploitation" is one of "community standards": what would the community tolerate others being exposed to on the basis of the degree of harm that such exposure may cause?[17] Community can be a difficult benchmark. Consider for example whether community standards will vary between rural Quebec and downtown Vancouver, or the backwoods of Tennessee and Hollywood, Los Angeles.[18] This notion becomes especially tenuous in the context of the information highway, which serves a "global community" with vastly varying values.

WHOSE COMMUNITY STANDARDS APPLY ON THE INTERNET?

In *U.S. v. Thomas* a couple created an adult-only bulletin board service providing pornographic material from Milpitas, California. They were prosecuted for disseminating obscene material in Memphis, Tennessee, where state prosecutors requested a Tennessee postal inspector to download the offensive images. The couple were judged guilty by a jury applying the more conservative Tennessee community standards to material that was judged legal by the more liberal California community standards.

In a more recent case, a major U.S.-based Internet provider deleted substantial amounts of adult audience material — acceptable in the U.S. — when it was prosecuted for obscenity in Bavaria, a strongly religious region of southern Germany.

Harm is determined by testing the results of the anti-social behaviours — the greater the risk of harm, the lesser the degree of community tolerance. The Supreme Court has established three categories of potentially harmful materials. Those manifesting:

- explicit sex with violence
- explicit sex without violence but which subjects people to degrading or dehumanizing treatment
- explicit sex that is neither degrading nor dehumanizing.

The first is almost always "undue"; the second is "undue" where the risk of harm is substantial; and the third is rarely "undue."

Once a court concludes that material is generally obscene it must then examine it in context. Here the court determines whether, within the entire work or communication, it plays a dominant or subsidiary but essential role. If it's both obscene and dominant, its publication, circulation, distribution, etc. is a criminal act.

But these *Criminal Code* prohibitions may be challenged as trespassing on constitutional guarantees of fundamental freedoms. To this challenge we now turn.

The *Charter of Rights and Freedoms*[19] was adopted in 1982. It guarantees in the Canadian Constitution certain fundamental rights and freedoms, including freedom of expression. By including certain rights in the Constitution they may be overridden only through an amendment requiring unique procedures and majorities, or by engaging the controversial "notwithstanding" clause, which must be re-engaged within five years for the override to continue. The Canadian Charter was one of the fundamental objectives of former prime minister Trudeau, who brought it into law with the amending formula to the Canadian Constitution by Act of the United Kingdom Parliament. The Charter applies to federal, provincial, and territorial governments. Accordingly, only state action or legislation can be challenged under the Charter.

Freedom of expression is not absolute; the Charter balances individual and collective rights. Thus, section 2(b) guarantees the fundamental "freedom of thought, belief, opinion and expression, including the freedom of the press and other media of communication." But section 1 qualifies this freedom. It authorizes the imposition of reasonable limits on these rights, provided the limits are sanctioned by law and "can be demonstrably justified in a free and democratic society." Two tests determine justification:

- Is the restriction of sufficient importance to justify overriding a constitutionally protected right and does it relate to a pressing and substantial social concern?
- Are the means to limit the right reasonable and proportionate to the object sought?[20]

The U.S. has struck a somewhat different balance between freedom and control. To this we now turn.

The U.S.: The First Amendment Constitutional Guarantees of Freedom of Speech

The United States has a much older constitutional guarantee of freedom of expression. Unlike Canada, the U.S. doesn't qualify the guarantee in the Constitution itself. But the courts have creatively done so through a series of tests that place boundaries on the "absolute" freedom. The Communications Decency Act (CDA), passed by Congress and signed into law by President Clinton in February 1996, was struck down scarcely six months later in a suit brought in Philadelphia by the American Civil Liberties Union against the U.S. Attorney General Janet Reno, who has the responsibility of enforcing this law. The Supreme Court confirmed its unconstitutionality in June 1997. The 1792 U.S. Constitution's First Amendment reads:

> Congress shall make no law respecting an establishment of religion, or prohibiting the free exercise thereof; or abridging the freedom of speech, or of the press; or the rights of people peaceably to assemble and to petition the government for a redress of grievances.[21]

The courts have permitted some governmental limitation on this freedom as necessary to protect social morals. The U.S. CDA simply went too far.

The European Union: Human Rights Convention

In the EU a wide-ranging group of nation states has created a common statement of community standards and individual freedoms. The European Convention for the Protection of Human Rights and Fundamental Freedoms[22] presents an interesting contrast to the Canadian and American constitutions because it provides a more explicit statement of the qualifications for the balance between individual and collective rights. Moreover, like the Canadian formulation, the Constitution itself contains these limits. It reads:

a) Everyone has the right to freedom of expression. This right shall include freedom to hold opinions and to receive and impart information and ideas without interference by public authority and regardless of frontiers. The Article shall not prevent States from requiring the licensing of broadcasting, television or cinema enterprises.

b) The exercise of these freedoms, since it carries with it duties and responsibilities, may be subject to such formalities, conditions, restrictions, or penalties as are prescribed by law and are necessary in a democratic society, in the interests of national security, territorial integrity or public safety, for the prevention of disorder or crime, for the protection of health or morals, for the protection of the rights of others, for preventing the disclosure of information in confidence, or for maintaining the authority and impartiality of the judiciary.

Another interesting feature of the European Convention is that it's supra-national. The United Kingdom is a member of the EU and a party to this Convention. Unlike the U.S., the U.K. doesn't guarantee such fundamental rights as freedom of speech in a written constitution. Its doctrine of parliamentary sovereignty (originally designed to check the absolute power of kings) gives supremacy to the lawmaker — the legislature — to enact any law, although British courts and public conscience have been notably successful over the centuries in limiting the overwhelming reach of the sovereign or lawmaker.[23] But the Convention provides a parallel system of law for balancing state collective control and individual freedom. Thus, whether or not a British citizen has first challenged a British law on freedom of speech grounds in the U.K., she may seek to do so under the European Convention, proceed to Strasbourg to petition the European Court of Human Rights, and seek enforcement against the U.K. Parliament through the EU in Brussels. Here we see one more model in the balance between control and freedom.

Conclusion

This brief review of criminal obscenity and freedom of speech guarantees in three jurisdictions illustrates the variances in the standards for the crime, the protective defence threshold, and the mechanism for interpretation. Moreover, electronic commerce will increasingly bring these individual and collective rights and responsibilities into conflict. This will likely underline the limitations of older types of regulation, and encourage greater reliance on less formal and less traditional forms.

Alternate Forms of Regulation

It is cyberspace's transjurisdictional nature that renders traditional national modes of legislation ineffective in deterring undesirable conduct. What's considered desirable and what's not differs across cultural and national boundaries. This sense of lawlessness has given rise to the frequent analogy drawn between cyberspace and the "wild West." That analogy is surprisingly good when one considers that the settling of the North American West involved an exploration and settling of new areas that attracted people from various backgrounds, cultures, and nationalities. And as with the settling of the West, a certain cyberspace "frontier justice" has developed so that order may be maintained. As we observe this frontier justice and its move toward more formalized norms we have an opportunity to redefine not only our methods of enforcement, but the very nature of laws themselves.

Consider the following problem: dissemination of child pornography has increased dramatically with the Internet's growth. Almost every jurisdiction has laws to deter pornography, yet enforcement is difficult. The law's purpose is to protect children from being forced to engage in sexual acts. Textual representations of sexual activity with children, for example, don't fall under some jurisdictions' criminal code prohibition of child pornography because mere text doesn't offend the law's underlying purpose. Conversely, pictorial manifestations have traditionally almost always fallen under the law's umbrella.

To further complicate matters a new form of pornography involving children is emerging in the digital age. It's now possible to digitally manipulate pictures (and any form of digital information) so that evidence of manipulation is virtually undetectable in the resulting image. Readily available drawing software permits one to take legalized pornography, i.e. where those depicted are of age, and to superimpose the face of a minor on the original person. One may further manipulate the picture to alter body parts so that they appear more childlike. Does the resulting image constitute child pornography? If one accepts the premise that the law was enacted to protect children from actual harm, then here no one is harmed and no law is breached.

A more difficult issue — one rife with freedom of expression problems — is whether to prevent the dissemination of this new material because it may lead to the harm of a child. Different jurisdictions, with different tolerances for state interference with liberty, will likely reach different conclusions. This and many other such issues raised by new technologies are years away from resolution. Indeed, they may never be harmonized at a global level. What happens in the meantime?

Often the knee-jerk response to these types of problems is a cry for government intervention. But given government downsizing and deregulation, the technological difficulties of controlling cyberspace, and free speech demands that this new environment be allowed to flourish "naturally," it's not clear that large-scale government intervention is the wisest approach. What has begun to emerge instead are alternate forms of regulation that are "true" to the techno-culture from which cyberspace has sprung.

Rules crafted in cyberspace are often market-driven, calibrated to user needs, and constrained by available resources. Further, user groups often comprise academics and researchers with relatively liberal values. The result is an environment that cherishes free thinking and expression and is relatively tolerant of behaviour that may, in conventional society, be considered offensive or injurious. This environment encourages the enhancement of knowledge and progress, and recoils from political correctness. Yet it's not anarchical, as some may believe. Some forms of control, instrumental in shaping the cyber-environment, have clearly emerged. Here we discuss three forms of alternate, non-governmental regulation: self-regulation, private regulation, and vigilanteism.

Self-Regulation

Self-regulation provides an entirely new control ethic whereby the power of regulation is placed in the individual user's hands. It's often proffered as the answer to the intricate problem of content control in modern society.

Free speech advocates have long argued that regulation should be self-imposed to encourage diversity of views and tolerance. Most jurisdictions support some form of plain view doctrine. This allows some free speech restrictions to be imposed so that people aren't forced to face materials that are socially questionable. However, modes in cyberspace, including the Web and USENET, often require a user to actively seek out these materials. Typically these are not in "plain view."

Greater difficulty arises with children, the Achilles' heel of free speech. Self-regulation simply doesn't work where children are concerned. However, newly developed access control products may provide a long-sought answer. Parents, schools, libraries, retailers — anyone who sets up a computer connected to cyberspace — now have tools to prevent minors' unwanted access. Although an infant technology, its acceptance is rapidly accelerating. Government, too, has embraced this technology. Technologically driven self-regulation may become cyberspace's predominant content regulation form.

Information providers catering to the adult market have created software-based products similar to the V-chip. Examples include Cyber Patrol, Surfwatch, and Net Nanny. In addition to blocking out pornography and hate literature, these products can restrict access based on whatever

The V-Chip

Once installed in a TV set, the newly invented Canadian V-chip allows a rating signal, which is transmitted with each television broadcast, to activate a block-out function. This will block either a whole show, or only its violent or sexual portions. The V-chip enables parents to set their own standards for what their children may watch at home.

criteria a user sets. Use of these products on one's local computer will work in conjunction with supported Web sites, enabling parents to restrict access to these sites. Many adult information providers have voluntarily supported the server end of this equation. Most products work on the USENET as well, and some will work on any information coming from cyberspace regardless of the mode, e.g. chat or e-mail. At present these products detect only text. The technology to detect graphics and sounds is currently being developed.

Private Regulation

Private regulation is relatively new. Although all the alternate regulation we discuss here properly forms a subset of private regulation, we use the term to denote non-governmental organizations that exercise control of cyberspace. Control may be either "hard," i.e. coercive, or "soft," e.g. standards setting.

First, soft. Standards-setting organizations include both policy- and technology-based groups. At the international level these include the International Telecommunications Union (ITU), the International Consultative Committee on Telephone and Telegraphy (CCITT), the International Standards Organization (ISO), and the International Electrotechnical Commission (IEC). National examples include the Canadian Standards Association (CSA) and the American National Standards Institute (ANSI). Lesser-known groups, such as industry groups and professional associations, e.g. the Order of Engineers, are key contributors to standards development. These organizations perform important work in place of government, often formalized in policy or even law. One example comes from the Canadian government's Information Highway Advisory Council and its privacy recommendations. It proposes that the federal government enact privacy protection according to the CSA's draft *Model Code for the Protection of Personal Information.*[24] Government policy in this area is increasingly reliant on such private sector work.

In cyberspace private regulation is increasingly "coercive" in nature, i.e. one must adhere to it. And often "soft" norms can become "hard" rules. Examples include the policies of Internet service providers (ISPs) and other cyberspace on-ramps such as universities, as well as the domain name system (DNS).

As cyberspace becomes an essential part of daily functioning (both in business and beyond) it increasingly adopts a public space character. Allowing private concerns to control access and use poses interesting legal questions. Traditionally governments control public spaces. The Canadian *Charter of Rights and Freedoms* and the U.S. Constitution set out the fundamental rights of citizens. These are rules for what law can and can't control. Where private organizations are concerned, however, these fundamental constraints don't directly apply. And without laws dictating the acceptable behaviour of these private organizations they have substantial freedom within their domains over what terms they can dictate. Although this isn't yet cause for conflict, the explosive growth of cyberspace creates the opportunity.

For the most part, private organizations whose sole purpose is to provide access to cyberspace (e.g. ISPs) are commercially driven. They adopt a market-based approach in formulating policy. Other organizations don't, and may operate using a different ethic. The access policies of universities, for example, are rooted in their primary goal of advancing knowledge. In business the primary goal is pursuit of profit, and this will be reflected in their employee cyberspace access policies, which may for example prohibit cyberspace game playing.

Of the three organizations — ISPs, universities, and business — ISPs are of most immediate concern. Why? Because society accepts that organizations with distinctive goals may set distinctive policies to achieve them, and will often strike a balance when several conflicting goals are present. Labour laws that set out employer and employees' respective roles and rights are an example. The role of ISPs, however, isn't as clearly demarcated. They provide access, set policies for their members, and exercise great societal control of cyberspace. They weren't given authority to exercise this control; the power has fallen into their lap. Since ISPs are primarily market-driven it's obviously not in their interest to set restrictive policies that will lose them customers. But they're particularly vulnerable to boycotts and pressure by conservative forces and radical fringe groups. Whereas unduly restrictive government intervention is traditionally overseen by a critical free press, monitoring of the ISP industry may be prudent to ensure that the access provided is consistent with our understanding and respect for freedom.

Cyberspace is becoming an essential part of communication. Power over communications shouldn't be lightly given into the hands of private organizations whose goals aren't always clear or, if clear, strike an inappropriate balance between individual freedom and public order. This issue merits further review.

The same argument applies to our second example, domain name systems (DNS). As described in Chapter 2, DNS is the system for registering and locating cyberspace addresses. The system is maintained by various organizations, each of which controls one or several domain groups, e.g. .com or .ca. There's no prescribed form for these organizations. They may be private not-for-profit or for-profit commercial organizations, or government agencies. Each organization will distribute the addresses it controls based on its policies, and some may even charge modest fees. Typically ISPs, which have their own address, will provide users with sub-addresses. However, even ISPs are subject to policies and control by higher-level organizations, e.g. Canada's CA*Net and the United States' InterNic and Network Solutions Inc. Are these policies fair? Should private organizations have ultimate cyberspace control? And finally, is there a new private monopoly in the making?

In order to address some of these problems, the World Intellectual Property Organization (WIPO) and the International Telecommunications Union (ITU) have recently implemented Administrative Domain Name Challenge Panels. This mechanism, designed to address second-level domain name conflicts, e.g. where domain names conflict with another's intellectual property rights, operates by securing agreements from domain name issuing organizations. Once they agree to participate, these organizations implement the mechanism into their Charter. Any time a dispute arises concerning a name under their control, the Challenge Panel mechanism kicks in. The procedure for forming these Challenge Panels and their rules will be controlled by WIPO. This provides an important stepping stone for the global harmonization of cyberspace rules. However, this mechanism is not law. It derives its effect from private agreements between WIPO and the domain name issuing organizations. It obtains its force through the application agreements signed by the domain name issuing organizations and the domain name applicants, e.g. companies. One can still apply to a national court in the case of a dispute. The court's decision will triumph over that of a Challenge Panel. It is likely, however, that over time courts will begin to look to WIPO Challenge Panel decisions for guidance, as these panels will amass a body of jurisprudence and expertise that can help guide courts in cyber-decision-making.

Vigilanteism and Netiquette

A final form of regulation of surprising effectiveness and power in cyber-

FRONTIER JUSTICE

In 1993 Lawrence Canter and Martha Siegel, a husband and wife team of lawyers, used the Internet's USENET news service to advertise their immigration advisory services. Although advertising of goods or services on the USENET was at that time considered to be largely unacceptable it was nevertheless beginning to appear in certain newsgroups. The difference here was that the two lawyers posted their ad to thousands of newsgroups around the world. While their cyber-marketing netted them some extra business, it also incensed some USENET readers — who promptly set out to rectify the situation.

They employed the more traditional pranks of having magazine subscriptions and pizza deliveries sent to the couple. But they also launched some high-tech retaliation. One user created a program known as a "cancelbot," which searched out and destroyed all messages posted by the lawyers to the USENET. The couple also suffered "spamming," cyberspace language for repeated sending of e-mail messages (the Bible — because of its length and meaning — is often a document of choice) with the intent of crippling their receiving system. The couple's ISP, inundated with complaints and spams, finally terminated their account.

The story, however, doesn't end there. The lawyers, quickly rebounding from the retaliatory shock, cashed in on their new-found notoriety and published a book about cyberspace marketing!

space is vigilanteism — individuals without the sanction of law using coercive measures to enforce their perception of just behaviour. This technique of regulation has dropped dramatically with the Internet's institutionalization. Stories largely of mythical proportion circulate today about a time when the untamed frontier of cyberspace was lawless and policing was left up to self-appointed posses.

Notwithstanding the experience of the two lawyers, the message was clear: commerce was coming to cyberspace, and there was little anyone could do to stop it.[25] The use of vigilanteism was effective as a stop-gap measure. While it was successful in raising awareness, it revealed new markets to those formerly unaware of cyberspace. It also revealed a lacuna in the ability to control cyberspace, by law and other means. To some it appeared that cyberspace was becoming a modern "wild West."

This fear, though, has proven to be largely unfounded. Cyberspace's continued growth and its increased use by business, which abhors uncertainty, serves as testimony. This successful growth results from the underestimated ability of people to organize themselves and adopt rules at a grassroots level. No central authority or control has thus far been needed, and it remains an open question whether one ever will be.

The rules of cyberspace are largely user-based; new users often receive them through Web sites and frequently asked question (FAQ) documents. "Netiquette," which defines the range of acceptable behaviour in cyberspace, began as a system of rules designed to make computer use at localized facilities "comfortable" and "secure" for average users. Today it's composed of rules that have evolved over time and that originate from all parts of the world. These rules are often posted on Web sites for the world to see, and are typically drafted by organizations that desire to control the behaviour of their users.

Today many access providers require users to adhere to contractual terms that govern behaviour. Some set out specific codes of conduct, while others simply make reference to such terms as "netiquette" and "acceptable behaviour in cyberspace." But whatever the rigidity of these contracts might be, it's clear that vigilanteism has been largely replaced by an institutionalized form of behaviour that's becoming more concrete with each passing day.

Conclusion

As commerce arrives in cyberspace it brings with it an understandable tension between the need for flexibility on the one hand and predictability on the other. Although informal, less rigid approaches to control seem more suitable in times of rapid change, there has been an inevitable movement toward more formal control as creative minds fix on "best solutions" and emphasize the need for certainty over flexibility.

7

Intellectual Property

Introduction[1]

With information doubling every few years, the 500-channel universe bursting upon us, and the Internet's octopus-like growth, consumer information habits are changing. People want information — lots of it — and they want it quickly. (One suspects that retention rates are constantly declining.) With so much information available the need to revisit works already consumed such as books or videos will diminish, since it's impractical to keep one's own expansive depository of books when libraries and video stores are easily accessible. And with new high bandwidth digital cable through which information of all types — from telephone conversations to films, books, and software on demand — will be quickly made available, the need and ability to permanently store information at one's site will further diminish. The immense amount of data required to reproduce digital information in high quality resolution means that the storing of a work is very expensive relative to its telecommunication. As a result, memory in the home or workplace will be severely limited compared to the volume of information that's consumed.

In short, we'll become information users, not keepers. What does this mean for ownership and property laws? Is the current law set up to take into account these changes wrought by technology?

Unsurprisingly, intellectual property (IP) is the area of law that's attracting the most cyberspace attention. IP is the legal protection (usually in the form of exclusive rights) governing works that result from some creative work process. Examples include copyright, trademark, patent, goodwill, trade secret, semi-conductor chip design, industrial design, and sometimes simply one's labour. Cyberspace lends itself to IP protection because it serves as a framework for compiling information flowing from one point to another.

IP is protected by a specific set of laws, both statutory and common, that impart exclusivity to the rights holder. IP isn't protected by general property regimes, i.e. real property rules for land or personal property rules for computers, cash, or cars. Rather, IP laws are generally narrow in scope and apply to specific subject matter. For example, the *Trade-Marks Act* applies to trade names and marks; the *Patent Act* to inventions; the *Copyright Act* to literary, musical, dramatic, and artistic works; and the *Integrated Circuit Topography Act* to semi-conductor chips.

IP is protected because it's easily appropriated. Without protection this highly useful subject matter would thin to a trickle, since creators couldn't recover their cost of creation, let alone gain some economic reward. To economists IP is a public good, characterized by non-exclusive and non-rivalrous use. Non-exclusive use means that once the good is created, everyone may freely use it irrespective of his or her contribution to creating the good. Non-rivalrous use occurs when one's use doesn't affect another's use of that good. Investing time, energy, money, and effort to create an informational product doesn't guarantee that one will control that product or be paid for its creation. Because the laws governing traditional property ignore these public goods characteristics they can't effectively apply to informational products. IP's intangible nature requires artificial compensation, e.g. by enacting laws, to promote its efficient use: hence the different legal regime for IP rights.

Here we examine copyright and trademarks, two IP regimes that are particularly crucial to commerce in cyberspace. We also briefly examine competition or anti-trust law. This isn't an IP law *per se*; rather it applies generally to all forms of commercial endeavour by attempting to restrict monopolistic practices. It's especially important with respect to IP rights because they are by their very nature monopoly rights. The interplay between IP rights and competition law is a delicate one, and not well understood.

Copyright

Copyright is the set of rules governing the right to copy a work; in Canada, the *Copyright Act* contains these rules. There is no common law of copyright. The statute gives the holder: (1) a time-limited exclusive right to make copies of a work, and (2) the right to exclude others from making copies. Copyright also protects the right to publish and perform a work, as well as other more specific manifestations, such as the right to make mechanical contrivances, telecommunicate works to the public, and authorize rentals of computer programs. Generally, copyright exists for the author's life plus 50 years.

While copyright protects the *expression* of ideas, it doesn't protect the *ideas* underlying that expression.[2] Thus the idea of a love story involving two young people is unprotected. However, if the actual text of *Romeo and Juliet* were written today it would be protected (there was no copyright law at the time of its writing; it is in the public domain and can be freely copied). Copyright laws currently apply to original literary, dramatic, musical, and artistic works. Examples of protected works include written text, tables, compilations (e.g. databases), photographs, paintings, translations and, most recently, computer programs. For copyright to subsist, the work must be original and expressed ("fixed") in some material form.

Fixation

As a general copyright principle, fixation derives from the common law. In other words, there's no "fixation" statement in the Canadian *Copyright Act*. Computer programs, however, are the exception. The Act explicitly requires that a computer program be "expressed, fixed, embodied or stored in any manner" for copyright protection to apply. The U.S. *Copyright Act* is slightly more specific. It requires a work to be expressed in a form sufficiently permanent and stable that it may be "perceived, reproduced, or otherwise communicated, either directly or with the aid of a machine or device."

What about an image that flashes across a TV screen? Is that fixed? What about the letter you typed and stored in a computer's random access memory (RAM)? Canadian courts have yet to address whether digital works (e.g. computer programs, graphics, or typed text) that sit only in a computer's RAM are sufficiently fixed. Fleeting images on a TV screen, for example, aren't sufficiently fixed to obtain copyright. In *Canadian Admiral Corporation v. Rediffusion Inc.* the Exchequer Court stated "that for copyright to subsist in a 'work' it must be expressed to some extent at least in some material form, capable of identification and having a more or less permanent endurance." Given that computers use memory chips to hold digital data, which can produce fleeting images placed on a screen, one wonders if the law's understanding of fixation should be revisited to cope with new technologies. Clarifying fixation is critical to IP law's evolution on the information highway.

Originality

The originality requirement has also undergone some change in light of new technologies. Until 1991, in order for a work to be original under Canadian and U.S. copyright law it seemed sufficient that it wasn't copied and that some labour — "sweat of the brow" — was expended in its creation. With the proliferation of computer databases, however, that principle has changed, at least under U.S. law. In *Feist v. Rural Telephone* the Supreme Court ruled that simply putting effort and cost into a work doesn't render it copyrightable. In the case of compilations — such as a telephone directory — there must be something more in terms of originality, i.e. "selection and arrangement." If there's a modicum of selection or arrangement that renders the work original beyond some court-determined threshold, then copyright applies.

Armed with this decision, U.S. trade negotiators began to push for similar provisions in international IP agreements. The effort was successful, at least for the North American Free Trade Agreement (NAFTA) and the General Agreement on Tariffs and Trade (GATT). Honouring

"SWEAT OF THE BROW" JUST ISN'T ENOUGH

In *Feist Publications Inc. v. Rural Telephone Service Inc.* Feist produced a telephone directory that was area-wide in scope as opposed to simply town- or city-based. To do this required the cooperation of the local telephone companies that produced the phone books based on and for their clientele. Of the 11 telephone companies that Feist approached only Rural refused to grant a copyright licence to use its listings. (Prior to the case it had been thought that copyright subsisted in these phone books.) Feist proceeded to produce its phone book despite Rural's refusal. Rural sued and obtained summary judgment at the District Court level. Feist's appeal was unsuccessful. Both Courts ruled that copyright could exist in a telephone directory, as consistent with other past lower court decisions.

But the U.S. Supreme Court reversed this, and ruled that in order to be original a work of compilation must have sufficient "selection or arrangement." The Court concluded that simple "sweat of the brow" isn't sufficient to protect a work.

these international obligations, countries such as Canada have enacted similar sections in their domestic legislation. Curiously, the new sections don't necessarily preclude the broader sweat of the brow test for originality, and Canadian courts have shown reluctance in eradicating this traditional test of originality. Recent jurisprudence suggests that in Canada there are two tests for originality: sweat of the brow and selection and arrangement. Demonstrating either will prove sufficient to obtain copyright protection under Canadian law.

The new split between affording protection for sweat of the brow versus selection or arrangement has great implications for the multimedia database industry. The selection and arrangement approach can lead to perverse results, stemming from the fact that many computer databases aren't structured in and of themselves. The data isn't ordered in a meaningful fashion; instead the user employs a search program to seek material. Thus the arrangement criteria has less relevance, leaving the creator with a requirement of selection in order to garner copyright protection. And to meet the U.S. originality requirement, the selection must go beyond simply providing the obvious. This raises the question of whether a comprehensive database — one that includes every piece of information about a subject — would pass the selection test. The designer of more complex databases decides what information to gather about the subject, e.g. Canadian musical artists, and may input some value-added information, e.g. a rating scheme. This is considered sufficient selection. However, where only purely factual data is used it's unclear whether a comprehensive collection will meet the selection criteria. If not, there is no copyright protection.

Note that even where no copyright protection exists there are other legal remedies if the work product is taken. The tort of passing off and the law of unfair competition are two examples. Unfair competition, based on common law, is underdeveloped in Canada and the U.S. The European Union (EU), on the other hand, recently passed its database directive which includes a "new right of unfair extraction" where a database is created but not protected by copyright. This right, held by the creator or owner of a database, arises where a database fails to reach the threshold necessary to garner copyright protection. It removes the protection of certain databases from the realm of copyright and clothes them with a new set of rights based on principles of unfair competition. Certain uses of database materials under this law, e.g. commercial use, are prohibited even though there's no copyright.

This type of rule solves the problem that threatens the North American database industry. The Directive adopts the selection and arrangement criteria, and recognizes that this standard will vary from state to state where approaches to IP differ. (For example, the requirements for copyright are fairly lax in the U.K., while France and Germany have more stringent requirements.)

Moral Rights

Moral rights are defined as the right to have one's name associated with a work (attribution), and the right not to have a work manipulated or distorted to the prejudice of the author (integrity). They exist in the Canadian copyright legislation, but not in that of the U.S. (with the exception of moral rights with respect to works of visual art). Moral rights are also accepted, in varying degrees, in virtually every jurisdiction in the world. With digital information the ability to manipulate an existing work that one has downloaded raises important moral rights issues. While this area has little case law, it's clear that in a moral rights jurisdiction one does not have the right to redistribute a work without the author's name or to change the name of the author. Similarly, without permission, one can't alter a work, either by insertion or deletion, if it will harm the reputation of the author. This test is highly subjective — a court will make the determination.

Copyright and Browsing

Much heated cyberspace copyright debate concerns digital browsing. Also called "surfing the Net," it typically refers to accessing Web sites. Each time a site is accessed something is copied (downloaded), in the form of text, pictures, sounds, or animation sequences (combinations of these types are referred to as "multimedia"). A "Web browser" is software resident on the browser's computer that interprets the data and presents it to the user in the intended format. (Popular Web browsers today include Netscape's Navigator and Microsoft's Internet Explorer.)

Copyright rules only apply when works are copied. The independent creation of a similar work isn't covered by copyright. The Act's infringement provisions apply where an entire work, or a substantial part of it, has been copied.[3] Whether the amount copied is substantial is the first copyright hurdle that must be cleared, and is determined case by case. In determining substantiality courts focus not only on the quantity of the parts copied but also on their quality, i.e. whether the downloaded part is substantial in the context of the entire site.

Copyright rules only apply when works are copied. The independent creation of a similar work isn't covered by copyright.

We begin with the classic *copyright browsing problem*. An author places her work on a Web site. This alone isn't a problem, but once she places her work on a publicly accessible site where any user may access the

Reaping Where One Hasn't Sown

In *International News Service v. Associated Press*, the U.S. Supreme Court extended IP protection based on "reaping where one has not sown" to uncopyrightable materials. In that case, Associated Press sued International News Service for copying its news reports and releasing them prior to Associated Press' full market release of the reports. The central issue was whether there was some IP protection in factual material. Copyright wasn't in issue, since International News Service wrote its own material using factual material gathered by Associated Press. The Court stated that its decision was based on principles of unfair competition, also known as the doctrine of misappropriation. Brandeis J. delivered a strong dissenting opinion identifying the slippery slope upon which the Court was embarking. He stated:

> An essential element of individual property is the legal right to exclude others from enjoying it. If the property is private, the right of exclusion may be absolute; if the property is affected with a public interest, the right of exclusion is qualified. (But the fact that a product of the mind has cost its producer money and labor, and has a value for which others are willing to pay, is not sufficient to ensure to it this legal attribute of property. The general rule of law is, that the noblest of human productions — knowledge, truths ascertained, conceptions, and ideas — become, after voluntary communication to others, free as the air to common use. Upon these incorporeal productions the attribute of property is continued after such communication only in certain classes of cases where public policy has seemed to demand it.) These exceptions are confined to productions which, in some degree, involve creation, invention, or discovery. But by no means all such are endowed with this attribute of property.
>
> . . . The rule for which the plaintiff contends would effect an important extension of property rights and a corresponding curtailment of the free use of knowledge and ideas; and the facts of this case admonish us of the danger involved in recognizing such a property right in news . . .

material, and the material is housed in such a manner as to encourage its downloading, then she has implicitly authorized copying. Remember that technology permits Web sites to remain password protected, thereby refusing access to the public at large. But since providing global public access is generally the purpose for placing material on the Web, to date the number of Web sites that are password protected make up only a small proportion of the total.

There's a further complication. Although the Act requires that any assignment or licence of copyright be made *in writing signed by the owner of the right*,[4] there is no such agreement in most browsing cases. But the Act further states that the owner may *authorize* the reproduction of the work in any material form. This means that it's possible to use the material, i.e. reproduce it, without owning or licensing the copyright. It's arguable that where browsing has been *authorized*, expressly or implicitly, the author isn't "transferring" her proprietary rights. Authorization, under this reasoning, is different from licensing or assigning rights. Consider an analogy. When you host a dinner party you allow visitors to make use of your property, e.g. house, plates, etc. This authorization doesn't allow the visitors to do anything further; nor does it deprive you of your proprietary rights. Under this interpretation, a grant of a licence (or an assignment) allows the licensee/assignee to transfer an interest in the work to a subsequent licensee. Of course, the competing view is simple and clear: a licence is a grant of any interest, including an interest to use a work.

In the case of copyright, the permissive view — that allowing the digital browsing of a work avoids the Act's signature provision — is likely to prevail. Generally, where a strict interpretation of the law doesn't yield a clear answer to a question the intention or purpose of the legislation is examined. Copyright was designed to encourage both the dissemination of works and their creation through granting authors time-limited monopoly rights. To restrict an entire genre of works by imposing a signature requirement violates the Act's spirit. In sum, placing material on a Web site doesn't grant an *implicit licence* to browse, but rather an *implicit authorization*.

Beware that this view of the spirit of copyright isn't universally accepted. There are many competing views, including, for instance, that of *droit d'auteur* jurisdictions such as France and Germany, which tend to view protection of one's creations as based on natural law principles.

Protecting an author's creation is thus a fundamental right, a form of human right. Conversely, Article 1 of the American Constitution clearly enunciates that Congress' copyright powers are based on utilitarian principles. Canada's situation isn't as clear. Although Canadians lack a strong purposive statement (such as a declaration in the Constitution) to anchor the law, it's nevertheless apparent from examining Anglo-Canadian copyright jurisprudence that both the U.K. and Canadian copyright laws have continually sought a utilitarian underpinning similar to that of the U.S.

Browsing Limitations

While the implicit authorization to browse may be a sufficient justification for the browser who downloads material for her own review, questions of further use of the material by that user remain. If there's no express statement allowing or excluding further use — to incorporate material into a business document, say, or to pass it on to friends — what rights are implied? We don't know. Similarly, other terms of the authorization, such as the length of time that a user may store downloaded material, remain unresolved. For example, must the user have to delete it within a given period of time? Several provisions in the *Copyright Act* partially address this problem.

First, if the portion of the work downloaded isn't a *substantial part* of the work as a whole, measured in qualitative terms by a court, the Act doesn't apply. An example of a qualitative part of a work would be the "hook" or "catchy riff" in a song. Similarly, choosing only those parts of a book that summarize the entire book runs the risk of infringing the work's copyright. Downloading an entire work, e.g. a journal article, will definitely bring the rules of the Act to bear.

Second, although downloading a substantial portion of the work for personal use is implicitly authorized, use of the work beyond simply reviewing it is not. There is no universally acceptable explanation to support an implicit authorization to further distribute the work. If one copies the work beyond "personal browsing" infringement may result. However, the *Copyright Act* contains several exceptions to infringement, which may operate as defences once infringement has occurred.[5] We deal with these defences below. Where a substantial part is downloaded the author's moral rights also kick in. The author's name must be given mention in association with the work if it was so included. Similarly, one cannot manipulate or in any way alter the work if it harms the author's reputation.

For businesses operating on the Internet a few tips are useful. First, in order to guard against copyright infringement all use of materials found on the Web should be appropriately cited. This will prevent an author from claiming that his or her work was "stolen" — and is a good business practice notwithstanding copyright. Second, where a substantial amount is used, e.g. in a marketing brochure, it's prudent to contact the author and request a licence to copy the work. Contacting the author is usually easy, since many Web sites provide e-mail addresses for authors. Further, the cost may be nil, whereas a copyright suit costs money and is embarrassing. A good practice for businesses using the Web to publish their own materials is to include a statement that indicates the acceptable use of the work. These don't have to take any specific form or employ legal jargon. Statements such as "You are free to use this material in any way" or "You may browse but not reproduce the material found here in any other way" suffice. Finally, if you want to change the work in a way that might harm the author's reputation, you should seek permission. Although moral rights with respect to material found in cyberspace don't apply in the U.S., causing harm to a creator's reputation may infringe other legal rights, e.g. defamation or unfair competition.

Browsing Works that Infringe Copyright

Browsing's most neglected and troubling aspect occurs where a user browses material placed on a site and the administrator has failed to obtain requisite authorization from the copyright holder. Here, the administrator knowingly or unknowingly has placed a work on her site for browsing without permission. The administrator might do so believing that the material is in the public domain, or she might be intentionally engaging in piracy. A work in the public domain is one that's free from copyright restriction, either because copyright has lapsed or the copyright holder has renounced his rights respecting the work. Here, the server administrator may find herself infringing copyright on several grounds. An unauthorized work placed on a server potentially violates several copy-rights: the reproduction right; the publication right (although it's not clear at law whether Web site creation and activation constitutes publication); performance (in the case of animation); and the right to communicate the work to the public by telecommunication.[6]

Although the administrator (whose intention is irrelevant in this inquiry) will likely be liable for infringement, is the browser? The *Copyright Act* is silent on whether the browser's intention is relevant to infringement in a civil context. Rather, once a copyrighted work is copied, the exceptions to infringement set out in the Act, and discussed below, provide the only relief. Absent a valid defence,[7] a browser who downloads copyrighted material placed on a site without the requisite authorization will likely be liable for infringement, irrespective of whether he had knowledge of the copyright in the work. In *Compo Co. Ltd. v. Blue Crest Music Inc.* the defendants were sued for making "mechanical contrivances" without the requisite authority from the copyright holder. The Supreme Court of Canada ruled that while intention is required for actions that raise criminal penalties under the Act such as *selling* infringing works, it's irrelevant for the purposes of civil infringement, which involves only *copying*.

Once infringement has been proven intention will be relevant to a defence and to the imposition of criminal sanctions of the *Copyright Act*.[8] The system allows those accused of infringement two kicks at the can. First, infringement must be proven by the copyright holder, or in the case of criminal sanctions, by the Crown. Even if that's done, there's the second possibility of raising a defence before remedies are imposed. We discuss these next. For criminal offences, one has the added protection that intention to copy must be proven. Furthermore, the Act's criminal offences concern commercial copying. They don't, for example, apply in situations where an individual browses a Web site.

Fair Dealing Exception

The *Copyright Act* contains both specific exceptions, e.g. making a backup copy of a computer program, and a more general defence — the fair dealing exception. (The U.S. *Copyright Act* contains a similar, but not identical, "fair use" section.[9] Fair dealing is often confused with its American cousin.)

This general defence allows "any fair dealing with any work for the purposes of private study [or] research" and "any fair dealing with any work for the purposes of criticism, review or newspaper summary" providing proper credit is given. Many believe that fair dealing should apply to browsing. But because of the paucity of case law interpreting this section's breadth, reliance on it is uncertain and should be avoided if possible.

Although the concepts of fair dealing and fair use are similar in that they provide a judicial safety valve, their exact scope may be different. Americans have a wealth of jurisprudence interpreting fair use. The U.S. Act sets out a four-part test to guide the courts; the Canadian Act does not. Thus Canadian business operates with anxious uncertainty where copyright questions are concerned. Copyright scholars have long debated amending the Canadian legislation to include a set of non-exhaustive factors. Most recently the Canadian IHAC took up the issue. While its copyright expert subcommittee recommended that the fair dealing exception not be touched, i.e. the Act required no additional text,[10] the non-specialist Council reversed the recommendation, stating:

> The section of the *Copyright Act* on fair dealing should be clarified. Specific criteria and guidelines as to the scope of the fair dealing exception should be provided in the Copyright Act, including explicit clarification that fair dealing applies to the making of an electronic copy of a work and to the storage and transmission of that copy by electronic means.[11]

The IHAC's position reflects that of business, whereas the committee of experts preferred flexible discretion for judges. The debate continues.

Public Interest Defence

Another general defence to copyright infringement that may exist in Canada is the public interest exception. Not grounded in statutory law, it exists through limited mention in case law. Under this defence the infringer claims that the purpose of the infringement served the public interest, overriding the private purposes of copyright law.

This exception has a more secure juridical history in the U.K., where it's also given legislative mention. The U.K. experience may assist Canadian courts in this exception's future.[12] (It has yet to be successfully raised in a Canadian court.) One area where it may prove useful is the infringement of Crown copyright. The "Crown" refers to a recognized level of government, whether it be federal, provincial, state, or municipal. Materials created by these governments, such as legislation, reports, or memoranda, are the subject of the Crown copyright in Canada. Consider legislation and case law placed on the Internet without government authorization. It could be argued that placing this information on the Internet without government authorization is in the public interest, thus overriding Crown copyright.

It's unclear whether a public interest defence applies only against the Crown or more broadly. If such an exception is founded on the theory that copyright is utilitarian and that social utility and public interest are mirror images, then a public interest defence should apply against any rights holder. If, however, the notion of public interest is restricted to a rule of law argument — democracy requires that the public have access to government materials — then the public interest copyright defence may be limited to Crown copyright.

Technological Trends and Consumer Habits

Browsing is but one manifestation of rapidly growing technology and fundamental changes in consumer habits that are pressuring copyright law to change. While enforcement of the law has proven difficult in the physical world, let alone cyberspace, law should nonetheless be in step with the reality it seeks to regulate.

Refer to the scenario at the beginning of this chapter. This exploding world has great implications for copyright law and its direction. Pressure for copyright reform is high; yet amendments have been slow. We suspect that a major overhaul of copyright, involving either a reform of existing legislation or the crafting of new legislation, will emerge within ten years. That may not be quick enough for some, but any change should be durable and made with care. Stable copyright law is essential for an information economy's growth, since it provides the backbone of the payments system for information use. Reform should provide greater certainty for business and encourage wealth creation and knowledge dissemination in this rapidly evolving environment.

Transjurisdictional Copyright Problems

Like other laws we discuss, intellectual property laws are only applicable in the jurisdiction within which they're in force, i.e. Canadian copyright and trademark laws don't operate in the U.S. and vice versa. This is especially problematic with respect to copyrighted works, which constitute much of cyberspace's content. Fortunately, several international treaties exist that harmonize some copyright rules and provide for reciprocal protection between member states. These treaties include the Berne Convention and its revisions, the Universal Copyright Convention, the General Agreement on Tariffs and Trade (GATT), and the North American Free Trade Agreement (NAFTA), to name a few. The best known is the Berne Convention, whose membership includes 125 countries. It's administered by the World Intellectual Property Organization (WIPO) in Geneva. WIPO also monitors the intellectual property field and proposes changes for consideration by member states. But as more states come on board, consensus becomes harder to achieve.

Both the Berne Convention and the Universal Copyright Convention operate under a principle of national treatment. Further, both GATT and NAFTA require accession to the Berne Convention. National treatment requires that a country protect foreign nationals of member states at least as well as it protects its own nationals. Thus, by creating a work in one member country, one is assured of protection in another. Such protection, however, will be in accordance with the second country's laws.

In December 1996, the WIPO Diplomatic Conference adopted the WIPO Copyright Treaty and the WIPO Performances and Phonograms Treaty. These two treaties update the Berne Convention to reflect newer technologies, including computer programs and digital works. They require accession by at least 30 WIPO member states, and will enter into force three months after achieving this threshold. (The treaties have a sunset clause whereby this level of membership must be reached by December 31, 1997.)

Among other things, the WIPO Copyright Treaty provides copyright holders with rights over computer programs (and their rentals), database creations, and works telecommunicated to the public. These rights already exist in Canadian law. The treaties also embrace the marking, e.g. digital coding, of information that can be transmitted in cyberspace. This marking allows information to be tracked once it's in circulation. Under the WIPO Copyright Treaty, interfering or changing marking information without the copyright holder's consent is prohibited, as is assisting or facilitating such acts. The WIPO Performances and Phonograms Treaty provides that performers be granted the exclusive rights over the recording and distribution of their performances regardless of the medium. Similarly, producers of phonograms (a term that encompasses digital sound recordings) are provided rights over distribution of their works regardless of form. Of course, in order for a phonogram to be produced, producers and artists must reach an agreement.

These treaties serve to internationalize existing trends in Canadian law. Once the treaties take effect and Canada's membership is confirmed, there will be little change to the law (with the exception of recognizing works distribution regardless of medium). Digital works will be expressly covered, as will marking.

Trademarks

We turn now to trademark law, important to business whether in cyberspace or the real world. A trademark consists of a symbol, design, word, or combination of these used to denote a particular ware, i.e. a good or service. Trademarks serve to distinguish one's goods or services in the marketplace, allowing consumers to identify them as being from a specific company. They may also be used to identify a good or service as being of a specific quality, since trademarks carry a certain goodwill or reputation built up by the company over time.

There are three trademark groups: ordinary trademarks, certification marks, and distinguishing guise. Ordinary trademarks are words or symbol marks associated with a good or service and held by individuals or organizations. (Coca-Cola is perhaps the best known.) Certification marks are names or symbols used by organizations to identify quality in a good or service. For example, the Canadian Standards Association uses the CSA mark to identify a good that satisfies its safety levels. Distinguishing guise, or "get up" as it's sometimes known, identifies a ware by its physical representation, such as its packaging or physical shape. (Coca-Cola's ribbed glass bottle with the curvy shape is a classic example.)

Trademarks, like copyrights, are considered IP. Trademarks differ from copyright, however, in that there are two applicable legal regimes depending on whether the trademark is registered or unregistered. A registered trademark complies with the federal *Trade-Marks Act* registration requirements and is inscribed in the trademark's register. It lasts for 15 years and is renewable. Registration costs several hundred dollars,[13] and renewal requires another fee. Once registered, the trademark holder has the exclusive right to use the trademark in the country of registration; no one else may use the trademark without the holder's permission. The holder may license or assign (transfer) it to others, and assignments must be registered with the Trade-Marks Office.

In Canada, trademarks may also be unregistered ("common law trademarks"). They derive their protection not from registration, but from use. No formal step is required. Unlike registered marks, unregistered marks don't necessarily apply across the country. They may be limited to the geographical area in which they're used and known. Generally, if one is serious about using a trademark to identify goods or services as being the product of a specific organization, or to denote a given quality, then the trademark should be registered. Reliance on an unregistered trademark is uncertain, and requires proof of use in court. If others use the same mark, or if the mark is registered by another, one may be forced to discontinue its use.

For a name or symbol to become a trademark certain characteristics must exist. If it's a name it can't be clearly descriptive of the good or service, since this would give a monopoly over characteristics native or generic to the good or service. This would cause unfair competition, which isn't the purpose of trademarks law. For example, a company offering online shopping couldn't register "Online Shopping." Similarly a trademark can't be clearly misdescriptive of the good or service. You couldn't, for example, register Joe's No-Meat Burgers if your burgers contained meat. Other prohibitions include misdescribing the location of origin of the good, e.g. it would be unacceptable to register "Canadian Cola" if it's made in France. Similarly, a word in a foreign language contained in a mark that describes the good or service can't be registered. Nor can a person's name, unless it's come to denote the good or service over time. Adidas shoes, named after the founder, Mr. Adidas, has come to represent his shoes and is registrable. Finally, certain marks set out in the Canadian *Trade-Marks Act* are prohibited from use.[14] These include, among others, the Canadian flag, the United Nations symbol, the Red Cross logo, and flags and symbols of other countries, provinces, and municipalities.

Trademarks are protected in order to avoid public confusion. Marks that cause confusion because they look or sound like other marks that represent similar goods or services can't be registered.

Finally, certain parts of a mark may be disclaimed, i.e. they may form part of one's mark but aren't protected. For example, "Superstar Internet Provider Service" would likely have to disclaim "Internet Provider Service" since it represents the nature of the service. If after much use the entire combination of words becomes sufficiently distinctive in representing one's goods or services then registration may be possible.

As with copyright, there is no marking requirement in identifying a trademark. Identifying the good or service using a ® or ™ or MC (*marque de commerce*) symbol is voluntary, though recommended. Note that the ® can only be used in the case of a registered mark, whereas the ™ or MC may be used with both a registered or unregistered mark.

Whether registered or unregistered, trademarks are only valid within the jurisdiction of the law that gives them force. A registered Canadian trademark isn't a registered trademark for U.S. law. If you run a business with international distribution, serious consideration should be given to registering your mark in each jurisdiction where your product or service is distributed.

The registration procedure may be broken down into several discrete stages: use, application, examination, and registration. Use refers to pre-application use (the *Trade-Marks Act* requires that a mark be used prior to registration). There's provision to make an application based on proposed use, but actual use of the trademark must occur before registration will be granted.

The application stage involves completing and submitting an application with the prescribed fee to the Trade-Marks Office with or without the help of a licensed trademarks agent. One usually searches the trademarks register prior to application to avoid immediate rejection. A public online register isn't yet in operation, and searching must be done in person at the Trade-Marks Office or through private firms offering this service.

Once submitted, the application will undergo several tests at the Trade-Marks Office. The trademarks register will be searched again, the trademark will be examined for compliance with the Act, and the proposed mark will be published in the Trade-Marks journal (issued weekly) as a public notice. At this point, anyone may file an opposition by submitting the prescribed form and paying a fee. This stage is important, since a dual (registered and unregistered) trademark system exists. It allows common law mark holders, for example, to prevent the registered mark from being issued based on prior use.

Finally, all going well, the trademark is registered upon payment of another fee and demonstration that the mark is in use (if the application was based on proposed use).

Cyberspace

Early cyber-commerce raises many novel trademark issues. We address three: domain names, cyberspace's transjurisdictional nature, and spillover and enforcement.

Domain Names

As discussed previously, cyberspace requires a special addressing system, known as the domain name system (DNS), which applies throughout cyberspace and doesn't recognize regional or national boundaries. It's administered by various agencies, such as the Internic and Network Solutions Inc. in the U.S. and the CA Domain Registrar in

DNS Policies

Section 5 of Network Solutions' (a.k.a. the Internic) Domain Name Dispute Policy (Revision 02, Effective September 9, 1996) deals with trademarks-DNS conflicts. It states:

5. Third Party Dispute Initiation. Registrant acknowledges and agrees that Network Solutions cannot act as an arbiter of disputes arising out of the registration of a Domain Name. At the same time, Registrant acknowledges that Network Solutions may be presented with information that a Domain Name registered by Registrant violates the legal rights of a third party. Such information includes, but is not limited to, evidence that the second-level Domain Name (i.e., not including .COM, .ORG, .NET, .EDU, or .GOV) is identical to a valid and subsisting foreign or United States federal Registration of a trademark or service mark on the Principal Register that is in full force and effect and owned by another person or entity ("Complainant"):

   a) Proof of such a trademark must be by submission of a certified copy, not more than six (6) months old, of a United States Principal or foreign registration (copies certified in accordance with 37 CFR 2.33(a)(1)(viii) or its successor will meet this standard for registrations in jurisdictions other than the United States ("Certified Registration")). Trademark or service mark registrations from the Supplemental Register of the United States, or from individual states (such as California) of the United States are not sufficient.
   b) In addition to the proof required by Section 5(a), the owner of a trademark or service mark registration must give prior notice to the Domain Name Registrant, specifying unequivocally and with particularity that the registration and use of the Registrant's Domain Name violates the legal rights of the trademark owner, and provide Network Solutions with a copy of such notice. Network Solutions will not undertake any separate investigation of the statements in such notice.
   c) In those instances (i) where the basis of the claim is other than a Certified Registration described above, or (ii) where the Complainant fails to provide the proof of notice required by Section 5(b), the third party procedures in Section 6 will not be applied.

Canada. Individuals and organizations register their cyberspace names with these organizations. DNS names are used to communicate with the name holder, so that in order to see IBM's Web page, for example, one must navigate to www.ibm.com; to send the company general e-mail, one sends it to info@ibm.com (see Chapter 2). But what if IBM wasn't the holder of the domain name ibm.com? Confusion would result — and the holder of the name would possess a valuable commodity. A further legal issue arises: does anyone but IBM (which holds the trademark to IBM) have the right to use the ibm.com domain name? What if the name in question isn't a registered trademark? What if it's only a corporate name? What if someone in a foreign jurisdiction registers a name either with the U.S. Internic or with another registration service such as Canada's CA Domain Registrar? Does this preclude future domestic trademark registration by another person?

These are unresolved questions. There's no cyberspace name statute, and little case law applying traditional law to this new environment. The rules of the game are left to the agencies (often private non-profit organizations) that register the names. To date they self-regulate using reactive, rather than proactive, policies; for example, each organization has formal domain name dispute resolution policies in place. Because business is just discovering cyberspace, conflicts have been minimal.

As cyberspace takes on public space characteristics, for policy reasons it's unclear whether the registration organizations will have the right to apply their rules, especially where they conflict with existing law or the public interest. Certainly the potential liability these organizations face

Business Names versus Domain Names

PEINET Inc. v. O'Brien was the first Canadian case to address the Internet domain names problem. The plaintiff, PEINET Inc., brought a motion to enjoin the defendant, O'Brien, a former employee, from using the Internet domain name PEI.NET or any similar name that could be confused with PEINET Inc. Following his dismissal O'Brien began his own firm, named Island Services Network, to compete with his former employer. Both companies were Internet service providers. PEINET Inc. had used the domain name PEINET.PE.CA as its Internet address. This was registered in

Canada with the CA*Net organization. Island Services Network registered the Internet domain name PEI.NET with the U.S. organization Internic. The defendant used the e-mail address info@pei.net on some literature. The plaintiff discovered this and sued the defendant for passing off.

This case didn't concern a registered trademark or even a common law trademark, but rather a weaker form of IP: one's business name. At issue was whether a domain name, if similar to a business name, could continue to be used by a competitor. Neither side presented expert evidence to assist the Court, and the defendant represented himself. This combination of circumstances led the Court to a peculiar decision. It concluded that because PEINET Inc. used uppercase letters for its corporate name, there would be no public confusion. The Court erroneously understood that the domain name PEI.NET was technologically limited to lowercase lettering. While it's true that the defendant's use of PEI.NET had appeared in lowercase lettering, the use of PEI.NET on the Internet can be lowercase, uppercase, or a combination of the two. A user looking for PEINET Inc.'s Internet address might very well assume that it uses the domain name PEI.NET. Further, the suffix used for ISPs is .NET, just as the suffix for businesses is typically .COM. It's reasonable to assume that IBM's domain is IBM.COM. It's not clear whether the Court took users in the online world, and the possibility of their confusion, into account in its decision. It seems likely that the Court didn't understand cyberspace and the domain name system's operation, i.e. that lower and uppercase both resolve to the same address. The judge hearing the case, in fact, recognized this possibility and commented:

> The whole area of the use of the Internet network and its conventions is new to the court. I find that the plaintiff has only made superficial submissions without explaining the Internet system. The plaintiff merely filed a short affidavit of its president, which leaves much to be desired in so far as an explanation of Internet is concerned. The plaintiff's president did not give viva voce evidence to further expand on his affidavit. . . . It must be remembered that the burden is upon the plaintiff to prove its case.

This cry for help is welcome. Courts can't be expected to be expert in areas concerning new technologies; yet we depend on them to decide their fate. Providing the court with clear technological expert evidence is essential to reliable cyberlaw.

mounts daily. For example, it would be easy for unscrupulous person A to find a company X that's about to go online and register X's name before it can. Once A is in possession of X's name, A may offer it back to X at a price.

To combat this form of cyber-blackmail, organizations such as Network Solutions Inc. have implemented policies to suspend the use of a name where an objection has been filed. Unfortunately they can do little else, given their limited resources and cyberspace's multi-jurisdictional nature. But, left unchanged, the current state of affairs is a recipe for disaster.

In order to assist these organizations, WIPO and the ITU have devised a dispute Challenge Panel mechanism, as discussed in the previous chapter. Where a dispute arises, it will be referred to a Challenge Panel by the domain name issuer. The panels, with a view to international harmonization of domain name issuing policies and with an attentiveness to intellectual property rights, will issue decisions which will then be implemented by the referring organization. The mechanism is so new that, at the time of this writing, it is just coming into force. There is no history by which it can be judged.

Transjurisdictional Problems with Trademarks

Another potential problem stems from the fact that trademarks only exist within national borders. Once outside the jurisdiction of registration, a trademark no longer applies and must be registered in the new jurisdiction. Consequently, in cyberspace there may be companies from different jurisdictions possessing the same trademarks. Whether or not a company is considering doing business in cyberspace, it should be aware of these potential difficulties. For example, if one has built up goodwill with one's goods or services, another company may try to entice consumers in one's own country to purchase similar goods or services using the same trademark. Preventing this may prove difficult and expensive, but nevertheless it's important. If one doesn't protect a trademark, one may lose it.

Similarly, if one places a trademark in cyberspace it may appear in another country without permission of the trademark holder there. In this case one would face a potential lawsuit in that other country for trademark infringement.

Enforcement of Trademarks in Cyberspace

In both cases, however, enforcement of one's rights is difficult. Companies abusing trademarks typically don't have worldwide operations and branch offices in other countries. Consequently judgments in lawsuits, though they may be filed and won, are difficult to enforce. Nevertheless, it's cold comfort knowing that one's organization faces an outstanding damages claim in another jurisdiction. This can hamper future expansion plans as well as disrupt the sale of the business.

How to solve this problem? Awareness is a good start. Those considering doing business in cyberspace would be wise to register their trademark in jurisdictions where the product will be sold. This will undoubtedly be costly, and will require a business decision weighing the costs and benefits of an international operation and the liability risks. If the trademark is already registered by a rival in the other jurisdiction, the business should consider adopting a new one to be registered in all relevant jurisdictions.

For businesses not considering marketing their products in cyberspace, awareness of others using similar trademarks is important. If a similar trademark is being used in one's jurisdiction a warning letter to the rival is useful. If that doesn't work it would be wise to consider filing a suit for trademark infringement. Although it may be difficult to collect any damages that are awarded, the outstanding court order will serve to protect the trademark. Absent these steps, if the trademark becomes associated with another's goods or services in the public's mind, then one may lose the trademark. The rival may apply to the Registrar of Trade-Marks to have the mark struck from the register. Once struck, the rival may apply to register its own trademark.

Cyber-age business requires both knowledge of IP rights and vigilance. Failure to protect one's rights is akin to leaving the doors of a warehouse open. IP law, while among the law's most technologically progressive areas, still lags behind commercial reality, especially in copyright. Trademarks don't fare any better.

Competition Law

Competition law impacts heavily on technology and business. Known as anti-trust law in the U.S., it prevents anti-competitive behaviour in the marketplace, restrains abuses of dominant market position, prevents the formation of monopolies, and proscribes anti-competitive trade practices. Price fixing, cartel formation, and predatory pricing are all examples of anti-competitive behaviour. Any industry whose market share is concentrated among a few players must be wary of this legislation, since these industries may fall under active government regulation.

Both telephone and cable telecommunications companies were traditionally monopolies, given that expensive, geographically specific switching systems made multiple local phone and cable companies infeasible. The resulting monopolies were heavily regulated, right down to prices charged and return on investment. But as technology leaps over expensive switches and invites competition into these industries, deregulation will occur. This will only happen, however, as the playing field levels.

IP by its very nature provides exclusive rights. It works on a monopoly basis, and is anti-competitive. But because IP rights are essential to the creation of IP products they're exempted, to a degree, from competition rules. Nevertheless, even IP rights may be abused in ways that offend competition rules. The latter will generally prevail in a dispute. In *Lasercomb America Inc. v. Reynolds* the U.S. Federal Court of Appeals applied the copyright "misuse doctrine," a legal mechanism used in cases where copyright and competition rules conflict. The Court held that the misuse doctrine extends to render "a copyright unenforceable against any person regardless of whether they entered into a contract containing the offending term." Even *attempting* to widen the scope of copyright protection, by contract, beyond its accepted limits is a bar to its use. Notwithstanding this decision, courts have scarcely considered the interplay between competition law and IP. One should not, however, underestimate the potential role of competition law in cyberspace evolution.

Microsoft: A Target for Anti-Competition Investigations

Since 1990 the U.S. Justice Department's anti-trust division has frequently targeted Microsoft Corporation, the world's largest software company. Microsoft produces the Windows and DOS operating systems used on a majority of the world's personal computers and other popular software. Justice's latest investigation into Microsoft's business practices concerns their Internet-based products, specifically their Web browser known as Internet Explorer 3.0. The investigation was launched after complaints by competitors, including Netscape Corp., the world's most successful browser manufacturer. Part of the problem lies in the fact that Microsoft is the creator of the operating system, in this case Windows, under which browsers run. The complaints accused Microsoft of providing Internet service providers with discounts on the operating system products and the ability to customize the screen to reflect the ISP's business if they officially endorsed the Microsoft Internet Explorer and, it was alleged, made competitor's browsers less accessible.

The investigation will be lengthy, and its result will profoundly affect software businesses. Another less apparent motivation for the complaint pertains to evolving software distribution methods. The present trend is to use the interconnectedness of cyberspace as critical to one's distribution strategy. Users of the Internet can download a software product for free, try it out, and if they like it, purchase it. In other cases, companies (most notably those that create computer games) provide part of the software — i.e. a scaled down version, or one episode of an episodic product — without charge. For example, Netscape Corp. allows users to download its browser, and some other products, for free. They may then use the software for a limited time and, if they decide to keep it, remit a fee. This is known as "shareware." Microsoft's Internet strategy is similar but with one important difference: it doesn't charge for its browser product. This is known as "freeware." Microsoft argues that this is part of the operating system for which it charges.

Whether Microsoft's strategy is anti-competitive remains to be seen. Since shareware and freeware distribution are an integral part of modern software distribution, labelling them anti-competitive will have dramatic effects on the software industry and on software prices.

Conclusion

To recap, intellectual property is the set of laws that gives intangibles their value. Because of its nature, information, e.g. in digital form, can easily be copied without depriving its owner of the information. Copyright laws are needed to artificially impose scarcity so that information can become the object of trade and commerce. We do this in order to encourage the creation of more information. As the primary, and often sole, form of statutory protection granted to authors of digital works, copyright will serve as the principle scheme of economic property rights in the developing information economy. However, copyright cannot do this effectively in its present state. It must be reformed if it is to co-exist comfortably with cyberspace.

Trademark laws are also encountering difficulties in cyberspace. With the rapid development of a global virtual marketplace, trademarks, which owe their existence to national laws, are coming into conflict. At present, a number of corporations and government agencies are responsible for issuing and maintaining cyberspace names. This cannot continue without some intervention, e.g. legislation. Lawsuits concerning trademarks are on the rise, and these organizations are not equipped with the necessary protections should they be on the losing end of these suits. Help, however, is on the way. WIPO and the ITU have together devised an international system of dispute resolution for domain name conflicts. The policy is new and it is not yet clear what effect it will have in creating an international body of domain name jurisprudence. Nevertheless it is an important first step.

Finally, competition law, a largely unexplored area of law in the context of intellectual property rights, is a potential weapon where these rights are being misused. As the importance of intellectual property in global commerce increases, so too will the importance of competition law.

8 CONTRACTS

INTRODUCTION

Consider the following problem. Two parties engage in a negotiation for the purchase of fabric for a shirt factory. The seller offers it at $5 per metre. The buyer refuses and states that it will pay only $4 per metre, and that it wants the seller to pay for shipping. The seller agrees. The transaction is completed, the fabric is shipped, and the money is transferred from the buyer's to the seller's account. This sounds like a typical business contract, but with one small exception. Whereas in the past the transaction involved human beings, in today's world this scenario might just as easily involve two computers. It's possible that no human being would participate in the transaction process. A contract is often defined as a "meeting of the minds." But what happens if the two contracting parties are computers? How have computers and cyberspace changed the ways we transact? What does this mean for the law? What if there's a dispute? Do traditional legal solutions apply? Should they? All these issues are facing any business seeking to transact in cyberspace.

In Chapter 5 we saw how technology can protect business. But what can the law do to protect business? With respect to transacting, "the law" usually means the rules that the parties to the transaction fashion between themselves — in other words, a contract. Just as contracts have been building blocks of business in the tangible world, so too will they be cornerstones in cyberspace. Any time a transaction is effected, e.g. a sale of a good, there's a contract. This should surprise few. The tricky part, however, is in applying existing contract rules to the cyberspace environment. Once again we evaluate the success of these rules against the yardstick of certainty. For if business is to move into cyberspace successfully, it must be comfortable in the knowledge that workable and enforceable rules exist.

In its broadest form, a contract is simply a promise made creating an obligation at law. It generally involves two parties, although it may involve more. In common law systems, general contract principles are often based on case law, i.e. previously decided cases, and not on legislation. Legislation is used to correct branches of the common law that no longer square with societal goals. Consequently, legislative provisions that affect contract law are scattered throughout various statutes, and are difficult to distill summarily.

The law of contracts forms part of the civil law, as opposed to the criminal law. It provides persons — whether individuals, corporations, or other commercial entities — with various legal rights that may be enforced against other persons in contractual situations. Other pertinent civil law areas include the law of property (Chapter 7) and torts (Chapter 9).

We begin this chapter with a discussion of the basics of contracts. We set out general contractual principles drawn from the common law across various jurisdictions. They are of so general a nature that they'll usually apply in civilian (as opposed to common law) jurisdictions, although their underlying sources will be different. We then move to a discussion of cyberspace contracts. What kinds exist? What challenges does cyberspace bring? We conclude with a discussion of new and proposed cyberspace legislation, and some of the transjurisdictional problems facing business in a virtual world that transcends national borders.

WHAT IS A CONTRACT?

A contract is struck when two or more persons agree to a certain course of conduct. I agree to sell you my car in exchange for a sum of money. Legal trends over the last several centuries have emphasized the parties' freedom to contract. The "law" will not interfere with contracts except in limited circumstances. The law is, therefore, used most often where one party has breached his obligations, or where there's been a misunderstanding with the result that one party is seeking to enforce the other's obligation under the agreement. If you and I agree that I'll pay you an advance of $50 to paint my house and you don't paint it, I may sue you

UNDERSTANDING "CIVIL LAW"

The term "civil law," used in comparison to criminal law is often confused with the civilian legal system, also referred to as "the civil law." Civilian systems of law are to be contrasted with common law legal systems. Unlike the common law, which draws its laws from the experience of past legal decisions that form the body of law, civil law regimes draw their legal effect from a civil code. This system, which dates back to Roman law, has its modern roots in the French Napoleonic Code. Civil law is still in force throughout much of the world, including France, Scotland, Louisiana, and Quebec. Common law jurisdictions include much of Canada, the United States, Australia, New Zealand, and England. Both systems possess a law of contracts that has evolved over time.

In sum, the common law of contracts has its roots in past decisions, whereas the basic principles of civil law (where contract law is also known as the law of obligations) descend from a civil code and related doctrine.

for breach of contract. In certain situations — such as those involving minors, or contracts with a criminal purpose, e.g. I'll pay you to help me rob a bank — the law may refuse to recognize the contract. In other cases, as in consumer transaction law, the law may require that businesses behave in a "higher" manner vis à vis the public. Here, contractual clauses entered into with a consumer that violate this "behaviour" may be unenforceable. For example, unless specified otherwise, a consumer purchasing a good at the retail level can assume that the product will function.

Contracts are essential to business. They allow firms to interact reliably with one another, e.g. for a retailer to purchase from a supplier or sell to a customer. Establishing a clear set of rules to apply where the contractual agreement doesn't operate as intended is therefore socially and economically valuable. Over time certainty in contract law has largely been achieved. Through many cases before the courts over many years an extensive body of law has developed that interprets frequently used words and clauses in business contracts. Today most business agreements are enforceable. The result? Lower risk and more efficient use of business resources.

Take a contract of sale for memory chips, between two parties who have an ongoing business relationship, where the price has been omitted. Both parties may act on the contract, one preparing for shipment, the other preparing sales. If either party objects to the price a court will fix one at the fair market value. The law expects that the parties have relied on a reasonable price, especially where there's an ongoing relationship and where the product is a commodity, i.e. there's an accepted standard price. If, however, the contract states that the price will be agreed upon at a future date the contract will be void. The law understands that the parties expected to negotiate a price agreeable to both. The court will not impose one.

This simple example reflects the general operation of contract law. It works according to what reasonable people expect of each other. In assessing reasonableness, the law uses such tools as inquiring who is the better risk bearer. Take a contract to sell computer disks, where the buyer has agreed to pay for the goods upon delivery and the goods currently sit in the seller's warehouse. The seller's warehouse burns down and the goods are destroyed. The buyer sues the seller, demanding performance. Unless a statute states otherwise, a court will examine the parties' conduct to see if the seller indicated a willingness to assume the risk of loss. The cause of the fire may itself be cause for a ruling against the seller — if, for example, the seller's warehouse was a fire hazard, and the seller had been warned but chose to ignore the warnings. If the loss was due to an unforeseen event, such as a jetliner crashing into the warehouse, the court will likely rule frustration, i.e. that the event was neither parties' fault and was unexpected, thereby excusing both parties from performance. And with no other intervening circumstances, the fact that the warehouse was under the seller's control, and the seller was better able to manage the risk, will favour the buyer.

In addition to attributing risk, contract law stipulates the relief available. The four types are: specific performance, expectation damages, reliance damages, and restitution. More detail is properly left to a specialized text. Suffice it to say that following a successful suit the court will usually award damages so that the aggrieved party will be put in the position that she would have been in had the contract been performed. These are known as expectation damages. They award the winning party that which she would have "expected" had everything gone according to plan. Generally courts will not force a party to actually perform the contract — the remedy known as specific performance — but will quantify the damages and force the loser to make a money payment to the victor. For example, assume that I agreed to give you my laser printer in return for some legal advice. You perform your part of the bargain, but I decide to give the printer to my brother. You sue me for breach of contract. Rather than forcing me to give you the printer, the court will likely quantify the damages, here the value of a laser printer, and require me to pay you that sum.

Ingredients

Under the common law there is no definitive or closed checklist as to what constitutes a contract. Our definition above is that it is a promise made between persons creating a legal obligation. In most cases, a contract is the result of a bargain. In determining whether a contractual bargain has been struck, the law will typically require these elements: *offer, acceptance,* and *consideration*. As most contracts in cyberspace will also be of the bargain variety, we'll shortly discuss these three points.

Formalities

But first we consider contractual formalities. Generally speaking, there are no specific terms that must appear in contracts. The same is true for other formalities, such as whether a contract must be in writing, have a seal affixed, or be signed by the parties. These elements aren't required because they don't harm contract enforceability. Rather, they simply bolster proof that the parties did indeed enter into an agreement. For example, where a standard form contract is used, i.e. one with pre-printed terms, the offeror may have difficulty demonstrating that the parties entered into a contract where the form remains unsigned. This is because the offeror has created the pre-printed formality of signing as an indicator of contractual agreement. Absent special circumstances, oral agreements have the same binding force as contracts that are written, signed, and sealed. For example, an agreement that I will sell you my notebook computer for $1000 will be enforceable even though we haven't written it out. Of course, if I deny it you'll require some proof, e.g. a witness, to convince a court that a contract exists.

But certain statutes have imposed formalities for particular types of contracts. For example, the *Statute of Frauds* requires that contracts for the sale of goods, where the value exceeds a given amount, or for the sale of land be made in writing and signed. The same is true for a copyright assignment: the *Copyright Act* requires that it be in writing and signed by the copyright holder. Thus one must check for required formalities, within the relevant statute and jurisdiction, prior to entering into agreements. It's always prudent to secure an evidentiary record by using a written signed contract, especially where large sums of money are concerned.

Contracts in Cyberspace

Legal rules applying to contracts have improved with time and experience. The modern law of contracts is highly sophisticated. When cases involving contractual disputes go before courts, judges usually have little difficulty in finding similar previous legal disputes to help them with their decision. Accordingly contractual certainty, i.e. predicting the result of a court challenge for a breach of contract, is high. With contracts created in cyberspace the basic rules are no different. There are, however, situations in cyberspace that are altogether new and to which no existing rules apply. Here uncertainty and business risk is high. Risk, a proxy for business cost, mounts when business must expend resources in guarding or insuring against potential liabilities.

We turn now to the elements of cyberspace bargains as they've traditionally been viewed by courts. As we have little cyber-experience to draw upon, we can only make educated guesses by analogizing existing legal theories to electronic commerce.

The Offer

An offer is an invitation to enter into a binding agreement. Its legal definition is consciously broad and vague; there are no magic offer words. An offer is only an offer if others would reasonably believe it to be. This is "the reasonable person" standard. Conduct that induces a reasonable

Telling your neighbour that you want to sell your 1993 Buick Century to her for $6000 is an example of an offer. If you e-mail her the message, the result is the same.

person to believe that the conduct is an invitation to enter into a binding agreement will generally be regarded as an offer. Telling your neighbour that you want to sell your 1993 Buick Century to her for $6000 is an example of an offer. If you e-mail her the message, the result is the same.

Of course, the situation can be much more complicated. Certain language and conduct may look like an offer in fact but may not be in law. For example, a statement indicating that one may make an offer, or an invitation seeking offers, doesn't constitute an offer. Similarly, an offer

Just So We Have It Straight

In contract language, an offeror is the one making an offer. The offeree is the person to whom the offer is directed. Once an offer is made, the offeree can choose whether or not to accept it.

made to a specific person may not be treated as an offer made to another person. For example, if you e-mailed the car sale offer to your neighbour but her brother read the message, it's not an offer to the brother. This raises the question of cyberspace message posting. For example, a newsgroup posting that states "1993 Buick Century for sale" will likely not be an offer. Since it doesn't identify the offeree, it's unlikely that a reasonable person would rely on it to his or her detriment. But conduct a little more specific may create an offer. For example, posting a message that says "1993 Buick Century for sale. Will take best offer received by 5 p.m. May 31, 1997" will likely be a valid offer, because an auction may be an offer.

Offers omitting terms that are central to a contract based on that offer aren't valid. Agreements to agree are one example of this phenomenon. Saying "I'll sell my car to Jane" doesn't constitute an offer. There's no mention of price, a central component to any contract of sale. Jane and I will likely have to haggle over the price, and the offer will arise at the haggling stage. Otherwise I have no obligation to act on my initial statement. However, omitting price in some cases may still produce an offer. Take two parties with an ongoing relationship where goods have been sold at the same price for years and the price is omitted on the most recent contract. A court will likely "fill in the gap" by ruling that the parties intended the price to be the one that was used in past agreements. Both sides can try to convince the court otherwise by introducing evidence to the contrary, e.g. that the cost of the goods has increased since the time of the last contract.

While the application of the offer rules may sound hopelessly uncertain and complicated, it's not. A simple rule of thumb is to examine every offer from the offeree's point of view. If a reasonable offeree would believe that an offer were made the law will likely agree. A cornerstone of contract law theory is that contracts should protect reasonable reliance. If a person makes an offer without realizing it, but reasonable people would rely on it and do, then the offeror is bound.

Revoking an offer is as simple as making it, with one important caveat: generally, a revocation must be received by the offeree prior to acceptance. The revocation, as can be expected, must be understood as being such by a reasonable person.

In some cases an offeree will return the offer with some additional terms. Here, the offeree may become the offeror. This depends on the nature of the additional terms. If the terms are inconsequential then the offeree may be considered to have accepted the offer. If the additional terms actually alter the nature of the offer then there is a counter-offer. The initial offeror becomes the offeree. This rule is significant for e-mail systems, given the nature of their edited-reply capabilities. Generally, a reply to an e-mailed offer that has been altered by inserting, changing, or deleting terms is a new offer. You can't change the terms and say "I accept" because there's no contract at this point, only a new offer. This brings us to what constitutes a valid acceptance.

The Acceptance

The rules of offer and acceptance are intertwined; one can't properly be considered without the other. Together they're often referred to as the rules of mutual assent. Once an offer is made the offeree must communicate his or her acceptance in order for there to be mutual assent, which is essential for the formation of a contract. Again, there's no rule that specifies what sort of communication constitutes acceptance. The offeror is free to establish what conduct he or she considers appropriate. Where no conduct is specified, the law will look to "reasonable behaviour." However, it's well settled that silence or lack of conduct can't constitute acceptance even if the offer states that without a reply there is a contract. Such unilateral offers, generally accompanied by unsolicited goods, don't constitute a contract. As well, many jurisdictions have legislation constraining this sort of business practice. One can't e-mail a document or software and demand payment without some agreement from the offeree.

As stated above, there are no magic words or conduct to indicate acceptance. Merely "going along" with the offer's terms may be sufficient. Suppose you download shareware software. The terms of the licence — which is a type of contract — state that should you wish to keep the software beyond 30 days you must send in a prescribed fee. Keeping the software for longer than 30 days is sufficient acceptance to create a contract under which the user must forward the fee. To do otherwise is to breach the agreement's terms. This is different from the silence example noted above. Here you've chosen to download the software, and so are therefore responsible for deleting it if you don't want to adhere to the terms offered.

Although the offeror may specify the terms and manner of acceptance, notification of acceptance sent to the offeror in a manner other than that specified but that is *no less advantageous* will be sufficient. Again, the law doesn't require parties to jump through a series of hoops; it expects reasonable behaviour.

Where a cyberspace offer is made, e.g. through e-mail or via a Web page, the offeror is free to indicate the manner of acceptance. Posting a message to a newsgroup that says "1993 Pontiac Sunbird for sale; $6000 firm; please respond by e-mail to j123@zoo.net" is quite acceptable. If no manner of response (e-mail in this example) is indicated in the offer, the question becomes what is reasonable in the circumstances. Generally a reply in the same manner as the offer, e.g. e-mail, is acceptable. Similarly, where an offer is made on the Web or in a newsgroup, and an e-mail address is located somewhere on the page or in the message header, an e-mail message of acceptance will likely suffice.

An offer may or may not specify a particular offeree. Where e-mail is concerned, it's reasonable to assume that the offer is directed to the e-mail account holder. If the post is widely made, e.g. via the Web or a newsgroup, one may reasonably assume that the offer is open to the public. What if the Pontiac Sunbird owner posts her message to a newsgroup? Does she have to satisfy all those who accept? Again, we rely on reasonableness. It's clear to anyone reading the message that the car is used and that there's only one unit for sale. It would be unreasonable to expect more than one car. Accordingly, a court will likely assume an implicit "first come first serve" term in the offer even though none was expressed.

The Mailbox Rule

Contract rules are concerned with the reasonable spreading of risk between contracting parties. The well-known *mailbox rule* was created with this in mind. The rule holds that an acceptance of an offer is effective upon posting, i.e. traditional mailing, of the acceptance. Historically this meant dropping a piece of correspondence into a mailbox. But what if the response gets lost in the mail? Once posted, the risk of delay or non-receipt becomes the offeror's. The offeror can't revoke the offer once the acceptance has been posted. The offeror is, of course, free to guard against this by stipulating that the acceptance must be received by a certain day. Contract rules, such as the mailbox rule, are generally used to fill in gaps omitted by the parties who can't contemplate every possibility. The transaction costs of assessing every element of risk would make most contracts too expensive to undertake.

Does the mailbox rule apply in cyberspace? The rationale for the original rule was certainty. If the parties knew which way the law would decide a case they could knowingly decide whether or not to accept it. It was meant to alleviate the uncertainty associated with the delay between posting and receiving correspondence. The question in applying the mailbox or any other contractual rule to cyberspace depends on whether the circumstances relevant to the theory behind the rule still apply. Delay problems still apply in cyberspace, depending on the actual means chosen for response. If the choice is e-mail there may be a delay, since e-mail is often queued or may sit at an intermediate computer for some time prior to arriving at its destination. The rule may apply. If the choice is online contract creation — e.g. through a Web site that sets out terms and asks "Do you agree?" — there is no delay. The rule wouldn't apply. Although the mailbox rule has received much attention in cyberspace communication, largely as a result of the e-mail-mail analogy, it will likely fade from existence as bandwidth increases and as communication in cyberspace becomes more instantaneous.

Instantaneous Communications

The law governing formation of contracts made through instantaneous communications, such as over the telephone, functions as if the parties were "face to face." In cyber-commerce, communicating with a server using a program that makes offers and receives acceptances will likely be considered a "face to face" situation. This is quickly becoming the standard for cyber-commerce. Many Web sites currently employ forms to receive comments and sometimes commercial orders from browsers.

These sites allow browsers to fill in the forms and submit them, usually by clicking on a submit button. A reply usually appears instantly, stating that the form has been received.

How does this transaction fit into contract formation law? Fortunately, the technology employed eliminates almost all risk that the communication, once received, has somehow been altered. If a browsing party expects to receive a confirmation message, then this should make the transaction iron-clad. Prudent businesses in cyberspace will send an e-mail confirmation message when electronic acceptance is received. The mailbox rule is unnecessary where the offeree is protected against revocation and non-receipt of his acceptance. Of course questions as to who the parties are must still be resolved. Technology for determining this exists (see Chapter 5), but it has yet to be deployed widely.

EDI: Computer-Created Contracts

Electronic Data Interchange (EDI) technology is today's most advanced form of cyber-contracting. EDI is currently conducted between trading partners who have a prior negotiated trading agreement governing the relationship. Computers contact (and contract with) one another. Based on programmed instructions, they try to negotiate an agreement. Often EDI systems simply take human-entered orders and convert them into the appropriate data stream, which is then transmitted. A reply that rejects the offer may be received and a counter-offer proposed. This will continue until an agreement is reached or until one system stops the transaction process. EDI systems range in complexity; only the most sophisticated try to "negotiate" terms in this way.

Because of the large sums involved in EDI transacting, and the absence of an appropriate default legal framework, EDI agreements are generally comprehensive; little is left to chance. This has priced EDI out of many businesses' range. A new wave of low-cost EDI products is emerging, however, that will eventually make EDI widespread, although it may take on another name.

With low-cost, widespread use, these new EDI agreements are also bound to be less encompassing. The risk of disputes arising with no governing contractual terms will increase accordingly. In the absence of terms, these agreements will follow the existing default law of contracts. Courts adjudicating these cases will examine not only the agreement, but the data stream producing the dispute and its computer programs and internal logic. Courts will assess whether the contract was executed in a manner consistent with the parties' intention and, where there is no intention evident, in a reasonable fashion. Since courts are currently ill-equipped to conduct such an analysis the resulting uncertainty will inhibit widespread acceptance of low-cost EDI.

While there are already some standards governing the construction of EDI products, their implementation may vary. The use of differing products to transact electronically runs the risk that one EDI program may not mesh perfectly with another. For example, one program may transmit acceptance of one part of the agreement, which the other may interpret as a blanket assent to the entire agreement. Consider the analogy of a contract negotiated by two people who both speak English but come from different countries. Each might use the same expressions relevant to the negotiation, but with contrasting meanings. While the two people may be able to discover and reconcile their confusion and proceed with the negotiation, EDI systems lack such flexibility. A computer program can't figure out that it's not adhering to the same terms of reference as its counterpart and correct itself accordingly. Not yet!

Take a futuristic example to clarify these concepts. It's likely that given technology's course there will exist "agents" to seek out information in cyberspace tailored to our needs. These agents are nothing more than computer programs calibrated to anticipate our likes and dislikes. We're already witnessing the embryonic stages of this technology. The Pointcast Network (PCN) browser is an agent that collects information relating to business, entertainment, sports, weather, etc. based on each user's preferences. For example, I'm interested in the Montreal Canadiens hockey team; the PCN agent collects articles and scores related to this team and displays them on my computer. At present a limited number of central servers are used to collect information. Client software (that which sits on my machine) then connects to the server and downloads those parts I need.

We anticipate that standardization will allow these agents to roam through many cyberspace sites. If I want my agent to shop for something, I set it loose to find the product I seek at the lowest price and initiate a purchase. This increases competition and converts the global market into a virtual village. Legal difficulties arise where the transaction doesn't take place as planned or doesn't meet the parties' expectations. Suppose I send the shopping agent to buy a pair of running shoes. Assuming that the data transmission doesn't get garbled (technology can often guard against this), what if the shoes that are delivered are black and I wanted blue? What if the size 8 I specified differs from the size 8 according to the store? What if two shoe retailers that the agent visits both send shoes, stating that their systems reached an agreement with the agent? These difficulties can be worked out through law and technology — but it will take time. At present, neither supports the infrastructure capable of addressing these issues. Consequently the outcome of such disputes remains unclear.

An appropriate legal framework is needed. An electronic contracting law should impose default terms where no terms have been negotiated, since attributing the risk either to the offeror or offeree is better than leaving the law uncertain. A law targeting one or the other will alert that party and allow him or her to contract out of the term if it's undesirable. The recurring theme in contract law is certainty, which must, of course, be balanced with economic efficiency. And without legislation governing EDI there is no certainty.

Consideration

The final element of a bargain is consideration. Unlike its conventional meaning, consideration at law refers to the value of that which is exchanged. Under the common law, gratuitous one-way promises are not binding contracts. Something of value must be exchanged. A newsgroup posting stating that I will give my car to my neighbour doesn't in and of itself create an enforceable contract.

Not all that is of value, however, must be in, or easily convertible into, monetary terms. For example, inaction may in some circumstances be sufficient consideration. For example, if you agree not to complain about service, I'll agree to give you a rebate.

The exchange of value must also be done contemporaneously. Promises for past consideration, i.e. value given in the past, won't generally result in a contract, although they have in some limited cases. These latter contracts aren't properly bargains; they're part of a limited exceptional class of non-bargain promises that result in contract formation.

Remedies

Once a contract is formed, many possible events may disrupt its smooth execution. Where a contract or part thereof fails, the parties may bring the ensuing dispute before a court. Using rules accumulated over centuries, courts will assess who, if anyone, breached the contract and what remedy may be appropriate. There are three typical remedies for breach of contract: expectation damages, reliance damages, and specific performance.

The most common relief granted in contractual disputes where the plaintiff (the one suing) is victorious is an award of expectation damages. Here the courts award the winning side an amount of money, to be paid by the losing side (defendant), placing the winning side in the same position as if the contract had been properly executed. For example, I agree to buy a 1991 Ford Taurus from a colleague for $4000; a contract is thus formed. My colleague, however, decides to sell it to someone else. Frustrated, I decide to look for another 1991 Ford Taurus elsewhere. The cheapest available substitute, however, costs $4500. If I sue my colleague, the court will order her to pay me $500, which represents the expectation damages of the breach of the contract. As a result I'll effectively end up paying the same price for the available, but more expensive, 1991 Ford Taurus — the $4000 that I originally expected to pay my colleague plus the $500 awarded to me by the court in damages.

Reliance damages are money awards that reimburse the plaintiff for his expenditures, i.e. the money spent in reliance on the contract. They're awarded only in limited contractual situations, such as where one party has misrepresented a fact that induced the other party to enter into the contract. For example, I agree to buy a horse from a farmer for $1000. The next day, I buy $100 of hay in order to feed the horse upon its delivery to me. The farmer, however, decides to sell it to someone else; he has thus breached our contract. If I then decide that I don't want a horse, I can still sue the farmer. The court will order him to pay me $100. This will return me to the financial position I was in before I relied on the contract to buy a horse and purchased hay.

In specific performance awards the court orders that the defendant perform her end of the contract. Specific performance is seldom used, and largely limited to sales of unique goods. It will not be used for a service contract, because forcing someone to perform a service against her will offends public policy. Instead of service the court will likely award expectation damages. For example, a court could order my colleague to sell me his 1991 Ford Taurus for the agreed price of $4000 if my colleague hasn't yet disposed of it. If, however, the farmer and I had contracted for riding lessons, the court wouldn't order him to give me those lessons himself if the farmer refused to do so. The court would instead award me expectation damages if similar lessons were offered elsewhere, albeit at a higher price.

Finally, once a plaintiff is aware of a breach he must do all he can to reduce his damages. This is known as mitigation. For example, if I found out that the farmer had sold the horse to someone else before I bought the hay, I wouldn't be compensated if I were to proceed to buy the hay anyway.

Contract law is vast, for in law, questions can't always be tightly compartmentalized. For example, problems in areas such as misrepresentation — where someone induces me to enter a contract using false information either innocently or fraudulently — stray into the field of torts. (We discuss misrepresentation in Chapters 5 and 9.) Nevertheless, it's important to note that it also implicates contracts. Moreover, we've skipped by more involved areas of contract law such as mistake, the use of standard form agreements, unconscionability, and frustration. A wealth of jurisprudence deals with these issues. Here we've simply canvassed the most basic mechanics of contracts, touched on the policy issues involved, and discussed how courts approach disputes. We now turn our attention to some of the more common cyberspace issues that will soon emerge.

Cyberspace Legislation

Recall the discussion of formalities. In some cases they're required by legislation, while in other cases putting a contract in writing is simply prudent. This is because it provides an evidentiary record of the transaction, reduces the potential for misunderstandings, and imparts a level of seriousness to the parties entering into the agreement. This raises the question as to what can be done in cyberspace where formalities are required or an evidentiary record sought. Does a written contract or a signature in cyberspace meet existing legal requirements? Today there is no specific legislation dealing with digital signatures (see Chapter 5). It's likely that some electronic contracts will satisfy writing requirements, especially if they're printed onto paper at some point. The writing requirement is often imposed to make it difficult for parties to subsequently alter the agreement's terms. Where a paper copy exists, changes, even minor alterations, may be apparent. But since contracts in cyberspace exist in digital form untraceable alteration can be accomplished with relative ease.

In Canada there are both legislative and technological solutions to these problems. One who alters contracting terms and then seeks its enforcement commits fraud, perjury, and possibly contempt of court. Still, parties are wise to take steps to guard against such behaviour. But these steps involve transaction costs, and one of law's chief purposes is to reduce these expenditures and to make contracting as easy and inexpensive as possible. For this reason, as well as the desire to protect consumers, we need legislation governing electronic contracts.

Some jurisdictions have already begun the task through legislative proposals that typically address two concerns. First, electronic contract legislation may be of a new variety that imposes technical requirements for electronic contracting. These proposals have so far appeared as policy initiatives wherein certain technical standards are *suggested*. This is done to standardize the form of electronic agreements where the private sector has failed to do so. Governments may try to implement such policy by becoming model users. For example, both the Canadian and U.S. governments are currently studying the possibility of creating a public key infrastructure (PKI). Under such schemes, the government would likely assume the role of a public key certification authority. Through a hierarchy or pyramid of trust, the government would certify the next level of entities, e.g. individuals or organizations, which in turn would certify the next level and so on. With the public key infrastructure in place — recall that the PKI structure is designed to facilitate the use of digital signatures — electronic contracts are made more reliable. The level of faith one may place in a digitally signed contract, especially where it's certified by a trusted authority and a penalty is imposed for fraudulent use of a digital signature, is high. (See PKIs and digital signatures in Chapter 5.)

The implementation of a PKI raises issues for the second type of electronic contract legislation: who should bear the risk in various situations of contractual breach, and what should the law impose as default contractual terms where agreements don't set them out? This type of legislation fits contract law's traditional mould, and is relatively technology neutral. It creates a regime of default risk allocation that parties may freely contract out of. Its chief benefit? Certainty. For example, the legislation may require that where a contract is offered and accepted solely in cyberspace, the risk of fraudulent use of a digital signature is the offeror's. Suppose, for example, that Sears sells its wares through the Web and ships products immediately upon receiving a digital signature acceptance of its sales agreement. If someone uses my digital signature to accept the contract and Sears ships the goods, this law forces Sears to assume the loss. They couldn't sue me for compromising the signature. Today, even without legislation covering electronic commerce, this will likely be the result where transactions go awry.

Of course, legislation may proceed in the opposite fashion. The electronic commerce community recently focused on Utah's passage of a digital signature law[1] (see Chapter 5). The Utah law sets technical PKI standards and allocates risk. It addresses a third party, known as a certification authority (CA), central to the functioning of a PKI. It's not mandatory that a certification authority follow the Act's parameters. But where it does, the law provides a safe harbour for the person relying on the digital signature. The Act prescribes an optional set of guidelines for CAs. If the CA in question "opts in" it must comply with the Act's requirements. The legal effect of compliance is to reverse the burden of proving that the digital signature was forged. Consider this example. If Y attempts to purchase goods from X and uses a legally compliant CA, then X may rely on the certificate, knowing that if it's been forged it will be to Y's detriment. The Act shifts the risk of loss away from retailers and suppliers and imposes the burden on the key holder. If a key holder, here Y, should lose or divulge his key, he must inform the CA of the compromised key as soon as possible. He'll remain potentially liable for all transactions where his certificate is relied upon until he does so. Under the existing law, for example in credit card transactions, the party who relies upon a signature bears the onus of proving its authenticity. The Utah law reverses this.

Other legislative changes are required if cyber-commerce is to advance. For example, the *Statute of Frauds* alluded to earlier requires that certain types of contracts, such as those involving the sale of land or those whose value exceeds $500, be in writing and be signed. While it's fairly safe to assume that electronic contracts (i.e. those transmitted in bit form over a computer network or via fax) will satisfy the writing requirement, the signature requirement isn't as clear. The purpose of the *Statute of Frauds*, first enacted in England in 1677, was to prevent the foisting of contractual obligations on persons without this formalized consent. By forcing the parties to make a written record of the transaction joined by signatures to indicate acceptance, the Statute easily met its objectives. But with the speed of modern commerce, the instruments involved in transacting, and the large sums involved, the *Statute of Frauds* is an anachronism that threatens to stifle contracting in cyberspace. The Statute's purpose is still relevant; its methods are not. It should be modernized to reflect digital transactions as constituting valid writing and accept digital signatures as valid attestation, or forbear where another piece of legislation, e.g. the Utah digital signature law, replaces it. There are already U.S. proposals to amend the Uniform Commercial Code (UCC), a codification of the law governing commercial transactions in that country. The Statute of Frauds is but one part of the UCC being examined for change.

There are many other initiatives underway to adapt contract law to cyberspace. The most prominent is that of the United Nations Commission on International Trade Law (UNCITRAL). UNCITRAL's Model Law on Electronic Commerce[2] covers many topics, including risk allocation in PKI situations, digital signatures, and more specific commercial contract topics such as carriage of goods contracts. The UNCITRAL model is continually evolving, and provides a sound basis to update electronic contracts law.

Government as a Model User

One way to ensure that government participates in and understands the needs of the marketplace is to become a model user. In Canada, IHAC actively recommended this in its 1995 report. By using government procurement to increase government and private sector electronic commerce, government will learn the needs and pitfalls of doing business in cyberspace and hence reduce the learning curve for both parties.

To become a model cyberspace user, government must create an infrastructure for electronic commerce. Government departments will require standardized software for communication of information and orders, as well as rules and procedures that govern internal government and private-public sector communications. This model may eventually migrate into widespread private sector use. Minimally, it will permit evaluation of the techniques chosen. Firms that interact with government must adhere to these new technological standards, which should create efficiencies for these participants. Care will be needed to keep the costs of interacting to a minimum. Otherwise there's a risk that only those players who can afford the technology will interact, thereby limiting the number of suppliers and producing higher prices. While the benefits of government as a model user are substantial, issues such as private sector cost must be carefully monitored. In the U.S., to no one's surprise, California has enacted early public sector legislation so that the state government's model use will spur the private sector.[3]

Transjurisdictional Problems

One formidable challenge for cyberspace legislation extending well beyond electronic contracting is cyberspace's limitless frontier. Since cyberspace doesn't respect national borders it ignores national laws. Questions such as where the contract is signed, what law applies, and whether it will be enforceable in another jurisdiction don't yield easy answers. Typically courts will decide whether or not they have jurisdiction based on "the balancing of interest and expectations of the offeror and offeree."[4] This denies certainty to contracting parties. Cyberspace contracts often connect parties from different jurisdictions, whether national, state, or provincial. Each will have different expecta-

Since cyberspace doesn't respect national borders it ignores national laws. Questions such as where the contract is signed, what law applies, and whether it will be enforceable in another jurisdiction don't yield easy answers.

tions of the legal outcome should the contract be breached. One party to a contract may omit a term where they know that the law will favour it should the contract reach a court. This is a dangerous strategy in cyberspace, not simply because more than one legal system is potentially involved, but also because enforcement of court orders across borders is difficult and expensive. (See Chapter 10 for transjurisdictional conflicts.)

What can be done to guard against these jurisdictional problems? For a start, any lawyer will advise that a contract term should always address the law governing the contract. The clause may simply read:

> This agreement shall be governed by the laws of ______________, and both parties agree to attorn to the jurisdiction of the courts of ______________ in the event that any proceeding shall be brought under the terms of this agreement.

The blank is the jurisdiction agreed to by the parties.

While resolving the relevant jurisdiction problem may be simple, assuring oneself of smooth enforcement of a favourable judgment is more difficult. As contractual relations are generally unrestricted by law, one may freely assign the dispute, should one ever arise, to a third party arbiter. After finding a willing third party — many lawyers offer such services — one can reflect this in the contract itself in the same way as the clause above. One can then provide that one or both parties pay additional sums of money to the third party to be released upon completion of the contract to both parties' satisfaction. Where there's a dispute the third party can decide whether to pay out damages to the aggrieved side.

Alternately, the contract might even stipulate that one party pay a third party his or her consideration until the contractual obligation is discharged by the other party, whereupon the consideration is released. In a dispute, the arbiter can decide whether to pay out the full sum or whether only partial payment is to be made and the remainder returned to the payer.

There are disadvantages to this arrangement. The former method assumes that parties have cash available to ensure contractual performance. Many do not. Further, both methods involve transaction costs to pay the third party and set up the scheme. These may not be cost effective for contracts involving smaller sums. As well, the administration of this scheme by contracting parties may produce headaches.

That said, a similar version of this scheme is already globally in place. We each use it. In our case the third parties are credit card companies such as Visa, MasterCard, and American Express. Where a credit card is used to purchase goods or services and there's a dispute, the credit card companies, by virtue of their agreements with merchants and their card holders, resolve the dispute. In fact the major credit card companies force new merchants to post collateral, usually in the form of a cash amount tied to projected sales, so that the credit card companies have the ability to pay back customers who may dispute some elements of the sale where the merchant disagrees.

To date no infrastructure to facilitate cyberspace commerce has developed. Chief among the reasons for this delay are security concerns.

The playing field is currently wide open for private enterprise to impose a proprietary, technologically secure structure. Credit card companies are now competing to lead in cyberspace. For example, MasterCard has recently teamed up with GTE, and Visa with Verisign Inc., to develop a PKI under the Secure Electronic Transaction (SET) standard. (For the various initiatives, including the SET PKI, see Chapter 5.) Given the legal difficulties of legislating an enforceable regime of cyberspace contracts, these companies' solutions may be the key to cyber-commerce.

Conclusion

The law of contracts, fashioned over centuries to fit the needs of parties who transact, is rich in human experience. It would be presumptuous to assume that technological change will fundamentally alter the way we contract. It will not. Rather, contract law will adapt, as it always has, to accommodate cyberspace. Although contract law must change so that it provides certainty and enforceability over cyberspace transactions, technology must progress before this can happen. Cyberspace security problems must be resolved, for until transactions can be securely effected simply and with wide accessibility, business will lack the necessary comfort level. This may require patience. It's important that the market resolve the technological issues first, or we run the risk of law dictating technology — a sub-optimal solution. The contract law that will emerge won't be a "new" or revolutionary contract law *per se*. Rather it will apply old principles to the new environment, and over time will evolve to further reflect cyberspace's idiosyncrasies.

Contract law issues that require immediate legislative attention are: the status of digital signatures and their acceptability in contracts, amendments to the *Statute of Frauds*' writing and signing requirements, legal support of encryption use, and criminalization of crypto-attacks. Government should also give priority attention to public key infrastructure issues, such as the liability of certification authorities. Other than becoming a model user, it shouldn't mandate use of a particular PKI system at this time. The market should be left to make its own choices.

9 Tort Liability

Introduction

In December 1996, America Online (AOL), the world's largest Internet service provider, launched a $300-million marketing blitz to offer its subscribers unlimited access to the Internet for $19.95 U.S. a month. The flat rate meant that once a user had established a connection there was no financial reason to hang up. The result? A surge of new AOL subscribers and an explosion in the amount of time each subscriber spent online. AOL was literally overwhelmed by the consumer response. The modem lines became flooded with users and subscribers were unable to connect to their service provider, in some cases for weeks on end.

Frustrated consumers, including many major corporations, began to vent their anger. They launched a dozen lawsuits against AOL. The Attorneys-General of 20 states threatened to take action, and entered into negotiations with AOL to reach a settlement on behalf of consumers.

Finally, on January 29, 1997, AOL avoided a lawsuit by reaching agreement with as many as 37 Attorneys-General to refund subscribers for lost service. Customers who signed up for the $19.95 unlimited access plan had two options: one month free or a partial refund based on use in December and January. As well, AOL agreed to stop advertising the deal and to maintain its customer base at the current level of 8 million subscribers until it implemented the requisite technological upgrade of its network to handle increased use. AOL CEO Bob Pittman says that the company will invest $350 million to upgrade its networks.

It's not yet known how the settlement — reported to have cost AOL $24 million — will affect the outstanding class action suits launched by frustrated consumers.

AOL's misfortune serves as a useful entry into the arena of tort liability. It forces us to ask several important questions. What had AOL done wrong? What was AOL being sued for? Was this a contractual issue, a tort issue, or a consumer protection issue? Was it all three? Was AOL offering a product or a service? Might product liability be an issue as well? Who could sue AOL? For how much? What was the damage? If AOL's poor service meant that their clients lost contracts, could these clients sue for economic loss? Is there anything new about this kind of settlement? Has cyberspace altered the terms of tort law in any identifiable manner? What protection does AOL have against such suits? Were they insured? Could they get insurance protection? How could they have minimized their risk of claims against them?

While not organized to answer these questions directly, this chapter will provide a sufficient overview of tort law to allow the reader to understand the elements of a more complete response. We begin with a brief explanation of tort law in the abstract, distinguishing torts from breach of contract issues and crime, for instance. We then explore how cyberspace may alter traditional perspectives on tort. We follow with a more detailed analysis of the kinds of torts that business people might encounter while using new information technology; and close the chapter with a brief discussion of issues related to insurance and risk minimization.

Torts, Generally

At the most abstract, one can surmise the meaning of tort from its French origins. *Avoir tort* is simply "to be wrong." To commit a tort — *faire un tort* — is to wrong or injure another person. A tort, then, involves a breach of a duty one owes to another person. This conceptual simplicity masks the mystery of tort law — a complexity that results from its piecemeal development. The law of torts has evolved over hundreds of years. The writ of trespass, for example, was crafted in the thirteenth century in an attempt to preserve peace and order. Over time dozens of other torts have sprung up, each with its own specific procedural requirements, legal tests, and remedies. In fact, for a long time procedural issues dominated tort law. With the increased importance of the law of negligence (discussed below) focus has shifted to more substantive matters, such as the appropriate standard of care that citizens owe their fellows.

How does a tort differ from other legal concepts?

Torts and Breaches of Contract

When AOL failed to meet its subscribers' needs, had it committed a tort or breached a contract? Because of its settlement with the Attorneys-General the issue hasn't come before a court. But the answer may be that AOL had done both. As we saw in Chapter 8, according to contract law we'd have to look to the subscriber's agreements themselves to determine what AOL promised its customers and whether it met these contractual promises. Tort law functions differently, however. Torts involve a breach of general duties to third parties. The Attorneys-General of 20 states were threatening to sue AOL under state consumer protection laws, but they were also considering the validity of several consumer tort claims, including deceptive and fraudulent business practices and false advertising.

There are several ways to distinguish torts from breaches of contract. First, whereas contract law is concerned with enforcing specific promises that individuals make to each other, torts enforce more general duties imposed by the law. Unlike a breach of contract, the injured person doesn't generally have an established relationship with the person who commits the wrong. In a contract relationship the parties themselves set out their obligations to each other, and sometimes even the remedy in case those obligations aren't met. With torts, these obligations and remedies are set by the courts.

Second, because the law of contract concerns the enforcement of promises, the basic principle for assessing damages — the award given to the successful complainant — is that the person should be put into the position in which she would have been *had the contract been carried out*. By contrast, in tort the person is entitled to be put back in the position in which he would have been *had the tortious act not occurred*.

Third, there's often a difference in the time allowed before the cause of action expires. This is known as the limitation period.

Finally, contract law generally functions on a principle of strict liability: if you fail to perform the obligation promised you must pay the damages, regardless of whether the failure resulted from your own fault. In tort law, by contrast, fault is almost always a required factor. As we'll see, U.S. courts have abandoned this fault requirement in situations of product liability.

Courts formerly went to great lengths to keep tort and contract law as distinct as possible. One consequence was that if the parties involved in litigation had already established a contract relationship the plaintiff was prevented from suing at tort. This is no longer the case in Canada. In *Central Trust Co. v. Rafuse* the Supreme Court of Canada accepted the idea of "concurrent alternative liability," which means that under certain circumstances it's possible to sue in both contract and tort. This is significant, both for the remedies available to the plaintiff and the period of time during which the plaintiff may take an action. The doctrine of concurrent alternative liability aids the plaintiff wherever the ability to choose between tort and contract rules offers remedies that would otherwise be unavailable.

Torts and Crime

The differences between torts and crimes have garnered much public attention in the wake of the two O. J. Simpson trials. How is it possible that he could be found "innocent" in one, but "guilty" in the other? Quite apart from the issue of good lawyering, a significant reason for the different outcomes is that the two legal realms have developed different burdens of proof. In criminal matters one has to prove guilt "beyond a reasonable doubt," whereas in tort it's enough to win on the "balance of probabilities."

What's the justification for this lower standard in tort? Since torts involve a breach of a general duty toward third parties, one might question how they differ from criminal acts. The short answer is that the difference is one of degree. Fraud is an example of an offence that may be either a tort or a crime, depending on its seriousness. With a crime the breach of conduct is so egregious that it's considered to be an act against society itself, and not just the victim. Accordingly the state is always the complainant in criminal cases. The tort plaintiff, by contrast, is the individual who suffered the harm.

If the Attorneys-General had pursued their investigation of AOL's business practices they would have looked for evidence of criminal fraud. If on the other hand an individual customer were to take an action against AOL, it would have been on the basis of a tort-based fraud; that is, a fraud against that one consumer, and not a fraud against a community in general. In short, torts involve private wrongs and crimes involve public wrongs.

Moreover, remedies in tort cases, like those for breach of contract, are attempts to compensate the victim for the loss that he or she has suffered. Criminal proceedings focus far less on the victim, and instead impose punishment upon the wrongdoer. The fact that criminal prosecution can lead to imprisonment — the most serious denial of individual liberty apart from capital punishment — justifies the high standard of proof that prosecutors must bring to bear against the accused.

Torts and Civil Liability

In contrast to the common law, the civil law has established relative conceptual clarity and consistency with regard to "civil liability," the functional equivalent of torts within the civil law system. In Quebec, a person isn't liable in "trespass" or "assault" or any other specific category of wrongdoing; rather, the person has breached a general duty to treat his fellows appropriately. According to the Quebec Civil Code, article 1457:

> Every person has a duty to abide by the rules of conduct which lie upon him according to the circumstances, usage or law, so as not to cause injury to another.

> Where he is endowed with reason and fails in this duty, he is responsible for any injury he causes to another person and is liable to reparation for the injury, whether it be bodily, moral or material in nature.
>
> He is also liable, in certain cases, to reparation for injury caused to another by the act or fault of another person or by the act of things in his custody.

The broad, principled language means that it's relatively easy, for both the claimant and the defendant, to understand the law as it affects them. It also means that a claimant will not fail in an otherwise valid claim simply because she has brought an action using the wrong tort. Though the civil law's general duty lacks some of the precision of common law tort analysis, over time case law in Quebec has given specific meaning to the principal terms of this general duty.

Intentional Torts and Negligence

The principled language of civil liability finds numerous echoes in the legal tests that have been developed for the concept of "negligence" in tort law. Given that it's easier to set out a broad duty of appropriate conduct than to establish independent rules for all of life's varied indiscretions, it's perhaps not surprising that negligence has taken over much of the practice of the common law of torts. Instead of saying, for example, that we have a duty not to enter upon another person's land uninvited (trespass), not to hit another in a manner that causes harm (battery), and not to speak threateningly to others (assault), it makes more sense to say that we have a general duty not to injure. This general duty imposed in tort law led Lord Atkin of the English House of Lords to comment, "The rule that you are to love your neighbour becomes, in law, you must not injure your neighbour."[1]

Vicarious Liability

In general, an employer is responsible for the acts of an employee that actually or ostensibly occur in the course of employment. In the case of an independent contractor (as opposed to an employee), the person or company that hires the contractor isn't liable for the latter's acts of negligence, except to the extent that such acts of negligence were directed by the principal. The distinction between employee and contractor stems from old master/servant law, where the master was deemed responsible for all of the servant's actions. The analogy was carried over to the modern employment context, though not to the situation of an independent contractor, who sets the terms and conditions of his or her own work. The classic "borderline" cases in this area involve doctors working in hospitals, where it's difficult to determine the status of the negligent doctor: is she an employee of the hospital or an independent party? In the context of electronic commerce, the status of "computer experts" may be similarly unclear.

Altered Terms of Cyberspace: What's New, What's Not?

If torts involve legally imposed duties to avoid injuring third parties, has new information technology and electronic commerce fundamentally altered them? What's different about a tort in cyberspace as opposed to torts in "physical" space? The answer is that nothing is new, if cyberspace is just a place of communication between the parties involved. For example, if a doctor uses e-mail while giving a faulty diagnosis to a patient, the use of information technology hasn't altered tort issues. The damage done is in the physical world. There's no appreciable difference between giving faulty advice in person, over the phone, via e-mail, or from an online database. Similarly, if I sell a product on the Internet that's defective, the rules for strict product liability aren't likely to be altered. Or again, the fact that AOL is an Internet provider does not, in itself, mean that its false advertising is any different than any other company's.

What *is* different then?

- Differences may arise in the frequency of certain torts. For instance, because it's so easy to "publish" on the Internet defamation and the invasion of privacy have become controversial issues. Similarly, certain torts are particularly endemic to cyberspace. For example, a new tort issue involves the liability for encryption program writers: are they tortiously liable if their programs fail to protect?

- The shift from the physical to the virtual may alter our conception of certain torts. Is it possible to trespass in cyberspace, for instance?
- Because interactions in the digital world are so often and so easily anonymous, enforcement may become a more burdensome issue: how are we to find out who caused the damage?
- Torts often involve a breach of community standards, which vary according to context. Pornography and obscenity are oft-cited examples. In cyberspace, the question of determining who belongs to the community becomes quite thorny. Are New Yorkers, Singaporeans, North Dakotans, and Parisians all part of the same community if they participate in the same online discussion group? Is there such a thing as a cyber-community? Whose community standard should apply? Note that the international aspect of much digital interaction isn't new, but the frequency, scale, and ease of such interaction is.
- Torts in cyberspace may well be new if this digital world creates new perpetrators. For instance, will we come to say that the artificial intelligence of a computer means that the computer itself can be at fault in a tortious manner? One author has already argued for the legal personality of computers, a fiction that mirrors the "personality" given to corporations for the purposes of legal action.[2]

Despite all these changes, we must highlight the law's conservative nature here. Given a new situation, the typical legal response is always to find an analogy to a situation the law has already treated. Only when such analogies become untenably strained will the law develop a new approach to solving new legal conflicts. In the following section we examine how the altered terms of cyberspace operate in a few situations endemic to electronic commerce.

TORTS AND ELECTRONIC COMMERCE

Intentional Torts

Here we highlight several intentional torts that have already or may soon come to the fore with the expanding use of the Internet and new information technology.

Defamation

Imagine that, on a tip from your stockbroker, you invest $20 000 in a company that has just launched a public share offering to raise capital. You don't know much about the company, except that your broker recommends it and the company has a solid reputation, confirmed by its high-profile clients. Now imagine that ten days after the share offering the company acknowledges that it lost one of its biggest clients *before* going public. The stock drops dramatically and you lose a significant chunk of your investment before the week is out. You belong to a newsgroup on the Internet that discusses business issues. You've developed a rapport with several of the other users and wish to alert them to the shady circumstances of the share offering, while at the same time venting some of your anger toward your broker. You post a message on the BBS. You rant!

Have you gone too far? Might there be grounds for a defamation suit against you?

The Internet has provided for the possibility of what one commentator has described as "cheap speech."[3] It's never been easier to step up on a soapbox to voice grievances. Moreover, there's never been such a wide, varied, and captive audience. This is problematic because people are rarely as careful when they post their points of view on an electronic bulletin board service as they are when they publish an article in a newspaper, for instance. The Internet has a new frontier, no-holds-barred ethic. Freedom of speech advocates zealously insist that any commentary should be and is permitted. Moreover, even if what's said isn't meant to be taken as offensive, irony and humour don't always come across in electronic print. All these factors combined have resulted in defamation rapidly becoming a leading legal issue on the Internet.

THE TRUTH DEFENCE

Many people are familiar with the expression "truth is a complete defence to defamation." While accurate, the statement hides the difficulty of "proving" truth in a court of law, where subjectivity becomes so apparent. Moreover, the so-called truth defence does not apply to privacy-related offenses.

Defamation occurs in two forms: libel and slander. Traditionally, slander refers to oral communication while libel refers to published works.[4] Text on a computer screen shares more traits with libel than with slander.[5] In Canada, defamation has been variously defined as words that tend to bring the person named "into hatred, contempt or ridicule"; words tending "to lower the plaintiff in the estimation of right-thinking members of society generally"; and as "a false statement about a man to his discredit."[6] In the U.S., defamation is defined as communication that tends to harm the reputation of another so "as to lower him in the estimation of the community or to deter third persons from associating or dealing with him."[7] "Community" doesn't refer to the entire community, but rather to a "substantial and respectable minority" of the "relevant" community. Accordingly, with defamation, as with many torts, the issue of defining community standards is significant. If hyperbole and aggressively critical speech is the norm in certain parts of cyberspace, courts may find that such speech does not "defame."

A Tale of Two ISPs

The following two cases, with vastly differing results, present a key issue in defamation cases in the digital age: the legal status of the Internet service provider (ISP). The determination of whether an ISP is a distributor or publisher helps the court set an appropriate standard of care.

In *Cubby v. CompuServe* the plaintiff alleged that one electronic newspaper, named Rumorville USA (Rumorville), had defamed another named Skuttlebut. An article in Rumorville on the Internet described Skuttlebut as a "new start-up scam" that obtained most of its information from Rumorville. The plaintiff argued that not only Don Fitzpatrick Associates (DFA), the publisher of Rumorville, but also CompuServe, the Internet service provider on whose data banks the publication was uploaded, were libellous.

The court had to characterize the role of CompuServe in relation to the publication of Rumorville in order to determine the applicable standard of liability. Was CompuServe a publisher or just a distributor? The question is important, because publishers have to live up to a higher standard of care than distributors with respect to monitoring the content of their publications. Ordinarily, "one who repeats or otherwise republishes defamatory matter is subject to liability as if he had originally published it."[8] With respect to entities such as news vendors, bookstores, and libraries, however, "New York courts have long held that vendors and distributors of defamatory publications are not liable if they neither know nor have reason to know of the defamation."[9]

CompuServe's status as a potential publisher was further complicated under the circumstances by the fact that it had contracted with another company, Cameron Communications Inc. (CCI), to monitor the content of its online magazine.

Ultimately, the court characterized CompuServe as a distributor and not a publisher, hence dismissing the claim. CompuServe, the court found, "has no more editorial control over such a publication than does a public library, book store, or newsstand, and it would be no more feasible for CompuServe to examine every publication it carries for potentially defamatory statements than it would for any other distributor to do so. First Amendment guarantees have long been recognized as protecting distributors of publications . . ."

In contrast, consider *Stratton Oakmont, Inc. v. Prodigy Services Company*. At issue in the case are statements about the plaintiff (Stratton), a securities investment banking firm, made by an anonymous user of Prodigy's "Money talk" computer bulletin board service (BBS). The user alleged that Stratton disclosed that a client had lost its biggest customer only after it (Stratton) launched a public offering of shares in the client's company. The offering was a "major criminal fraud," wrote the user, and the plaintiff was a "cult of brokers who either lie for a living or get fired." Stratton sued both the unidentified user and Prodigy, the owner and operator of the computer network on which the statements appeared.

To accelerate litigation, Stratton asked the court to determine at the outset (on "summary judgment") whether (1) Prodigy may be considered a "publisher" of the aforementioned statements, and (2) the "Board Leader" for the computer bulletin board on which the statements were posted acted as Prodigy's "agent."

The court found for Stratton on both counts. Prodigy was a publisher and the Board Leader acted as Prodigy's "agent." Prodigy exercised editorial control over the content of all posted materials. The company held itself out as offering a service that screened such materials so as to avoid the publishing of "inappropriate" comments.

The Court didn't treat the issue of whether the statements were, in fact, defamatory. This will come at trial.

What was different about these cases, such that Prodigy was held responsible and CompuServe was not? The answer has to do with the legal arrangements each company took to shield themselves from liability and the degree of involvement that each company had with the content of their services. For instance, Cameron Communications, Inc. (CCI), which is independent of CompuServe, contracted with CompuServe to "manage, review, delete, edit and otherwise control the contents" of the Journalism Forum. Thus, CompuServe had no direct relationship with Rumorville's publisher, DFA. Moreover, CompuServe had no opportunity to review Rumorville's contents before DFA uploaded it onto CompuServe's computer data banks. By contrast, Prodigy began its Internet service with a policy of manually reviewing all messages prior to posting. This policy subsequently became infeasible due to the sheer volume of postings; however, Prodigy established a computer-run screening device designed to indicate the posting of inappropriate language and so on. Moreover, Prodigy had "Board Leaders" whose role was to monitor the postings and to block any that violated the Prodigy guidelines.

In *Prodigy* the Court distinguished between the cases on two counts. First, Prodigy held itself out to the public and its members as controlling the content of its computer bulletin boards. Second, Prodigy implemented this control through its automatic software screening program and through the guidelines, which addressed the nature of appropriate content and which Board Leaders were required to enforce. Thus, where CompuServe distanced itself from the content of its BBSs, Prodigy did much to involve itself in the control of its content.

Limits of the Analogy

These cases illustrate a typical legal strategy for addressing a new type of legal conflict: attempt to establish an analogy to well-established principles. They also illustrate the limits of this method, in that sometimes the analogy becomes strained. As one commentator has argued, these decisions are greatly flawed because they don't fully acknowledge the particularities of the new technology in issue.[10] Three criticisms of these judgments merit mention.

- The decisions attempt to determine whether an ISP is a publisher, distributor, seller, archivist, or common carrier for the purposes of establishing the appropriate standard of conduct. The problem is that an ISP may be all of these at once. Moreover, the phenomenon of converging media makes these distinctions questionable.
- Instead of determining liability on the basis of what the ISPs *could* be doing, the Court measured the defendants by their current practices.
- The two decisions have the perverse result of discouraging ISPs from monitoring their content at all. Nevertheless, they represent the current state of the law on the subject.

These and other defamation cases — along with obscenity and copyright infringement cases — highlight several leading legal issues on the Internet: just how are we to categorize the players? To what standard of conduct should they be held? Who is responsible for infringements, tortious or otherwise?

Invasion of Privacy

We treat privacy issues at length in Chapter 4; here we merely highlight privacy as a realm in which tort action is increasing as business implements information technology on a broader scale. In the U.S., where the right of privacy has received a great deal of legal attention, there are four actionable torts related to the invasion of privacy:

- an intrusion into the plaintiff's private affairs
- the public disclosure of private facts about an individual
- the appropriation of the plaintiff's personality
- publicity that places the plaintiff in a false light in the public eye.[11]

In Canada, where these four torts don't exist as such, others might be used or developed. For instance, torts related to trespass, nuisance, or injury causing nervous shock might be used instead of the first two torts. Defamation and libel, discussed above, cover much of the same ground as the latter two. English courts don't recognize a right of privacy *per se*.

The publisher/distributor distinction discussed above will likely be critical to the outcome of any tort case involving invasion of privacy on the Internet. This isn't because the status of the ISP will determine whether there's been an invasion of privacy or not, but rather because it will determine the possible degree of damages available in the event of a successful action (i.e. the service provider is likely to have far greater resources than the private individual who has presented the intrusive information).

Trespass

This tort involves intentional direct contact with the property of another, whether possession is lawful or unlawful. This has traditionally applied only to direct "physical" contact. Thus the question for the digital age becomes: what of virtual contact (e.g. hacking)? It's possible that intrusion in and damage to computer files, occurring when one obtains access to another person's computer, may provide grounds for tort action. On August 15, 1996 hackers successfully entered the U.S. Department of Justice's official Web site, replacing text with pornographic pictures, President Clinton's portrait with that of Hitler's, and the background graphics with swastikas. The immediate reaction of the Justice Department was to consider both trespass and the destruction of government property as avenues for legal action.[12]

We saw in Chapter 4 that hacking is also dealt with under the *Electronic Communications Privacy Act*. In Canada, hacking is a criminal offence under section 342.1 of the *Criminal Code*.

Conversion

The tort of conversion involves an intentional exercise of dominion or control over the goods ("chattels") of another, which so seriously interferes with the right of another to control them that the actor may justly be required to pay the other the full value of the chattels. As it relates to cyberspace, this tort might apply where a computer virus damages electronic files. In Canada, section 430 of the *Criminal Code* makes it a criminal offence to cause "mischief to data." The offence carries with it a maximum penalty of ten years in prison.

Fraud

In the U.S. the elements of fraud were most fully set out in *Clements Auto Company v. Service Bureau Corp*. A subsidiary of IBM represented to the plaintiff that it could provide automation equipment beyond the then state of the art. The court assiduously dissected the cause of action into 11 elements: (1) there must be a representation; (2) the representation must be false; (3) it must have to do with a past or present fact; (4) that fact must be material; (5) it must be susceptible of knowledge; (6) the representor must know it to be false, or in the alternative must assert it as of his own knowledge without knowing whether it is true or false; (7) the representor must intend the plaintiff to act, or be justified in acting; (8) the plaintiff must be so induced to act or so justified in acting; (9) the plaintiff's action must be in reliance upon the representation; (10) the plaintiff must suffer damage; (11) that damage must be attributable to the misrepresentation, i.e. the statement must be the proximate cause of the injury.

An action in fraud against AOL, for instance, would have to meet each of these conditions to be successful.

Passing Off

Let's say I pretend to represent your company in cyberspace. It's easy to do. Have I done anything wrong? Do you have a right of action? Yes to both. Why? Because I've "passed off." For all intents and purposes, passing off is a common law version of trademark protection discussed in Chapter 7. Its value lies in the fact that it may be used by those who haven't registered a trademark for their product or service. Passing off doesn't provide as complete protection as trademark registration, however. A trademark gives its owner a legal presumption that the product inspires public "goodwill" towards the product or the company throughout the entire jurisdiction; a claimant in "passing off" must prove goodwill with respect to the product in each and every area where an infringement is claimed.

The theory behind the tort of "passing off" is that it's important to avoid causing public confusion in the marketplace. Where such confusion is deliberately created in the mind of the public for the benefit of a private individual, the act is actionable at tort.

Negligence

Negligence is by far the most important tort field.[13] It's become a catch-all, and hence a conceptually unifying factor in the law of torts. Negligence is a conduct that falls below the standard accepted in the community. Unlike intentional torts, it's irrelevant whether the negligent party *meant* to act the way he did; what's important is that an unacceptable mistake was made.

To prove negligence one must show: (1) that the defendant (the alleged wrongdoer) had a *duty of care* to the plaintiff; (2) that the defendant's conduct breached the *standard of care* to which he was obliged to conform under the circumstances; (3) that the plaintiff suffered *damage*; (4) that the defendant's conduct was the *proximate cause* of that damage; (5) that the damage suffered was *foreseeable* by the defendant at the time of his conduct causing damage; and (6) that there's an absence of any conduct by the plaintiff that would preclude or limit recovery. We examine each of these points in turn, using the case of *Coastal States Trading, Inc. v. Shell Pipeline Corp*.

Coastal was in the oil trading business. Shell operated a pipeline that served as a conduit for offshore oil produced in the Gulf of Mexico to onshore terminals and other pipelines in Louisiana. Those who received the oil didn't have title to any specific barrel of oil, but simply to a specific percentage of each month's production. It wasn't unusual for the oil to be traded several times even before it was delivered to Shell's pipeline. Accordingly, Shell commenced a specific computerized procedure for submitting the written requests of its customers (a precursor to EDI). Shell's computer kept track of all transactions and was programmed to identify any mismatches or breaks in the chain. Due to a data entry error by a Shell computer employee, oil destined to go to one company ended up at another, without the "foolproof" computer system noticing. Before the error could be corrected the company that received the oil went bankrupt. Coastal, the company that should have received the oil, sued.

The Court found both a breach of contract and negligence by Shell. The latter point interests us here. Shell designed a system specifically to prevent the kind of problem that arose, and its customers relied on that system. Shell not only made an improper delivery, it failed to notify Coastal of the mismatch. These failures breached both contractual and tort duties, and were the proximate causes of Coastal's damage. Shell had to pay $1 412 350 in damages.

This case, which involves what one court has termed "computer induced negligence,"[14] may guide our understanding of negligence and the legal issues that are apt to arise when using information technology.

1. *The duty of care*: A duty of care is owed to anyone who can be reasonably anticipated to be affected by another's careless actions. It doesn't matter whether one knows the particular person. Rather, courts determine the ability of an average person in the defendant's position to anticipate the ultimate victim. So, as Knight and Fitzsimmonds argue, a supplier of computer software may or may not be responsible to the ultimate beneficiaries of data processing carried out using the software; it depends on the court's sense of the normal scope of the defendant's obligations.

   In the *Shell* case the court determined, unsurprisingly, that Shell owed a duty to those who were to receive the oil transferred through its pipeline and who thus relied on the efficacy of Shell's computer program.
2. *The standard of care*: Not all behaviour resulting in injury is "negligent" for the purposes of gaining compensation; a mistake isn't always

WAITER, THERE'S A FLY IN MY SOUP!

In 1932 a famous case in English law, *Donoghue v. Stevenson*, established in general terms those to whom one owes a duty. It's also a leading case on product liability.

Miss Donoghue went with a friend to a store, where the friend purchased a bottle of ginger beer. As the friend poured the last of the bottle, Miss Donoghue alleged that she saw the remains of a partially decomposed snail come out. She became violently ill and extremely upset. The question before the House of Lords was this: could Miss Donoghue sue the bottler for negligence? Miss Donoghue couldn't sue the shopkeeper under the Sale of Goods law, because she didn't buy the bottle and therefore wasn't party to the contract of sale. Miss Donoghue's friend wasn't injured, so had no reason to sue. The manufacturer couldn't be sued in contract for the same reasons. Therefore, in those days before consumer protection laws, the plaintiff's only chance was to use tort principles. This involved establishing that the manufacturer owed her a duty of care.

The Court found for Miss Donoghue, holding that a duty of care extended to any person whom the manufacturer could anticipate would consume the contents of the bottle.

a negligent mistake. The standard of care imposed is established according to the circumstances: the nature of the situation, how the injury occurred, and the sort of person alleged to have been negligent. Three examples help clarify: a computer programmer who makes a negligent mistake while helping a friend doesn't have the same standard of care as a programmer who sees a client in the course of work; a supplier of software only has to anticipate reasonable use of it, not extraordinary use; and finally, if I agree to have an amateur fix my computer, rather than one who holds himself out to be specially qualified, I am implicitly accepting a lower standard of skill.[15]

Shell is a large company, expert in the field. It designed a system specifically to prevent the kind of problem that arose. The Court thus expected a high standard of skill from the company, and didn't hesitate in finding a breach of this standard.

3. *Damage*: There must be some sort of damage caused by the negligent act. In the vast majority of cases this is self-evident, but at times issues

arise where negligent acts cause no real loss. In the *Shell* case it's clear that there was damage — the lost value of the rerouted oil. The problem for the Court was to identify precisely how much oil revenue was lost.

4. *Proximate cause*: The action of a person accused of negligence must be the real and proximate cause of the injury suffered. If the real cause is completely unpredictable, the intervening act of someone else, or in fact the victim's own doing, then the victim can't allege that the particular loss was suffered as a result of the negligence of the person so accused.

   There was little doubt that the inefficacy of Shell's computer tracking system caused the loss to Coastal. Moreover, there was no other intervening negligent act.

5. *Foreseeability*: A negligent person is only liable for the damage that was probable and foreseeable by any reasonable person in his position at the time of the negligence. As long as the damage is accordingly foreseeable, however, it's irrelevant if the extent or value of the damage is far greater than expected.

   Shell designed its computer system to avoid precisely the sort of problem it faced. We can assume that Shell should have foreseen the outcome.

6. *Absence of defence*: The plaintiff must show that the following circumstances don't apply in a manner that would mitigate or eliminate altogether a damage claim:

   - Voluntary assumption of risk: Where a person undertakes a particularly hazardous activity, and deliberately ignores safety procedures, then no duty of care is owed at all.
   - Contributory negligence: A court is usually permitted to allocate damages between the plaintiff and the defendant, depending on the degree to which the negligence of the victim contributed to her own loss.
   - Mitigation of loss: After the injury or loss has been inflicted the victim has a duty to minimize its impact, financial or otherwise. For example, if as a result of some negligence the victim's data

> processing capabilities are impaired, the victim must do everything reasonable to obtain substitute processing facilities. The victim can't simply allow a business to wither and claim a huge loss of profits. If the negligent party can show that the plaintiff could have taken steps to mitigate damages, then the victim will only be entitled to the lesser amount of damages that would have been payable.

Coastal didn't contribute to its damages in any way. By the time it discovered the loss the beneficiaries of the mistake were all bankrupt, thus precluding any form of mitigation.

Economic Loss

The law has always been very cautious about extending a remedy to any person who suffers "merely" economic loss (unaccompanied by physical damage) arising from the negligence, as opposed to deceit or other deliberate conduct, of others. Traditionally, mere economic loss has been deemed a matter for contract law, not tort.

This distinction has become increasingly strained. And in a recent Supreme Court of Canada case involving a partially collapsed condominium wall, the distinction was all but abandoned.[16] The cladding on the condominium's walls had been improperly installed. But contractual claims were no longer available because the original developer — i.e. one of the parties to the original contract — had already sold the building. Nevertheless, the Court found that the contractor owed a tort duty to subsequent purchasers of the building, where it was foreseeable that improper workmanship might subsequently cause injury. Even though no personal injury was suffered, the Court decided that masonry posed sufficient threat, and that it would be best to anticipate such an injury and repair the wall before it occurred.

The case is important for issues of electronic commerce because negligence involving information technology so often results in economic loss. Consider the AOL case. If a court had found that AOL had been negligent, could AOL clients sue for lost revenues that resulted from the stoppage of service?

It's not yet clear, however, whether courts will insist upon a finding of an impending threat of physical injury before awarding economic loss claims.

Negligent Misstatements

The courts of most common law countries have recently recognized a broad principle of liability for negligent misstatements. The principle is derived from professional negligence cases involving "professional advisors," such as lawyers, doctors, stockbrokers, and accountants, as well as statutory authorities having a responsibility to store and disseminate information (such as registries and local government bodies). The broader principle is that anyone — not just a person in the traditional categories of advisors — who gives advice with the expectation that it will be acted upon will be held liable for foreseeable economic loss consequent upon the giving of the advice negligently.[17] This principle is qualified to the extent that there must exist a "special relationship" between the giver and receiver of the advice, such that the former can expect the latter to rely on the advice given. The requisite special relationship may exist in situations as informal as a newsletter to clients.

MacKenzie Patten v. British Olivetti illustrates the principle in an information technology context. A salesman representing Olivetti went to a firm of solicitors and advised them that, notwithstanding the small size of the firm's business, the firm would be considerably advantaged by computerizing its accounting system. As it turned out, experts agreed in Court that the solicitors couldn't have benefited from such computerization; indeed, the computer equipment was simply never used. Olivetti was found liable for breach of warranty, i.e. for a breach of its contract with the solicitors. However, the Court also found that the plaintiff's partners were inexperienced in computers and had very reasonably relied on the advice given by Olivetti's salesman. In the circumstances, the salesman was found to have had a duty of care to advise truthfully and impartially in relation to the subject of computer systems. Thus Olivetti was also liable to the solicitors in tort for the damage suffered.

Remoteness

The problem of the recovery for "relational economic losses" has plagued tort law for years.[18] It's difficult to posit a fixed rule that limits the scope of damage awards once it's decided that economic losses resulting from property damage to another are recoverable. Take the following example.

In *CNR v. Norsk Pacific S.S. Co.* the plaintiff was the principal user of a railway bridge owned by Public Works Canada. The bridge was negligently damaged when the defendant's tug, towing a barge, collided with it. The accident forced the closure of the bridge for several weeks, causing extensive economic losses to the plaintiff, who was forced to make arrangements for other transportation routes. The issue was whether a person who contracts for the use of the property of another can sue a person who damages that property for losses resulting from his inability to use the property during the period of repair. Can purely economic losses such as this be recovered? The Court found that there was sufficient "proximity" between the negligent act and the damage suffered and that there were sufficient policy reasons for allowing recovery.

One might well agree with the Court that the tug operator's negligence caused CNR damage, which should be recoverable. But what of the economic loss suffered by CNR's clients? Should they be awarded damages also? Imagine, for example, that CNR was carrying computer timing equipment to Atlanta for the Olympic Games. Because of the damage to the bridge the shipment was a week delayed, by which time the delivery date for the equipment, specified in the contract of purchase, had lapsed and the contract was lost. Could IBM then sue the tugboat operator? At this point, the Supreme Court of Canada has answered no more precisely than to say that it's necessary that the damage be "proximate" and that an award be "practical."

The issue will certainly be revisited in the context of electronic commerce. Consider the following situations. On January 15, 1990 a computer malfunction locked up a major portion of the AT&T telephone network. On February 9, AT&T suffered a second accident, this one interrupting service to tens of thousands of WATS service callers. A technician had forgotten to program necessary information into a network computer.[19] Economic losses were certainly suffered as a result of this negligence. Should they be recoverable? Or again, more recently, on August 7, 1996 there was an online crash at AOL; thousands of companies were left without e-mail capabilities and a host of other services.[20] Many lost thousands of dollars as a result. Should these economic damages be recoverable by the AOL users? Should the economic losses of the clients of these AOL customers be recoverable?

Business is increasingly relying on the "electronic backbone" to carry on day-to-day operations. When the backbone is injured spasms may be felt far and wide, and in the most unlikely places. Accordingly, the issue of economic loss and remoteness will certainly require revisiting to determine the circumstances under which recovery is merited.

Strict Product Liability

Strict product liability doesn't exist in Canada outside Quebec.[21] Rather, defective products are treated under negligence law,[22] which is consistent with the notion that torts are fault-based. In the U.S., however, strict liability was born in 1944 when a Coke bottle exploded in a woman's hand.[23] It has developed rapidly ever since. The development of strict liability has been described as the "most rapid and spectacular overthrow of an established rule in the entire history of the law of torts."[24]

Product liability generally refers to the legal liability of manufacturers for personal injuries caused by their products. Strict product liability grew out of a societal judgment "that people need more protection from dangerous products than is afforded by the law of warranty."[25] Basically, strict product liability permits an injured consumer to recover damages for physical injury or property damages from a manufacturer upon showing that the manufacturer distributed a product containing a dangerous defect into the stream of commerce, and that the defective product caused the injury.[26] Neither negligence nor privity (the contract notion that a duty is owed only to those who have entered into a contract relation with one another) must be proved. This is the law in the U.S. and in civil law Quebec, but not in the rest of Canada where the common law requires proof of negligence.

Aetna Casualty and Surety Co. v. Jeppesen demonstrates one of the leading issues of product liability: namely, what is a "product"?

In 1964, an airplane crashed on its approach to Las Vegas. All aboard were killed. Wrongful death claims filed on behalf of the passengers were settled by the airline and paid by Aetna, the airline's insurer. Jeppesen is a company that publishes instrument approach charts to aid pilots in making instrument approaches to airports. Aetna contended that the chart for the Las Vegas airport was defective and that the defect was the cause of the crash. The Court in *Aetna* agreed that the charts *were* products. The defective nature of the product stemmed from the fact that the "plan" view of the approach, depicted as if one were looking down, and the "profile" view of the approach, depicted as a side view, weren't drawn to the same scale. Since the trial judge found that such inconsistency of scale marked a "radical departure" from customary chart design, and since it was plausibly demonstrated that the crash resulted from a reliance on the defective product, the Appeal Court maintained a finding of strict product liability against Jeppesen. The Appeal Court also found, however, that the pilots had negligently relied on the defective charts. Accordingly, both Jeppesen (the manufacturer of the defective products) and Bonanza (whose pilots were negligent) had to share in the liability claims. Under the applied law of California, a defendant remains strictly liable for injuries caused by a defective product, but a plaintiff's recovery is reduced to the extent that its lack of reasonable care contributed to the injury.

The *Aetna* Court's determination that the provision of landing charts constituted a product, rather than a service, has provided one of the few touchstones for subsequent decisions as to the legal nature of information. Remember: only defective "products" are germane to product liability. The distinction between products and services is often blurred in the information age, where a product is often information itself. For instance, the makers of Lotus 1-2-3 were sued for product liability when a "defect in structure" of a software program led to an incorrect cost/price calculation resulting in substantial loss on a government contract. The defect? An alleged deficiency in user documentation.

More recently, in *St. Albans City and District Council v. International Computers Ltd.*,[27] an English Court of Appeal had to determine whether a computer program was a "good" for the purposes of the U.K. *Sale of Goods Act*. The City of St. Albans, relying on a defective computer program, substantially miscalculated their budget. The trial judge decided that software was a "good," and awarded the city over £1 million (roughly $2 million Cdn.). On appeal in 1996, the Court found that a software program is like the information in a user's manual for a car. If the information contained in the manual is inaccurate, such that by following it I damage my car, then the manual is a defective good. It doesn't matter that the physical object — the manual — is in fine shape; its contents — the information — is not. Similarly, according to the judge's reasoning, if I buy a computer program on a disk, the good is still defective if the disk is fine but the information on it isn't. In such a circumstance the program — the information — is inseparable from the tangible object — the computer disk — in which it resides, and therefore the defective program is a "good." However, where the program exists independently of a purchased disk, as when it's been copied, the program isn't a "good."

The legal debate over the nature of a computer program is likely to continue. Is a program a product or a service? Perhaps courts will find, as some commentators argue, that it may be one or the other depending on its function.

Moreover, if computer programs are found to be products, to what standard will/should they be held? Programming errors or "bugs" are so prevalent — even in off-the-shelf software — as to have become the rule rather than the exception. Many software companies have turned this into an aspect of their marketing strategy, releasing "beta" (unfinished) versions of their products to the public at large and then requesting feedback from these customers as to bugs and inefficiencies in the design. On the other hand, modern software has become so powerful, ubiquitous, and essential to our daily functioning that it begins to invite complacency and reliance on the consumer's part.

Does it make sense to hold software designers to a standard of strict liability in personal injury cases? Might this not have the effect of stifling innovation? So far, society's and our courts' judgment on this issue has been that public safety takes precedence over innovation.

The *Aetna* case involves the sort of situation where an information product may cause personal injury. What other such situations might arise? In his 1995 *High Technology Law Journal* article, which analyzed strict liability for encryption software programmers, Professor Michael Rustad described the following hypothetical situations as examples of further instances in which strict liability might be invoked: (1) An energy management system in a high school that was programmed to be inoperable until 6:30 a.m. and that prevented an exhaust fan in a chemistry lab from working, thus causing an early arriving teacher to inhale chlorine gas. (2) A computer system that generated a prescription drug's warning label, which was inadequate and which the pharmacist failed to use anyway. (3) A computer system used by a pre-trial service agency that failed to warn an arraignment judge that an arrestee was out on bond for two previous armed robberies, a circumstance that resulted in the release of the arrestee and grave injuries to a person wounded in another armed robbery attempt. (4) A defective computer and software program that were used to assist in calculating doses of radiation received for patients who were being seeded with radioactive implants to treat prostate cancer.

Insurance and Risk Management

What protection does a company have against a potential onslaught of lawsuits? How can a corporation minimize its risk of claims against it? Is there insurance? Quite frankly, not enough has changed in the realm of tort liability to warrant a radical rethinking of standard business practices. A few obvious suggestions come to mind.

As always, companies should avoid holding themselves out as offering goods or services that they aren't willing or able to provide. As always, companies should warn consumers as to potential defects and/or dangerous uses of their products.

Since tort law is underdeveloped in the realm of electronic commerce and cyberspace in general, the best legal offence is a responsible busi-

All Grace Periods Must Come to an End

A paper given at a 1992 International Association of Science and Technology for Development (IASTED) conference had this to say about the embryonic state of laws governing software:

> Today, software developers are living in a liability "grace period" ironically afforded to them by the legal profession. This is most likely because the legal system does not yet understand how software works and the insurance sector doesn't yet understand how software's potential risks can be assessed. Furthermore, the courts have not demanded of software practitioners the absolute level of professionalism that is required of engineering disciplines. As the aphorism says, "All good things must come to an end." It is prudent to recognize this unusual period of non-liability in [the software] profession's history for what it is — temporary.[28]

ness practice defence. Those companies that deal with confidential information related to their clients should protect it as effectively as they can, providing employees with clear guidelines on proper handling of the information. Companies that deal in data processing should always have backup copies of all files, preferably off-site. Banks and financial centres, for instance, must prepare themselves not only against traditional real-world "disasters" such as floods, earthquakes, and terrorists; but now against such virtual-world disasters as hacking and computer viruses. Businesses should think now about the best ways to mitigate damage in case of calamity.

Insurance coverage is available for both hardware and software contingencies. One financial institution with which we spoke, for instance, covered its electronic data processing hardware for $20 million and their software, against viruses, for $5 million. Backup facilities, with a complete set of data files, were established in two different cities, 200 kilometres apart.

Insurance is similarly available in the event of liability claims against one's business for cyber-indiscretions, such as AOL's recent blunder. Risk assessment remains an imprecise art at this point, given the paucity of tort claims awarded. The insurance industry is compelled to anticipate where the law is going in terms of risk of liability and size of damage awards. In this sense, the industry has to stay one step ahead of the law.

Conclusion

The law of torts has evolved over centuries, and will continue to evolve. During the Industrial Revolution, the law of torts underwent some fundamental changes, moving from a procedure-focused, strict liability regime to a more flexible, substantive, negligence-based regime. Tort law was perhaps the epicentre of legal dynamism at the time, in large measure because the era of railway capitalism and industrial accidents resulted in so many personal injuries. By contrast, the Information Revolution is less likely to revolutionize torts than to bring certain issues — liability of Internet service providers, remoteness, and economic loss, for instance — into focus.

10 CONFLICT OF LAWS

INTRODUCTION

In few areas are the effects of new technology and globalization more clearly seen and more disruptive than the conflict of laws, or private international law. And in no other area are the answers of traditional law so unsatisfactory if one looks to the rule of law for stability, predictability, fairness, cheapness, and speed.

Why? First, electronic commerce has dramatically telescoped time and space. It's thrown different peoples, cultures, and legal systems into contact, which occasionally produces conflict in their commercial relationships. Second, this is simply a notoriously difficult area of law. As a leading Canadian scholar has observed, "In no other field of law is there so much uncertainty with respect to basic theories, methods or interests at stake."[1]

In this chapter we attempt a brief introduction to the complexity of conflict of laws, and its adequacy in responding to the challenges of electronic commerce.

PRIVATE INTERNATIONAL LAW

Every legal jurisdiction in the world has at least two sets of laws. The first — substantive laws — states the rules of appropriate interaction among the members of its society. Most of this book is devoted to these. The second — conflict laws or private international law — determines which jurisdiction's laws should apply when the laws of two or more clash. For instance, if person A from country X breaches a contract with, or commits a wrong against, person B from country Y, which country's court will hear the dispute? Which law will be applied? How will the judgment be enforced? These are the three classic conflicts of law questions.

The hypothetical airplane crash example is unusual in the number of countries with legal points of contact to the incident. But it illustrates legal problems that increasingly arise when electronic commerce brings individuals, firms, and nation states in frequent and close legal contact.

An International Incident

Consider the following scenario. A Boeing 777 airplane leased by a Brazilian airliner from its owner, an Irish airline consortium, and financed by a Japanese bank, which has transferred the mortgage or first charge on the plane to a Kuwaiti financier, crashes in Paraguay. All lives are lost, and a village is destroyed. The majority of the passengers are Argentine. But the crash victims include citizens of many other South American nations, as well as the U.S., Canada, Spain, and Portugal. A Swiss firm leads the airline's insurers. The contract of sale was made between the Seattle headquarters of Boeing and the Dublin airplane consortium through a London financial agent for a Brussels incorporated airplane broker.

The investigation — shared by the Paraguayan Ministry of Transport and the U.S. Civil Aviation Authority, with assistance from the International Civil Aviation Organization (ICAO) and the International Air Transport Association (IATA) (U.N.- and airlines-sponsored agencies both headquartered in Montreal) shows that the crash resulted from an unusual fault associated with automatic pilot software. It was produced in Toulouse, France, under licence arrangements with its developer, a German software engineering firm who has purchased its patent from an Italian inventor. The software is routinely used in European Airbus airplanes, but not in Boeing planes. Boeing recommends software exclusively designed by or for Boeing in its airplanes. The software lost contact with an air traffic control station in Uruguay just before the crash.

The initial temptation for any court faced with a plaintiff is simply to apply its own jurisdiction's laws. After all, the court knows them best. But this isn't always an effective solution to the conflict problem. Here's why.

First, what if the defendant just doesn't show up? How will the judgment be enforced *in abstentia*? The principle of "territorial sovereignty," borrowed from public international law, says that while states have sovereign authority within their borders they have no authority beyond them. Courts are forced to justify their assertions of jurisdiction in international disputes.

Second, it's chauvinistic always to apply one's own laws, since it suggests that they're always better than everyone else's. In international affairs this isn't an attractive attitude to present to the world. The principle of "comity" holds that while technically foreign states have no authority in nation A's jurisdiction, out of respect nation A frequently recognizes the legitimacy of the foreign authority.

Third, such recognition makes most sense when virtually every aspect of the legal controversy is related to the foreign jurisdiction: the injury was suffered there, the fault was committed there, the wrongdoer lives there, etc. The legal matter has a "closer connection" to the foreign nation's laws than it does to one's own.

Fourth, if nation A applies only its own laws it must accept that foreign jurisdictions will follow suit, potentially to the detriment of nation

---

"Conflict of laws" rules of each jurisdiction determine when, why, and how a court should decide to apply either its own laws or those of another jurisdiction.

A's citizens. The principle of "reciprocity" suggests that, at least in some circumstances, one should apply and respect foreign laws and judgments. "Conflict of laws" rules of each jurisdiction determine when, why, and how a court should decide to apply either its own laws or those of another jurisdiction. The four notions raised above — territorial sovereignty, comity, close connection, and reciprocity — explain conflict of laws' whole domain. Despite ambiguity in their application to individual cases, they illuminate the path.

Let's return to the Brazilian airliner crash. If a Canadian plaintiff launched a lawsuit in Montreal a Canadian court would first determine the issue in conflict. Is this breach of contract? A tort case in wrongful death? Product liability? The court would then examine the parties involved and the specific facts. Who are they? Where do they live? If one party is a company, where's its head office located? Where did the events most significant to the case's outcome occur? These three factors — particular legal issues involved, parties to the dispute, and specific facts — will determine if the court should hear the case, which country's law the court should apply, and whether courts of other jurisdictions will recognize and enforce the decision taken by the court of first instance.

How? The leading concept in private international law is "close connection." If the family of the sole Canadian to die in the crash were to sue for wrongful death, a Canadian court might agree to hear the case. If the family were from Paraguay, on the other hand, and came to Canada simply because the laws here are more favourable to plane crash victims, the court would likely refuse. There isn't a sufficiently close connection to the court's place of jurisdiction to justify hearing that complaint. Once the court decides to hear the case, however, the second issue is to determine whether Canadian laws regarding wrongful death apply. In this example? Unlikely. Every element of the case — damage, fault, location of most of the parties — is foreign. A court would thus apply the laws of the country with the closest connection to the legal issue in question. Finally, once foreign law is applied, what remains is whether the courts of the wrongdoer's jurisdiction would enforce the Canadian court's judgment. If the decision is unfavourable, the defendant might argue that the Canadian court erred in accepting jurisdiction in the first place, that Canada didn't have a close enough connection to the issues involved, or that it was an unsuitable forum (*forum non conveniens*).

These are the conflict of laws issues. Who should hear the case? What laws should apply? Which judgments should be enforced? Why?

The conflict of laws isn't a body of substantive rules. It's a technique that courts use to choose the appropriate forum and the relevant applicable substantive law. Its rules and principles don't therefore provide a direct solution to a dispute; they merely indicate where to look for the solution. In federal states (e.g. Canada and the U.S.) that comprise several legal jurisdictions (provinces and states), conflict of laws issues arise intra-nationally as well as internationally. Take our Brazilian airliner crash again. We have a further complication: if the suit is first launched in Montreal, where the ICAO investigation experts are located, it will be considered under the civil law of Quebec derived from France and European civil law. If the suit were first launched in Toronto, as the place of domicile of the heirs of the deceased Canadian crash victim, it would be considered under the common law of Ontario derived from England and English common law.

Some History

Conflict of laws' history can be traced back to the Ptolemies of ancient Egypt, then to special accommodation for foreigners in early Greece, and onto the Roman Empire's benevolent recognition of native laws in its conquered provinces. The "modern" period begins in the north of Italy 800 years ago, later expanding into France and the Netherlands and finally entering English common law 250 years ago.[2]

Over these centuries the question "Under what circumstances should one legal jurisdiction apply the laws of another?" has often been posed. Each answer finds an echo in contemporary approaches to the problem.

The Greeks and Romans developed specific rules for many situations involving foreigners; for example, non-residents were allowed to sue, and international custom regulated international transactions.[3] The rules were rooted in common practice rather than in theory. In the Middle Ages a theory of the "personality of laws" developed, whereby different laws applied to different people within the same territory.[4] This created difficulties in relationships involving people of different groups. In some cases, contracts were valid only if they were applicable to both parties' laws. This theory was gradually replaced with a theory of "territoriality." The law of the jurisdiction applied to everyone in it, irrespective of the citizenship of the parties to the dispute.

None of these theories responded fully to international trade complexities. For they lacked the key initiative: that in certain situations it makes sense for a court to apply foreign laws or to refuse to hear the case outright.

Conflict of laws proper emerged in the twelfth century, in what is now Northern Italy. Why? Each city state had its own laws, but a lot of commercial activities took place between them. The so-called "Statutist" method evolved to deal with the conflicts that arose. It rested on the premise that all laws fall within two broad categories: personal laws related to people and "real" laws related to property.[5] For each of the two categories a particular conflict rule applies: if a law is a real law, then the law of the place where the object is situated applies; if it's a personal law, then the law of the place of domicile applies.

But this simple either/or choice was insufficient. A German, Savigny, expanded the Statutist's two categories into several more: property, personal, contract, and civil responsibility. For each category there's "a natural seat of jurisdiction." For property, it's where the asset is situated; for persons, it's their domicile; for a contract, it's where it was concluded. The court must analyze the local law and the competing foreign law to establish the category and thus the jurisdiction. Savigny's extension, now with the respect of age called the "traditional" method, is applied in Canada and most jurisdictions.

The traditional method is even-handed. It accords foreign law the same importance as local law. Moreover, it's relatively simple and consistent in result. Over the last 25 years, however, it has come under attack. First, the method accords no consideration to the result of its choice of law, even if the result is manifestly unjust. Moreover, it disregards local interests, even where there are strong policy reasons for promoting them. Finally, the method is deemed inflexible, insofar as it ignores the fact that certain legal questions invoke several legal categories. The Brazilian airliner crash scenario illustrates these shortcomings, since its multi-point fact situation produces multiple legal categories. Consider for example the desire of the South American domiciled victims to have their claims tried in their national South American courts versus the desire of the French software manufacturer, the German developers, the Swiss insurer, or the U.S. plane builder to have the suit heard in a French, German, Swiss, or U.S. court.

The Current State of the Law

We now explore the three fundamental "conflicts" issues: what courts will hear the case, which laws apply, and who will enforce any judgment.

Jurisdiction

A series of U.S. Supreme Court cases provides some classic tests for the choice of jurisdiction.[6] Courts ask: (1) Is there a close connection between the events that have occurred and our jurisdiction? (2) Is it fair to hear the case here? (3) Will hearing the case here affirm the goals of fairness, judicial administration, and international comity?

Choice of Law

Unless the parties have mutually agreed to the applicable law in advance, the choice of law is determined by "the closest connection" test. The relevant contacts include: place of contracting, negotiation, or performance; creation of the subject matter of the contract; and the domicile, residence, nationality, or place of incorporation or business of the parties.[7] For instance, when a dispute arises over whether and when a contract was properly formed (as in the purchase of the Boeing 777 airplane), the choice of law is the place where the parties transacted. In our example this could be Seattle, Dublin, London, or Brussels.

But there are many difficulties in characterizing and weighing these points of connection. Two vastly different approaches to this problem have emerged.

Choice-Influencing Factors

The American *Restatement (Second) of Conflict of Laws (1971)* presents legislators and courts with policy considerations to guide them in the choice of the appropriate laws.[8] The most relevant and oft-cited choice-influencing considerations used in Canada include:

- coordination of legal systems
- justice of the end result
- protection of justified expectations
- predictability and uniformity of results or of legal consequences
- convenience, simplicity, ease in the determination, and application of the law to be applied.[9]

The "Government Interest" Method

But the American Restatement isn't universally accepted; one respected U.S. scholar proposed its total rejection.[10] In lieu of a series of choice of law rules, he contended that courts should look instead to competing "government interests." If two states have an interest in a conflict, the law of the state where the litigation is initiated should apply. "However, in determining whether the interests of the two states are actually in conflict, the forum should be prepared, when circumstances warrant, to give a moderate and restrained interpretation to the policy or interest of one state or the other and thus avoid conflict."[11] This approach, though influential in the U.S., has been highly criticized. Among many other faults, the government interest method is considered highly chauvinistic; it's too political for a field mostly concerned with private relations; it encourages forum-shopping; and it prevents uniformity of result. It's not followed in Canada.

Enforcement

Finally there is enforcement of a legal judgment. This usually takes the form of a claim for monetary damages. But it can also be a fine or even a jail sentence in criminal proceedings. It might involve a revocation of a licence to do business or of some other privilege granted by the state. Or it might result in an order for specific performance of a contract, or an injunction forbidding certain conduct in the future (such as copyright infringement). The crucial question is whether there are assets or persons in the jurisdiction to whom such sanctions can be attached.

Is there, for instance, a bank account or some valuable assets that a sheriff acting under the court's authority can seize? The answer will often determine whether an action is brought in the first place and whether a court of law will accept jurisdiction. There's little point in seeking a favourable judgment if there's little possibility of enforcing it.

Federal states (e.g. Canada, the U.S., and Australia) have organized reciprocal enforcement of judgments given by provincial or state courts within their borders.[12] Thus within most federal states enforcement presents no problems. The situation is different between nations.

U.S. VERSUS CHINA

An epic dispute over alleged copyright violation in recent years pits the U.S. against China. American authorities have documented wide-scale Chinese pirating of U.S. copyrighted software programs, musical compact discs and cassettes, and movie videos. The battle is sufficiently serious that U.S. authorities have threatened to withhold "most favored nation" trading status for Chinese exports to the U.S. and to impose specific trade sanctions. On two occasions the matter was temporarily put to rest. The Chinese authorities sharpened their copyright protection laws and agreed to enforce them more vigorously. They closed down a number of factories producing and distributing pirated materials in China and abroad, but the "cure" wasn't permanent.

The saga continues, reflecting not only traditional conflict of law principles, but different conceptions of private versus public property as well as China's developing state aspirations to catch up to the economically developed world without the same legal framework.

Private International Law in Quebec

With the adoption of the new Civil Code of Quebec (CCQ) legislators in Quebec completely overhauled private international law in the province. As a recent, concerted effort to reform conflict of law, the new rules warrant attention.

The CCQ uses the traditional (Savigny) method for its underlying structure: each category of law has a natural seat. But the CCQ expands the number of legal categories to 50, assuming that greater specificity ensures greater certainty of result.[13] Second, in numerous instances

Quebec law is imposed simply to safeguard the particular law's policy goal (e.g. protection of vulnerable parties, such as consumers or youth).[14] This responds to the criticism that the traditional method lacks sensitivity for the justice of the result. Third, the specific rules often allow for alternative choice of laws so as to ensure the validity of the legal transaction.[15] Fourth, the CCQ allows that with most contracts, the parties may choose the applicable law to protect their justified expectations.[16] Finally, in order to coordinate legal systems the notion of *forum non conveniens* and the "closest connection" principle are cast as discretionary principles to be used by the courts to ensure logical results.[17]

Assuming a Quebec court accepted jurisdiction for a suit in the Brazilian airliner crash, it might apply the law of many different jurisdictions depending on which of 50 legal categories the fact situation dictates. But we conclude that the Quebec Civil Code provisions respond to most serious concerns in international commerce disputes. They provide a relatively high degree of certainty and respect for public policy concerns while maintaining enough flexibility to respect the interests of contracting parties.

Altered Terms of Cyberspace

Does electronic commerce raise novel legal questions for private international law? Perhaps in degree but not in kind, as this excursion through history has shown us. The Brazilian airliner crash scenario illustrates the multiple actors involved in modern commercial transactions made possible by near instantaneous communication. Just as debate once flared over emerging air and space law after World War II (and over accelerated trading between the prosperous twelfth century Italian city states), so it continues today over how serious is the challenge that electronic commerce poses for traditional law. Is modest tinkering the best approach, or is a fundamental overhaul necessary? Most prefer evolution or adjustment rather than radical redesign, contending that these questions have arisen for centuries — as long as people have traded or travelled across national borders.

The Law Merchant

During the Roman Empire's long rule Pax Romana provided a consistent unitary law over much of Europe. But with the Roman Empire's collapse and trade's later advance, particularly with technological improvements in sailing ships, new legal structures across national borders were required. It was on this stage that the Law Merchant gradually appeared in the Middle Ages. Its focus was the "trade fair." Merchants from all European nations and some from Asia gathered in one city at one regular time to exchange goods and order more for transport back to their home countries. Customary rules fashioned for these transactions developed irrespective of the laws of the cities and nations where the trade fair happened to occur. They were relied on by the merchants.

These increasingly well-established trade customs between merchants were accepted by individual nations as the applicable or overriding law in cases where the individual nation's law might prescribe differently. In fact not only the choice of law, but also the choice of court and the method of enforcement of decisions came within the Law Merchant framework. Form followed function.[18]

Two signal changes wrought by electronic commerce need to be addressed by the reform of private international law. The first is the dramatic reduction of time and space that can quickly bring so many

The sheer volume of transnational transactions in the information age compels new solutions to these centuries-old questions.

different people and jurisdictions together in legal interaction. The sheer volume of transnational transactions in the information age compels new solutions to these centuries-old questions.

The second change is what we call the "banality of international exchange." It used to be simply impractical to trade internationally unless one dealt in large quantities or in high-value goods. Now anything can be traded. Think of our first chapter's blue jeans — even something as banal as this can become the source of an international contractual dispute. But because the goods' value is low the parties aren't likely to spend the time and money required to launch a court action when a breach occurs. However, plaintiffs who are unwilling to bear the legal expense unwittingly sanction their own mistreatment.

Solutions

What to do? First, harmonize laws through treaties. This is done increasingly. Take our air crash scenario, where international treaties govern many aspects of the carriage of passengers and goods by air. Treaty provisions are incorporated into the terms and conditions of the contract for passage formed when a passenger buys a ticket. Telephone tariffs and standards across national boundaries are widely governed by treaties initiated by the ITU. Copyright is significantly regulated by successive versions of the Berne Convention currently administered by WIPO.

But some nations don't adhere to these conventions. Consider China and the pirated software. And some courts may decide that a particular fault — perhaps a defective computer software program in our Brazilian

What's clear is that the escalation and intensification of global commerce, and the increase in disputes implicating two or more nations' laws, will require greater efforts in striking bilateral and multinational treaties, at least to settle in advance questions of the applicable law.

airliner — isn't governed by the exclusionary or loss provisions of conventional air passage contracts. What's clear is that the escalation and intensification of global commerce, and the increase in disputes implicating two or more nations' laws, will require greater efforts in striking bilateral and multinational treaties, at least to settle in advance questions of the applicable law.

Second, the parties themselves should determine in advance which law shall apply, which court or arbitrator shall decide, who shall enforce or "execute judgment," and what assets can be seized to "secure judgment." This isn't always practicable, however. Often people with potential legal claims haven't participated in negotiating the contract. Take the families of victims in the Paraguayan village destroyed by the airplane crash. They were ignorant of the software contract. They're "third parties" — strangers to the contract whose terms will not apply to them. Accordingly, any contractual determination of conflicts of law issues may be unsatisfactory.

Moreover, there may be legal issues not directly covered by any contract; for example, a breakdown in the communication signals between the airplane's automatic pilot system and the Uruguay air traffic control centre to which the aircraft was connected when the system failed. Or there may be substantial inequalities between the contract's parties, e.g. in their economic power or knowledge. Thus consent to its terms couldn't reasonably and prudently be given. The law often protects the vulnerable party in such situations.

Third is a "return to the Law Merchant," whereby a "cyber small claims court" is required. Trotter Hardy proposes an intriguing solution: instead of travelling "back to the future" we move "forward to the past." The Law Merchant didn't spring from a statute or a nation's rule;[19] it existed apart from the law of the city hosting a trade fair. Its "courts" were composed of merchants themselves. Since time is money, it promised speedy resolution of disputes. Because its rules emerged from trade custom its judgments were practical and flexible. While its courts eventually disappeared, the Law Merchant, in reverse osmosis, gradually became part of English common law.

Today speed, frequently changing commercial parties, and interaction over vast distances crossing national boundaries and time zones are characteristics of commerce in cyberspace. Speedy, predictable, inexpensive, fair, and enforceable resolution of disputes is increasingly needed. Do online discussion groups and their "netiquette" provide the basics for "a cyber small claims court"?[20] At least with respect to the banality problem, a bottom-up approach is preferable to a top-down one.

Conclusion

Conflict of laws is a field of considerable uncertainty. Courts are called upon to answer three questions when faced with a legal question involving more than one jurisdiction. Which court should take jurisdiction? Which jurisdiction's laws should apply? How will the judgment be enforced? Four general terms summarize the key elements of the answer:

- Territorial sovereignty: States are sovereign within their own borders, but are powerless beyond.
- Comity: Out of respect for foreign states, one sometimes must recognize the legitimacy of foreign authority.
- Close connection: The jurisdiction of the court that hears the dispute and whose law is applied must have a close connection to the dispute itself.
- Reciprocity: If one state hopes to have its judgments enforced elsewhere, it must similarly respect and allow the enforcement of foreign judgments.

We highlight these basic principles in order to help clarify the issues arising in electronic commerce. But perhaps the best advice for business is to "put it in the contract"! And perhaps the best conclusion one can make at this point is that, without further effort to adjust and refine the conflict of laws, the stability, certainty, and fairness traditionally sought by the rule of law will become increasingly elusive.

11 Where Do We Go from Here?

Electronic commerce and the law have lagged to date in welcoming in the digital revolution. But are they quickly catching up? Will they now lag, lead, or simply be swept along?

Where Do We Go from Here?

Where is the law going in the new information economy? For a glimpse of where the information age might take business and the law, we look to the characteristics of its driving force: information. Information is by nature immaterial and non-proprietary. Two broad conclusions follow. First, the law will be most transformed where it treats with information exchange most directly. Second, the land-based and proprietary metaphors of fences, barriers, controls, enclaves, and hierarchies will all quietly diminish, perhaps dissipate, even disappear. Regulation and the law generally, as well as business practices, will have to adapt to the open, porous, enlightening nature of information. Both points require further explanation.

The most dramatic shift exemplified by the new economy lies in the nature of society's principle economic engine. Wealth creation now stems primarily from ideas and knowledge, rather than from anything material. Just as the Industrial Revolution marked a shift in principal location of value from land to goods (or, in legal parlance, from "immovables" to "movables"), so the information revolution marks a fundamental shift from goods to ideas. The nineteenth century had its great steam engines; until recently the twentieth century has been dominated by electricity and the automobile. And now it in turn has been replaced — not only by computers themselves, but even more significantly, by computer software. Almost 60 percent of all American workers are knowledge workers. Eight out ten new jobs are in information-intensive sectors of the economy.[1] Incredibly, more Americans make computers than cars, and more work in data processing than in petroleum refining.[2]

From Lord Inbred to Union Pacific to Consolidated Edison to General Motors to Microsoft to Netscape (a company whose entire existence is tied to the virtual world of the Internet): this has been the evolution of our economic engines.

Each fundamental change in the economy produces a corresponding shift in legal focus. In the age when land was prized above all, legal rules governing succession and inheritance were at once far more strict and more developed with respect to immovables than they were to movables. Similarly, laws related to civil liability and insurance have evolved enormously in this century, simply because so many people get into car accidents. Unsurprisingly then, the area of law that's under the greatest strain these days is that of intellectual property: copyright, patents, and trademarks. The law of copyright took substance and structure in an age when the best way to determine how original ideas were spread throughout society was to keep track of which printing presses were copying which works. Copyright law provided a pretext both for the establishment of monopoly rights in a work of art and for a mode of censorship. But in an age wherein anyone can make copies easily and inexpensively one is hard-pressed to follow the logic of the current copyright regime.

An information-based economy is by nature open, porous, ubiquitous, and unbounded by state, space, and time. Such an economy and the laws that support it simply don't lend themselves to either the old-style, put-a-fence-around-it type business or state, or the military

A Doomsday Scenario for the Coming Millennium?

Permit us one final example of how cyberspace and the law are colliding with some potentially nasty results. This example brings together virtually all the legal concepts discussed throughout the book, as well as all the peculiarities that result from our overwhelming dependence upon digital information in the current economy. It's the so-called "year 2000 problem" (a.k.a. Y2000).

The problem is simple. The date fields in many computer programs are limited to two digits, indicating the decade and the year. Programmers hadn't bothered to include the "19" in "1997" because it took up memory space and seemed unnecessary. The result? Many important computer systems around the world are unable to recognize dates beyond the millennium — the year 2000 is interpreted as the year 1900 or as meaningless. Additionally, some programmers used "99" as a default number in the date field, so the problem could arise even sooner.

It all sounds ridiculous, but the potential consequences aren't funny at all. Doomsayers predict a meltdown in the financial sector; chaos on air-traffic routes, rail lines and even highways; elevators that stop running; government benefits and pay cheques that don't get sent; and medical and pharmaceutical records that are lost. Potentially everyone will be affected. As Jon Newberry reports in his article "Beat the Clock," Unum Corp., a Portland, Maine, insurer, already lost thousands of policy files in 1995 due to a Y2000 failure. A computer program designed to remove dormant files would add five years to the last payment and examine whether the figure generated was before the current year. When the program added five years to payments made in 1995, it assumed that the last activity had occurred in 1900. The consequence? Important insurance records were deleted.

There appears to be no easy way to solve the problem. Software for most large corporations is custom designed. The source code in which the date fields are defined differs from one program to the next, so that it's not possible to simply write a single antidote. Available solutions tend to be labour-intensive and expensive.

Estimates are that 80 to 90 percent of desktop computers will be affected; for mainframes the percentage is even higher. The Gartner Group, a Connecticut-based international information technology consulting firm, estimates the cost to fix Y2000 worldwide at US $300-600 billion. A typical estimate of repair costs is $1.00–1.10 per line of source code. At that rate, the Prudential Life Insurance Company reportedly expects to spend US$150 million to achieve Y2000 compliance.

Potential sources of liability include vendors' breach of express or implied warranty, terms, copyright infringements in the course of attempting to correct the problem, directors' liability if the costs are not disclosed or if the problem is not corrected in time, or vendors' tort liability as a result of fraud, negligent misrepresentation, professional malpractice, or product liability.

What should be done? Before scouting out firms which promise to eliminate Y2000 problems (over 40 U.S. vendors market in excess of 100 software tools to correct the problem — see www.mstnet.com/year2000), many experts, including Jeff Jinnett of the law firm Lebeouf, Lamb, Greene and MacRae (see www.year2000.com and www.comlinks.com/legal), suggest that the first step in addressing the problem is to conduct a hardware and software audit so as to assess the magnitude of the problem for your firm, determine the best path forward, and protect the firm against potential future liability claims:

1. Prepare an inventory of hardware and software being used.
2. Prepare a data processing flow chart to determine how information moves through the firm's computer architecture.
3. Identify all software known to be owned or licensed.
4. Identify all undocumented software (e.g. "legacy" software, brought in by staff).
5. Track down companies whose names have changed or which have been subject to a take-over.
6. Determine what level of customization is involved in your firm's software and what computer languages are used. (Many languages are dying or are obsolete, and finding programmers who are qualified to review the source code will become increasingly difficult as time passes and as other firms scramble to engage their services.)
7. Begin the process now and remember that you must allot time to test your systems thoroughly before the year 2000, or potentially, 1999. (The U.S. Office of the Comptroller of Currency sent a letter to all U.S. national banks on June 17, 1996, advising them to correct the Y2000 problem by the end of 1998, leaving one year for testing.)

The next step involves conducting a legal audit:

1. Review licence agreements and long-term maintenance agreements relating to third-party licensed software.
2. Determine if these agreements contain express or implied warranties to cure "bugs" or "defects" into the next century.
3. Review confidentiality provisions to determine whether you are precluded from using outside help to fix potential problems.
4. Review "force majeure" provisions to determine whether Y2000 counts as "an Act of God"!
5. Consider the effect of copyright restrictions on creating derivative programs (e.g. in the course of altering the source code) or of providing reproductions of the software to third-party Y2000 "fix it" companies.
6. Consider the effect of statutory export restrictions on cryptography, if you use it and plan to use a firm from a foreign country (e.g. in India or the Philippines) to review your source code.
7. Consider the effect of statutory disclosure requirements on financial statements and in the course of due diligence exercises. (How much money is your company going to be forced to set aside to fix the problem?)
8. Consider the tax implications of these measures; on July 18, 1996, the U.S. Emerging Issues Task Force of the Financial Accounting Standards Board decided that companies in the process of implementing a Y2000 corrective plan should currently deduct the costs rather than capitalizing it.
9. Review your insurance policies. (How are you covered against potential liability?)
10. Establish a paper trail, documenting all measures undertaken to address the Y2000 problem in your firm.

As always, the best solution is to prepare as far in advance as possible (for some, it may already be too late to avoid the problem altogether) and fix it first, instead of looking to sue or be sued.

command structure of government or business management. Flattened enterprises, the elimination of hierarchies and borders, networking, partnership, and communication flow facilitation: these are the current business paradigms. Open government, streamlining, real democracy, public/private/social sector cooperation, government as facilitator, "model user," partner, and internationalism: this is the buzz in our capitals. The law, like business, will have to dust itself off, open itself up, and justify its inefficiency, its inefficacy, and its inaccessibility.

What Compass Can We Use in Getting There?

Perhaps the metaphor of the compass is an appropriate one as we look ahead to the journey of digital law and electronic commerce in cyberspace. For while a compass gives us our general direction, it needs regular resetting and frequent overseeing. What follows are several observations that may establish our bearings and set us on our course.

First, law is conservative by nature. It looks backward, either to precedent or to its doctrinal principles. Its machinery for change is heavy, multi-layered, and replete with checks and balances.

Second, we're facing extraordinary change in the information age — and electronic commerce is at the leading edge of this change. But that shouldn't seduce us into thinking the rule of law could or should disappear. Shakespeare's declaration in *Henry VI* — "The first thing we do, let's kill all the lawyers" — may have a popular appeal. But these words were said by conspirators who were attempting to bring in a totalitarian order and who found it necessary to eliminate the natural custodians of order first. The absence of all law is the negation of freedom.

Third, business looks to law for two sets of somewhat conflicting values: predictability and enforceability versus fairness, flexibility, and efficiency. How best can we resolve these tensions? Several conclusions emerge from our passage through the previous ten chapters:

- We should be prudent in identifying what really *is* changing. Some things aren't, and should be left alone. The first principle of medicine comes to mind: Do no harm. And the second: Assist the inherent healing of the body itself.
- We should make the disciplined effort to understand what's changing and how and why. With that base of comprehension we should look to a solution that best fits the nature of the problem. We should

ensure that form (law) follows function (commerce). Moreover, we should take pains not to oversolve, recognizing that solutions may not have their traditional period of permanence or durability.

- We should allow for informal, normative mechanisms to flourish where change is greatest, where creativity is critical, and where the public interest isn't particularly threatened.
- Taking our cue from the tendencies of the information age to flatten and dissolve hierarchies, we should allow the "best solution" to emerge organically ("bottom up") instead of imposing a "top down" solution before all the variables are known. Informal solutions tend to crystallize over time, as "best solutions" emerge and as the need for certainty begins to outweigh the need for flexibility.
- Just as in that period of great commercial and legal change in Europe when the national frontier-crossing Law Merchant sprang into being, we should stay closely tuned to the creators of change themselves so as to ensure that the solutions fit naturally with their new practices. Moreover, we should challenge them to craft rules that are both suitable to themselves and harmonious with the broad public interest.

How well does this set of prescriptions fit our discussion in the previous ten chapters? In Chapter 1 we saw how the chip has ushered in dramatic change, with broad and deep transformative effects on our economic, social, and cultural institutions. So profound is that change that the phrase "chips for neurons" is increasingly invoked. Chapter 2 described what the transformative instruments were and the science on which they rested, while Chapter 3 examined the resulting changes in the marketplace.

In Chapter 4, the first of the law chapters, we looked at some of the privacy concerns that stem from these transformative effects, and the early combinations of old and new law, and formal and voluntary constraints, that have been employed to resolve them. We also saw how business could impose certain constraints on itself in order to ameliorate these privacy concerns and hence win new customers.

In Chapter 5 we identified a combination of technological and legal constraints and barriers that provides system assurance. Getting this security calibration right will be a continuing challenge.

Chapter 6 traced the sweeping wave of deregulation, and contrasted traditional regulation with the new, alternative forms designed to provide less rigid rules of the road. An important part of the solution will lie in getting that balance right.

Chapter 7 portrayed intellectual property as the area of law under greatest stress. We understand that a fertile social and economic environment for rapidly evolving ideas and innovation creates wealth. The effort to protect these ideas and facilitate their expression through traditional rules of property law produces an enormous tension. Solutions here will be found by a willingness to look beyond the traditional rules.

In Chapter 8 we discerned an easier marriage between electronic commerce and cyber-law in the area of contracts, probably because this area has had the most intense activity and concentrated attention of the parties involved.

In Chapter 9 we saw that predictability and enforceability have a precarious existence in the area of tort liability. The anchor points are changing rapidly, but this was true of twentieth century tort law well before electronic commerce. Flexibility and fairness have been and increasingly will be in the fore until a new equilibrium sets in. Efficiency has been pushed to the sidelines, at least if it's measured by predictable, quantifiable, and contained legal costs.

Finally, in Chapter 10 we saw how electronic commerce's conquest of time and space has created enormous pressure on our rules for dealing with legal problems that cross over national boundaries. While umbrella treaties are increasingly inventive, they're simply having a tough time keeping up.

The prescriptive observations set out earlier have clear application in each of these areas of law. If many of our institutions — and especially the rule of law — seem to be in disarray in the digital age, it's because we haven't had the time nor the attendant wisdom to adapt them to the new technologies. How to achieve such adaptation is a worthy agenda for social science for the beginning of the twenty-first century. Confusion should evaporate once technology and our legal institutions come into synchrony again.

We end with the maxim from our generation that seems particularly apt to this analysis of electronic commerce and digital law: "Some people see things as they are and wonder why. We dream of things that ought to be and ask why not."

Notes

Chapter One

1 Don Tapscott, *The Digital Economy: Promise and Peril in the Age of Networked Intelligence* (New York: McGraw-Hill, 1996).

Chapter Two

1 See Chapter 7.

Chapter Three

1 The Society of Management Accountants of Canada, *Electronic Commerce* (Hamilton: SMAC, 1994) at 2.

2 Marleen O'Conner, "The Human Capital Era: Reconceptualizing Corporate Law to Facilitate Labor-Management Cooperation," (1993) 78 *Cornell Law Review* 899.

3 John A. Byrne, "Strategic Planning: After a Decade of Gritty Downsizing, Big Thinkers Are Back in Corporate Vogue," *Business Week*, August 26, 1996.

4 Don Tapscott, *The Digital Economy: Promise and Peril in the Age of Networked Intelligence* (New York: McGraw-Hill, 1996) at 46.

5 Information Highway Advisory Council (IHAC) Final Report, *The Challenge of the Information Highway* (Ottawa: Supplies & Services, 1995) at xv.

6 James and Theodore Barr, cited in Tapscott, *supra* at 93.

7 Jeremy Rifkin, *The End of Work: The Decline of the Global Labor Force and the Dawn of the Post-Market Era* (New York: G.P. Putnam & Sons, 1995).

8 Forum discussion between Paul Tough, a senior editor of *Harper's Magazine*; Ronald Blackwell, chief economist of UNITE, a trade union; Albert Dunlap, known affectionately as "Chainsaw Al," who has "restructured" nine different companies, including Scott Paper, where he laid off 11 000 workers and increased the company's stock value by 225 percent, and most recently Sunbeam, where he intends to lay off 6000 of the 12 000 employees and to triple the stock value; George Gilder, who wrote the "bible" of the Reagan revolution, *Wealth & Poverty*; Edward Luttwak, consultant and author of "The Middle-Class Backlash"; and Robert Reich, U.S. Secretary of Labor. The Forum was

entitled "Does America Still Work? On the Turbulent Energies of the New Capitalism," *Harper's Magazine*, May 1996, 35 at 41 & 43 [hereinafter *Does America Still Work?*].

9 According to a 1996 *New York Times* poll, one-third of all American households have experienced a layoff since 1980. One in ten admitted that a layoff has precipitated a major family crisis. Louis Uchitelle and N.R. Kleinfield, "On the Battlefields of Business, Millions of Casualties," *New York Times*, March 3, 1996.

10 See e.g. John Berry, "Restructuring's Toll on Workers Slowing," *Washington Post*, August 23, 1996 at F1.

11 *NLRA*, Ss. 2(5) and 8(a)(2).

12 Michael Leroy, "Can Team Work? Implications of Electromation and Dupont Compliance Analysis for the Team Act," (1996) 71 *Notre Dame Law Review* 215. See also Samuel Estreicher, "Employee Involvement and the 'Company Union' Prohibition: The Case for a Partial Repeal of Section 8(a)(2) of the *NLRA*," (1994) *New York University Law Review* 125.

13 S. 295, 104th Cong., 1st Sess. (1995); H.R. 743, 104th Cong., 1st Sess. (1995).

14 Leroy, *supra* at 256.

15 *Teck Corporation Limited v. Millar*, [1973] 2 W.W.R. 385, 33 D.L.R. (3rd) 288 (B.C.S.C.) at 314.

16 Marleen O'Conner, *supra* at 958.

17 *CBCA*, s. 122 (1)(a).

18 Joel Rogers and Wolfgang Streek, "Workplace Representation Overseas: The Works Councils Story," *Working Under Different Rules* (New York, Russell Sage Foundation 1994), edited by Richard Freeman at 104.

19 Rifkin, *supra* at 223.

20 Rifkin, *supra*.

Chapter Four

1 Daniel B. Klein, "Promise Keeping in the Great Society: A Model of Credit Information Sharing," (1992) 4 *Economics and Politics* 117.

2 Steven Bibas, (1994) 17 *Harvard Journal of Law and Public Policy* 591.

3 Judith Prowda, "Privacy and the Security of Data" (1995) 64 *Fordham Law Review* 738 at 741.

4 "Privacy and the Canadian Information Highway" (Ottawa: Supply & Services, 1995) at 7.

5 Rose Aguilar, "Research Services Raise Privacy Fears," *c!net news*, June 10, 1996. Lexis-Nexis defends its P-TRAK service, saying the company can't be responsible for what's done with the information it provides. "Our company's policy has been, and continues to be, that this product is to be used in a legal manner, and that's one thing that we try to stress with our customers," said Judith Schultz, public relations manager for Lexis-Nexis. "If something did happen, we wouldn't deal with it because we are a third party."

6 Cited in Cavoukian and Tapscott, *Who Knows: Safeguarding Your Privacy in a Networked World* (Toronto: Random House, 1995) at 171.

7 Tom Wright, "Privacy Makes Good Business Sense" (Toronto: Information and Privacy Commission/Ontario, 1994) at 2.

8 Art. 5: [Translation] Every person has the right to the respect of his private life.

9 S.Q. 1993, c. 17. Note that not all provisions came into effect immediately. Some took effect in July 1994, so as to give the business community an opportunity to ensure that their practices conformed with the law. Note also that the new Civil Code of Quebec (CCQ) took effect at the same time.

10 R.S.Q., c. A-2.1

11 From a business perspective, Peter Martin, lawyer with McCarthy Tétrault in Montreal, finds that the law as it now stands is clearly an improvement over the initially proposed legislation. If the law were taken at its word, however, the costs to business would be overwhelming. Many of its provisions are quietly ignored, simply because they don't correspond to business practice.

From the point of view of some privacy advocates, on the other hand, the last-minute modifications to the law weakened it unduly. René Laperrière writes in "La protection des renseignements personnels dans le secteur privé et la loi québécoise de 1993" in *La vie privée sous surveillance* (Cowansville: Yvon Blais, 1994) at 80:
[Translation] "The new law posits . . . general guidelines and broad principles; but unfortunately it includes too many exceptions, leaves open huge gaps and legitimizes practices which are widespread but dangerous. The deficiencies of the juridical framework for the sectors which treat personal information are such that all too often the loopholes constitute an invitation to pirate people's identity."

12 18 U.S.C. ss. 2510-2520.

13 Cavazos and Morin, *Cyber-Space and the Law: Your Rights and Duties in the On-Line World* (Cambridge: MIT Press, 1994) at 18.

14 18 U.S.C. s. 2701(a)

15 *Cyber-Space and the Law*, *supra* at 23.

16 Commission of the European Communities, 1995 OJ2 281, 95/489/EC.

17 A workbook on the implementation of the principles is available to organizations intending to adopt the CSA standard. The complete text of the Model Code is available from the Canadian Standards Association, 178 Rexdale Boulevard, Etobicoke, Ontario, M9W 1R3.

18 IHAC Final Report, *supra* at 141.

Chapter Five

1 *Cryptography's Role in Securing the Information Society* (Washington, D.C.: National Academy Press, 1996).

2 *Criminal Code* R.S.C. 1985, c.C-42, s. 334.

3 *Criminal Code*, s. 184. Additionally, s. 184.5 applies specifically to radio-based telephone communications.

4 *Criminal Code*, ss. 184(1) and 184.5(1).

5 Senator Patrick J. Leahy, Statements On Introduced Bills And Joint Resolutions (Senate — March 5, 1996): *The Encrypted Communications Privacy Act of 1996* at S1517.

6 "[T]he creation of system-based assurances of authenticity constitutes a condition precedent for continued expansion in the modern use of the systems in important marketplaces." Raymond T. Nimmer, Patricia Krauthouse, "Electronic Commerce: New Paradigms in Information Law," (1995) 31 *Idaho Law Review* 937 at 945.

7 See McBurnett, *PGP Web of Trust Statistics* (January 1996, http://bcn.boulder.co.us/~neal/pgpstat/).

8 *Utah Digital Signature Act*, Utah Code Annotated Title 46, Chapter 3 (1996).

9 UNCITRAL, *Model Law on Electronic Commerce*, U.N. Doc. A/51/17 (1996), Article 13.

10 According to Nimmer and Krauthouse, *supra* note 6 at 944-45: "A statute of frauds serves an evidentiary function aimed at establishing the existence of a contract. This encompasses three items of authentication: (1) that a promise or commitment was actually made; (2) the basic terms (e.g. price and quantity); and (3) the source of the commitment.

"On the first two, a rule that conditions enforceability on compliance with a particular method of authentication constitutes overkill in modern commerce. There are many different ways to authenticate or, at least, create an inference of authenticity, but the statute of frauds approach emphasizes only one. The better approach treats authentication as an issue of burden of proof, not enforceability."

11 U.C.C. section 2-201(1) (1991).

12 The law of negligent misrepresentation grew out of the English Law through cases such as *Hedley Byrne & Co. v. Heller & Partners Ltd.*, [1964] A.C. 465, [1963] 2 All E.R. 575. It has evolved naturally in Canadian jurisprudence, and its principles seem similar to those in many common law jurisdictions.

13 *Brocklesby v. Jeppesen*, 767 F.21 1288 (9th Cir. 1985) at 1294-95.

14 *Aetna Causalty and Surety v. Jeppesen, supra.*

15 John T. Soma and Jay Batson, "The Legal Environment of Commercial Database Administration," Spring 1987 *Jurimetrics Journal* 642 F.2d 339 (9th Cir. 1981) 297 at 312.

16 The IHAC Report, *supra* at 145, states: "It is likely that broad-based security will be achieved through several PKIs, to be built by different public and private entities. The federal government notes PKI will probably be the first in Canada. An unfragmented 'electronic market' on the Information Highway, offering maximum consumer choice, will be possible only if PKI interoperability standards issues are fully addressed."

Chapter Six

1 S.C. 1993, c. 38.

2 *Alberta Government Telephones v. CRTC*, [1989] 2 S.C.R. 225. See also *Teléphone Guèvrement v. Québec*, [1994] 1 S.C.R. 878.

3 The one exception is the Saskatchewan Telephone company, which was grandfathered as a provincially owned telecommunications carrier. It's scheduled to pass under federal jurisdiction in 1998. This was a compromise between the federal and the Saskatchewan governments for the latter's support of the Charlottetown constitutional accord in 1992.

4 R.S.C. 1985, c. C-46.

5 R.S.C. 1985, c. C-34, as renamed and amended by S.C. 1986, c. 26, Part II.

6 R.S.C. 1991, c. 11 B-9.01.

7 *Ibid.* c. 3 (I)(d)(iii): (8).

8 See e.g. IHAC Report, rec. 2.18 at p. 102.

9 R.S.C. 1985, c. R-2.

10 To make matters worse, the law is uncertain. (*Globe and Mail*, June 28, 1997, B3.) The Federal Court of Canada ruled that receiving a U.S.-based satellite television service violates the *Radiocommunications Act*. The case was brought against satellite system retailers and is now under appeal to the Federal Court of Appeal. The ruling conflicts with a Saskatchewan Court of Queen's Bench (Klebuc J.) which ruled that receiving U.S. satellite service does not violate the Act.

11 *Globe and Mail*, Feb. 20, 1997, at B9.

12 *American Civil Liberties Union v. Janet Reno, Attorney General of the United States*, 929 F.Supp. 824 (United States District Court, E.D. Pennsylvania) and *Joe Shea et al. v. Janet Reno, Attorney General of the United States*, 930 F.Supp. 916 (United States District Court, S.D. New York, 1996). The Attorney General has advised that she intends to appeal to the U.S. Supreme Court to determine the issue of the unconstitutionality of the CDA.

13 *Reno, Attorney General of the United States, et al. v. American Civil Liberties Union et al.*, 1997 U.S. Lexis 4037.

14 R.S.C. 1985, c. C-46.
15 S. 163.
16 S. 163 (8).
17 *Ibid*. "Sadly, we are running up against the dark side of human nature" — Canadian Foreign Affairs Minister Lloyd Axworthy, suggesting that national and international controls are needed to prevent the Internet from becoming a haven for child-pornographers, drug-traffickers, merchants of hate, and terrorists, in the Montreal *Gazette*, June 29, 1997, A8.
18 These tests were largely formulated by the Supreme Court in *R. v. Butler* [1992] S.C.R. 452.
19 Part I of the *Constitution Act*, 1982, Schedule B of the *Canada Act*, 1982 (UK), 1982, c. II.
20 *R. v. Oakes*, [1986] 1 S.C.R. 103.
21 U.S. Constitutional Amendment I.
22 Opened for signature 4 November 1950, Article 10.
23 For a contrary current view see *The Economist*, Feb. 15-21, 1997, p. 16. "The threat to British Liberty. Both Labour and Tories are happy to whittle freedoms away. Britain needs a bill of rights."
24 Canadian Standards Association, *Model Code for the Protection of Personal Information* (Canada: CSA, 1996). CSA document no.: CAN/CSA-q830-96.
25 Michael Cowpland, head of Corel, predicts business on the Internet will soar to $200 billion by 2000 from $15 billion in 1996, based on a current monthly growth rate of 20%. *Ottawa Citizen*, May 2, 1997, C3.

Chapter Seven

1 Some of this chapter appears in: Sunny Handa, "Copyright Liability when Browsing on the Information Highway," (1996) 29 *Law/Technology Journal* 11.
2 This is a long-established legal principle. See: *Jefferys v. Boosey* (1855), 4 H.L.C. 815; *Cartwright v. Wharton* (1912), 25 O.L.R. 357 (S.C.); *Stevenson v. Crook et al.* [1938], 4 D.L.R. 294 (Ex. Ct.); and *Moreau v. St. Vincent*, [1950] Ex. C.R. 198.
3 *Copyright Act*, ss. 3(1) and 27(1).
4 *Copyright Act*, s. 13(4).
5 *Copyright Act*, s. 27(2).
6 *Copyright Act*, s. 3(1).
7 Such as under either under s. 27(2) of the Act or under the public interest exception (if it indeed exists in Canada).
8 *Copyright Act*, s. 42.
9 U.S. *Copyright Act*, 17 U.S.C. s. 107 (1994).
10 *Copyright and the Information Highway: Final Report of the Copyright SubCommittee*, 1995, Information Highway Advisory Council, Government of Canada.
11 *The Challenge of the Information Highway: Final Report of the Information Highway Advisory Council* (Government of Canada, 1995) at Recommendation 6.5, p. 116.
12 It gained judicial recognition in *R. v. James Lorimer & Co.*, [1984] 1 F.C. 1065, 77 C.P.R. (2d) 262 (C.A.). It was considered at greater length by the U.K. courts: *Hubbard v. Vosper*, [1972] 1 All E.R. 1023 (C.A.); *Beloff v. Pressdram*, [1973] 1 All E.R. 241 (Ch. D.); and *Lion Laboratories Ltd. v. Evans*, [1985] Q.B. 526 (C.A.).
13 In Canada the costs of registration are $150 for each trademark application filed, $200 for the certificate of registration. If extra documents are required, i.e. an application is incomplete, the cost is an additional $50.
14 *Trade-Marks Act*, s. 9(1).

Notes

Chapter Eight

1 *Utah Digital Signature Act*, Utah Code Annotated Title 46, Chapter 3 (1996).
2 UNCITRAL, Model Law on Electronic Commerce, U.N. Doc. A/51/17 (1996).
3 Cal Gov Code @ 16.5 (1996) reads:
(a) In any written communication with a public entity, as defined in Section 811.2, in which a signature is required or used, any party to the communication may affix a signature by use of a digital signature that complies with the requirements of this section. The use of a digital signature shall have the same force and effect as the use of a manual signature if and only if it embodies all of the following attributes:
1) It is unique to the person using it.
2) It is capable of verification.
3) It is under the sole control of the person using it.
4) It is linked to data in such a manner that if the data are changed, the digital signature is invalidated.
5) It conforms to regulations adopted by the Secretary of State . . .
b) The use or acceptance of a digital signature shall be at the option of the parties. Nothing in this section shall require a public entity to use or permit the use of a digital signature.
d) "Digital signature" means an electronic identifier, created by computer, intended by the party using it to have the same force and effect as the use of a manual signature.
4 S. Waddams, *The Law of Contracts* (Toronto: Canada Law Book, 1984) at 81.

Chapter Nine

1 *M'Alister (or Donoghue) v. Stevenson*, [1932] A.C. 562 (H of L).
2 Leon E. Wein, "The Responsibility of Intelligent Artifacts: Toward an Automation Jurisprudence," 6 *Harvard Journal of Law and Technology*. Note that the corporation has "neither a soul to be damned nor a body to be kicked," but it does have a distinctive personality to sue or be sued.
3 Eugene Volokh, "Cheap Speech and What It Will Do," (1995) 104 *Yale Law Journal* 1805.
4 Most commentators find the distinction superficial and unhelpful, but it's largely maintained nonetheless.
5 David Loundy, "E-Law: Legal Issues Affecting Computer Information Systems," (1993) 12 *Computer Law Review* 101 at 112.
6 A.M. Linden and L.N.Klar, *Canadian Tort Law* (Toronto: Butterworths, 1994) at 704.
7 Restatement (Second) of Torts, s. 568 cmt. b (1989).
8 *Cianci v. New York Times Publishing Co.*, 639 F.2d 54, 61 (2d Cir. 1980) (quoting Restatement (Second) of Torts, s. 578 (1977)).
9 *Lerman v. Chukkleberry Publishing, Inc.*, 521 F.Supp. 228, 325 (S.D.N.Y. 1981).
10 Frank Darr, "A Proposed Defamation Standard for Commercial Computer Information Systems," (1996) 18 Hastings *Entertainment Law Journal* 267.
11 William Prosser, "Privacy" (1960), *California Law Review*, 383, at 389.
12 *CNN US News* Web site (http://www.cnn.com), August 16, 1996.
13 A.M. Linden and L.N. Klar, *Canadian Tort Law* (Toronto: Butterworths, 1994) at 155.
14 *Bank Leumi Trust v. Bally's Park Place*, 528 F.Supp. 349 (1981).
15 Peter Knight and James Fitzsimmonds in *The Legal Environment of Computing* (Sydney: Addison-Wesley Publishing, 1990).
16 *Winnipeg Condominium Corporation No. 36 v. Bird Construction*, [1995] 1 S.C.R. 85.
17 See *Hedley Byrne & Co. v. Heller & Partners Ltd.*, [1964] A.C. 465, [1963] 2 All E.R. 575.

18 A.M. Linden and L.N. Klar, *Canadian Tort Law* (Toronto: Butterworths, 1994).

19 Benjamin Wright, *The Law of Electronic Commerce* (Boston: Little, Brown & Co., 1991) at 334.

20 *New York Times*, August 8, 1996.

21 Article 1468 of the Civil Code of Quebec (CCQ) states:
"The manufacturer of a movable property is liable to reparation for injury caused to a third person by reason of a safety defect in the thing, even if it is incorporated with or placed in an immovable for the service or operation of the immovable.
"The same rule applies to a person who distributes the thing under his name or as his own and to any supplier of the thing, whether a wholesaler or a retailer and whether or not he imported the thing."
Article 1469 CCQ states:
"A thing has a safety defect where, having regard to all circumstances, it does not afford the safety which a person is normally entitled to expect, particularly by reason of a defect in the design or manufacture of the thing, poor preservation or presentation of the thing, or the lack of sufficient indications as to the risks and dangers it involves or as to safety precautions."

22 *Rae v. T. Eaton Co.* (1961), 28 D.L.R. (2d) 522 at 528 expresses the current Canadian common law:
"... The test of liability is not whether the product sold was or was not a 'dangerous thing,' but considering its nature and all relevant circumstances whether there has been a breach of duty by the manufacturer which he owed to the injured person."

23 *Escola v. Coca Cola Bottling Co. of Fresno*, 150 P. 2d 436 (1944). Mr. Justice Traynor wrote: "I believe the manufacturer's negligence should no longer be singled out as the basis of the plaintiff's right to recover on cases like the present one. In my opinion it should now be recognized that a manufacturer incurs absolute liability when an article that he has placed on the market, knowing that it is to be used without inspection, proves to have a defect which causes injury to human beings."

24 See Prosser, "The Fall of the Citadel," (1966) 50 *Minnesota Law Review* 791.

25 *East River S.S. Corp. v. Transamerica Delaval, Inc.* 476 U.S. 858 at 866 (1986).

26 Restatement (Second) of Torts, s. 402A (1964)

27 [1996] 4 All ER 481 (C.A.). The Court of Appeal upheld the trial judge's decision by holding that the contract contained implied terms of warranty.

28 J.M. Voas, L.K. Voas and K.M. Miller, "A Model for Assessing the Liability of Seemingly Correct Software," Proc. of the IASTED Conference of Reliability, Quality Control and Risk Assessment (Tysons Corner, VA, 1992) 32-35, reprinted at http://www.rstcorp.com/liability.html.

Chapter Ten

1 J.-G. Castel, *Canadian Conflict of Laws* (Toronto: Butterworths, 1994) at 20.

2 From Castel, *supra* at 19.

3 From the classes of Professor Talpis of the Université de Montréal.

4 In Canada even today aboriginal peoples are subject to different laws than other Canadians.

5 Think of the term "*real* estate," for instance.

6 See *International Shoe Co. v. Washington*, 326 U.S. 310 (1945); *Burger King Corp. v.*

Rudzewicz, 471 U.S. 462 (1985); *World-Wide Volkswagen Corp. v. Woodson*, 444 U.S. 286 (1980); *Asahi Metal Industry Co. v. Superior Court*, 480 U.S. 102 (1987).

7 See U.S. Second Restatement of Conflict of Law section 188(1) and (2).

8 Professor Yntema, in an oft-cited article "The Objectives of Private International Law," (1957) 35 *Canadian Bar Review* 721 at 734-35, states that these policy considerations include "uniformity of legal consequences, minimization of conflict of laws, predictability of legal consequences, the reasonable expectations of the parties, uniformity of social and economic consequences, validation of transactions, relative significance of contacts, recognition of the 'stronger' law, co-operation among states, respect for interests of other states, justice of the end results, respect for policies of domestic law, internal harmony of the substantive rules to be applied, location or nature of the transaction, private utility, homogeneity of national law, ultimate recourse of the *lex fori*, and the like."

9 Castel, *supra*.

10 Currie, "Notes on Methods and Objectives in the Conflict of Laws," [1959] *Duke Law Journal* 171.

11 David F. Cavers, *The Choice of Law Process* (Ann Arbor: University of Michigan Press, 1965) at 63-64.

12 In Canada, see *Morguard Investments Ltd. v. De Savoye*, [1990] 3 S.C.R. 1077.

13 See 3083-3133 CCQ.

14 See e.g. 3085 CCQ.

15 See e.g. 3088 CCQ.

16 See e.g. 3111 CCQ.

17 See e.g. 3082 CCQ.

18 Taken from Trotter Hardy, "The Proper Legal Regime for Cyberspace," (1994) 55 *University of Pittsburgh Law Review* 993.

19 *Ibid.*

20 *Ibid.*

Chapter Eleven

1 Don Tapscott, *The Digital Economy: Promise and Peril in the Age of Networked Intelligence* (New York: McGraw-Hill, 1996) at 7.

2 Nuala Beck, *Shifting Gears: Thriving in the New Economy* (New York: HarperCollins, 1992), cited by Tapscott, *supra* note 1 at 9.

Glossary

AECA — *Arms Export Controls Act* (U.S.).

ANSI — American National Standards Association.

ATM — 1) Asynchronous Transfer Mode: a high-speed networking technology for broadband communications.
2) Automated Teller Machine: an unattended terminal-type device that provides simple banking services such as cash withdrawals, transfers of funds between accounts and account balances.

Bandwidth — The range of frequencies required for the transmission of a signal, usually given in hertz. More bandwidth is required for carrying more complex signals. For example, more bandwidth is required to carry full-motion video than simple voice messages.

BBS — See electronic bulletin board.

Binary — Where only two values or states are possible for a particular condition, such as "ON" or "OFF," or "1" or "0."

Bit — A contraction of the term "binary digit." A unit of information represented by a 0 or 1. The speed of information transmission is measured in bits per seconds (bps).

Bottleneck — A local communications company network service, function, or facility currently subject to some degree of monopoly control, that competitors cannot economically duplicate but require access to in order to compete.

Broadband services — A range of communications services that require and use larger bandwidth than traditional voice messaging. A broadband communication system can simultaneously accommodate television, voice, data, and many other services.

Broadcasting — Any transmission of programs, whether or not encrypted, by radiowaves or other means of telecommunication, for reception by the public by means of a broadcasting receiving apparatus. Does not include any such transmission of programs that is made solely for performance or display in a public place.

BT — British Telecom.

Bundling — The practice of combining separate hardware, software, and services into a package offered at a single price.

CA — Certification Authority: a trusted authority that assigns a unique name to each user and issues a certificate containing the name and the user's public key for purposes of security of messaging.

CA Domain Registrar — An organization in Canada that administers second-level domain names using the ".ca" suffix.

CAI — Commission d'accès à l'information: the agency overseeing privacy protection in Quebec.

CBA — Canadian Bankers Association.

CCITT — International Consultative Committee on Telephone and Telegraphy (now known as the ITU): see ITU.

CCTV — Closed Circuit Television.

CDA — Communications Decency Act (U.S.).

CDMA — Canadian Direct Marketing Association.

CD-ROM — Compact Disc with Read-Only Memory. Compatible with computers, compact discs are inexpensive high-capacity storage devices for data, text, and video.

CFAA — Computer Fraud and Abuse Act (U.S.).

Chat — See IRC.

Convergence — The "coming together" of formerly distinct technologies, industries or activities; most common usage refers to the convergence of computing, communications, and broadcasting technologies.

CRL — Certificate Revocation List: a list of public-key certificates that have been revoked before they expire.

Cross-certification — Occurs when a corporation which is legally certified to provide products and service in one industry (or marketplace) is also certified (as a legitimate or legal entity) to provide products or services in another industry.

Cross-ownership — The practice of one corporation exercising partial or complete control of the operation of another, through purchase or ownership of stock in the latter corporation.

Cross-subsidization — The practice of applying revenues of an operation or line of business to another operation, to lower the price of the latter operation. For example, local telephone rates have remained low because they were subsidized by long-distance revenues.

CRTC — Canadian Radio-Television and Telecommunications Commission.

Cryptographic algorithm — A mathematical function used for encoding and decoding a message. Also called a cipher.

CSA — Canadian Standards Association: one of five standards-writing organizations in Canada that are accredited by the Standards Council of Canada.

Cyberspace — The three-dimensional expanse of computer networks in which all audio and video electronic signals travel and users can, with the proper addresses and codes, explore and download information.

Digital — Being expressed in binary patterns of 1s and 0s.

Digital radio — Microwave transmission of digital data via radio transmitters or radio broadcasting using a digital signal.

Digital scanner — A device that allows users to monitor radiocommunication frequencies automatically.

Digital signature — Data, appended to a part of a message, that enables a recipient to verify the integrity and origins of a message.

Digitization — The conversion of analog or continuous signal into a series of 1s and 0s, i.e., into a digital format.

Direct-to-home (DTH) — A TV signal broadcast by satellite and received directly in a subscriber's home via a small dish antenna.

Distance education (tele-education) — Education using different media (correspondence, radio, television and others) but requiring little or no physical attendance at the institution offering the courses and accredited certification.

DNS — Domain Names System: a system that equates alpha-numeric names with computer addresses used on the Internet. The DNS is administered by various organizations such as Network Solutions Inc. in the United States and the CA Domain Registrar in Canada.

Domain name — An alpha-numeric representation of a computer or group of computers in the Internet Domain Names System.

ECPA — *Electronic Communications Privacy Act* (U.S.).

EDI — Electronic Data Interchange: electronic preparation, communication, and processing of business transactions in a predefined structured format, using computers and telecommunications.

Electronic bulletin board — An electronic messaging system and an information storage area shared by several users, each having access to all information left in a posted area.

Electronic commerce — Consumer and business transactions conducted over a network, using computers and telecommunications.

E-mail — A medium through which textual messages can be sent to a specific recipient, transmitted almost instantly, regardless of the physical distance between the sender and receiver.

Encryption — The coding of data for privacy protection or security considerations when transmitted over telecommunications links, so that only the person to whom it is sent can read it.

EPIC — Electronic Privacy Information Center (U.S.).

EU — European Union.

FAA — Federal Aviation Administration (U.S.).

FCC — Federal Communication Commission (U.S.).

Fibre-optic communications — A modern transmission technology using lasers to produce a beam of light which can be modulated to carry large amounts of information through fine glass or acrylic fibres.

FidoNet — A standardized system whereby BBSs phone one another and relay e-mail.

Freenet — A non-profit community organization that provides free access to electronic mail and information services and to computer networks such as the Internet.

Freeware — Software that users can freely download and distribute without having to pay any licence fees.

FTA — Canada–United States Free Trade Agreement.

FTP — File Transfer Protocol: a standard by which users can transfer computer files to one another.

Full-motion video — Video that is perceived to provide smooth and continuous motion.

GATT — General Agreement on Tariffs and Trade.

GII — Global Information Infrastructure: a global information highway initiative put forward by the United States to G7 countries.

Gopher — An information service that is similar to the WWW but is more rudimentary in its features.

HDTV — High-Definition Television: television with greater resolution than the current 525-line television standard.

Hertz — A unit of frequency; one cycle per second.

Home page — A World Wide Web site (or "website") with a specific address.

Hot chat — Chat used for sexual gratification.

Hypermedia — Use of data, text, graphics, video, and voice as elements in a hypertext system. All the forms of information are linked together so that a user can move easily from one to another.

Hypertext — Text that contains embedded links to other documents or information.

IATA — International Air Transport Authority.

ICAO — International Civil Aviation Organization.

IEC — International Electrotechnical Commission.

IHAC — Information Highway Advisory Council of the government of Canada.

Intellectual property (IP) — A collective term used to refer to new ideas, inventions, designs, writings, films, etc., and is protected by copyrights, patents, trademarks, etc.

Internet — A vast international network of networks that enables computers of all kinds to share services and communicate directly.

IRC — Internet Relay Chat (or simply chat): a textual form of real-time communication between two or more users.

ISDN — Integrated Services Digital Network: a set of digital telecommunications network standards.

ISO — International Organization for Standardization: a specialized international agency for standardization, with a membership of standards bodies in 89 countries.

ISP — Internet Service Provider: a company that provides an access point to the Internet.

ITAR — International Traffic in Arms Regulations (U.S.).

ITU — International Telecommunications Union: an international telecommunications standards organization.

Key escrow policy — A United States policy concerning the technology developed to address the concern that widespread use of encryption would make lawfully authorized electronic surveillance more difficult. It involves granting designated third parties special keys needed for law enforcement agencies to gain access, under court warrant, to encrypted communication or transactions.

LMCS — Local Multipoint Communication Services: A service that uses a combination of wired and wireless communication to provide two-way multimedia services at the community level in Canada.

Local Area Network (LAN) — A private data network in which special serial transmission is used without store and forward techniques for direct data communication among stations located within the user's premises.

Local loop — The part of a communications circuit between the subscriber's equipment and the line termination equipment in the exchange facility.

Logon — The act of connecting to an internet service provider.

Modem — A contraction of the words *mo*dulator and *dem*odulator. An accessory that allows computers and terminal equipment to communicate through telephone lines or cable. The modem converts analog data to the digital language of computers.

NAFTA — North American Free Trade Agreement.

Narrowband — A relatively restricted frequency band normally used for a single purpose or made available to a single user.

NBER — National Board of Economic Research (U.S.).

Network Solutions Inc. — An organization in the U.S. that administers the second-level domain names ending with ".net", ".com", ".org", ".edu", and others.

NLRA — National Labor Relations Act (U.S.).

NSF — National Science Foundation (U.S.).

Number portability — The ability to maintain the same user number when transferring among various networks and service providers.

OECD — Organization for Economic Cooperation and Development: an international cooperation organization, of which Canada is a member. The OECD is responsible for issues in international development including information and communications technologies and related standards.

Pay server — An Internet server that restricts access to paid members, who are provided with a password.

PCS — Personal Communications Services: a family of radiocommunication services provided through personal user radio terminals operating in a mobile portable mode.

PCTV — Personal Computer Television.

PGP — Pretty Good Privacy: a widespread public-key cryptography system based on the RSA algorithm and used on the Internet.

PKI — Public Key Infrastructure: a system for the publication and distribution of cryptographic keys.

PKIX — Public Key Infrastructure using X.509: a draft Internet standard for a PKI based on X.509.

PPA — Privacy Protection Act (U.S.).

Protocols — Sets of technology language rules that determine how various components of communications systems interact.

Rate rebalancing — A process aimed at increasing prices for local telephone service subsidized by long-distance revenues and reducing subsidies paid by long-distance service providers. See also cross-subsidization.

RSA — Rivest, Shamir, Adleman: the name of a public-key cryptography system invented by Rivest, Shamir, and Adleman.

SDSI — Simple Distributed Security Infrastructure ("sudsy"): a PKI proposal by Rivest and Lampson.

SET — Secure Electronic Transaction: an X.509-based PKI for online credit-card transactions.

Shareware — A software product that can be freely downloaded and distributed ("shared") by users. Users may have to pay a licence fee to keep using the product beyond a certain free period.

SHRM — Society for Human Resources Management.

Spectrum — The range of electromagnetic frequencies capable of traversing space without the benefit of physical interconnection.

SPKI — Simple Public Key Infrastructure ("spicky"): a draft Internet standard for a PKI.

Structural separation — The creation or existence of a separate but affiliated company to provide a specific line of business. Structural separation is one approach to dealing with cross-subsidization of undue preference.

Switched communications system — A communications system that allows the two-way, point-to-point exchange of information.

Telnet — Computer software that allows a remote terminal or computer to access another computer.

TLA — Three-Letter Acronym ;-)

TSACC — Telecommunications Standards Advisory Council of Canada: a government/industry-led body establishing commonality of standards.

UCC — 1) Uniform Commercial Code (U.S.).
2) Universal Copyright Convention.

Unbundled — Services, software, and training sold separately from the hardware.

UNCITRAL — United Nations Commission on International Trade Laws.

Universal access — The ability to get online to a network from anywhere.

Universal service — A policy that local telephone rates should be kept low enough to ensure that the maximum number of persons are able to afford basic service.

URL — Universal Resource Locator: a World Wide Web address.

USENET News — A distributed message base, one of the various modes of the Internet, currently with 20 000 various subjects, or "newsgroups," for discussion.

Video compression — The process of contracting data so that more can be stored and transmitted.

Video-dial-tone (VDT) — The two-way, or "switched," broadband carriage of information. VDT technology will provide the platform for video-on-demand services.

Video-on-demand service — A service that allows the user to dial in to a video-dial-tone system, choose a video, and play it.

Virtual reality — An interactive, simultaneous electronic representation of a real or imaginary world where, through sight, sound, and even touch, the user is given the impression of becoming part of what is represented.

Wide Area Network (WAN) — A communications network made up of Local Area

Networks (LANs) and/or Metropolitan Area Networks (MANs), allowing access to data physically located at great distances.

WIPO — World Intellectual Property Organization: A Geneva-based organization of states and non-governmental organizations that proposes and administers international intellectual property treaties.

WTO — World Trade Organization.

WWW — World Wide Web, or "the Web": the Internet's most rapidly growing mode, through which text graphics, video sequences, sounds, and animation can be conveyed.

X.500 — A set of ITU standards for a worldwide electronic directory service, akin to the white pages.

X.509 — The part of the X.500 standard that pertains to PKIs.

Bibliography

Books

Barber, Benjamin. *Strong Democracy*. Berkeley: University of California Press, 1984.

Beck, Nuala. *Shifting Gears: Thriving in the New Economy*. New York: HarperCollins, 1992.

Brière, Jean-Yves, and Jean-Pierre Villagi. *La protection des renseignements personnels dans le secteur privé*. Montreal: Les publications CCH, 1995.

Carroll, Jim, and Rick Broadhead. *Canadian Internet Handbook*. Scarborough, Ont.: Prentice Hall Canada, 1996.

Castel, J.-G. *Canadian Conflict of Laws*. Toronto: Butterworths, 1994.

Cavazos, Edward A., and Gavino Morin. *Cyber-Space and the Law: Your Rights and Duties in the On-Line World*. Cambridge: MIT Press, 1994.

Cavers, David F. *The Choice of Law Process*. Ann Arbor: University of Michigan Press, 1965.

Cavoukian, Ann, and Don Tapscott. *Who Knows: Safeguarding Your Privacy in a Networked World*. Toronto: Random House, 1995.

Dam, Kenneth W., and Herbert S. Lin, eds. *Cryptography's Role in Securing the Information Society*. Washington, D.C.: National Academy Press, 1996.

Davis, Kenneth W., and Herbert S. Lin. *The Monster Under the Bed*. New York: Simon & Schuster, 1994.

Drucker, Peter F. *Post-Capitalist Society*. New York: Harper Business, 1993.

Flaherty, David. *Protecting Privacy in Surveillance Societies: The Federal Republic of Germany, Sweden, France, Canada and the United States*. Chapel Hill: University of North Carolina Press, 1989.

Fox, H.G. *Canadian Law of Copyright and Industrial Designs*. Toronto: Carswell, 1967.

Freeman, Richard, ed. *Working Under Different Rules*. Russell Sage Foundation: New York, 1994.

Fridman, Gerald H.L. *The Law of Torts in Canada*. Toronto: Carswell, 1990.

Gibson, William. *Neuromancer*. New York: Ace Books, 1984.

Goldstein, Paul. *Copyright's Highway: From Gutenberg to the Celestial Jukebox*. New York: Hill & Wang, 1994.

Jackson, M. Drew, and Timothy L. Taylor. *The Internet Handbook for Canadian Lawyers*. Toronto: Carswell, 1996.

Johnston, David, Deborah Johnston and Sunny Handa. *Getting Canada Online: Understanding the Information Highway*. Toronto: Stoddart, 1995.

Knight, Peter, and James Fitzsimons, eds. *The Legal Environment of Computing*. Sydney: Addison-Wesley Publishing, 1990.

Laperrière, René. *La vie privée sous surveillance*. Cowansville, Que.: Yvan Blais, 1994.

Larson, Erik. *The Naked Consumer: How Our Private Lives Become Public Commodities*. New York: Henry Holt & Company, 1992.

Lawson, Ian. *Privacy and Free Enterprise*. Ottawa: Public Interest Advocacy Centre, 1992.

Linden, A.M., and L.N. Klar. *Canadian Tort Law*. Toronto: Butterworths, 1994.

MacPherson, C.B. *The Life and Times of Liberal Democracy*. Toronto: Oxford University Press, 1970.

Negroponte, Nicholas. *Being Digital*. New York: Alfred A. Knopf, 1995.

Pateman, Carole. *Participation and Democratic Theory*. Cambridge: Cambridge University Press, 1970.

Posner, Richard. *Economic Analysis of Law*, 4th ed. Boston: Little, Brown & Co., 1992.

Rifkin, Jeremy. *The End of Work: The Decline of the Global Labor Force and the Dawn of the Post-Market Era*. New York: G.P. Putnam & Sons, 1995.

Rothfedder, Jeffery. *Privacy for Sale: How Computerization Has Made Everyone's Private Life an Open Secret*. New York: Simon & Schuster, 1992.

Tapscott, Don. *The Digital Economy: Promise and Peril in the Age of Networked Intelligence*. New York: McGraw-Hill, 1996.

Waddams, S. *The Law of Contracts*. Toronto: Canada Law Book, 1984.

Wright, Benjamin. *The Law of Electronic Commerce*. Boston: Little, Brown & Co., 1991.

Articles

Aguilar, Rose. "Research Services Raise Privacy Fears." *c!net news*, 10 June 1996.

Alsop, Stewart. "The Cable Industry's Big Dream." *Fortune*, 13 January 1997.

Bareburg, Mark. "Democracy and Domination in the Law of Workplace Cooperation: from Bureaucratic to Flexible Production." 94 *Colum. L. Rev.* 753 (1994).

Barlow, John Perry. "The Economy of Ideas: A Framework for Rethinking Patents and Copyrights in the Digital Age (Everything You Know About Intellectual Property Is Wrong)." *Wired* 3.03, 1994.

______. "Selling Wine Without Bottles: The Economy of Mind on the Global Network." New Mexico: Ojo Caliente, 1992. Published online @ http://www.eff.org.

Berry, John. "Restructuring's Toll on Workers Slowing." *Washington Post*, 23 August 1996, F1.

Bibas, Steven. "A Contractual Approach to Data Privacy." 17 *Harv. L.J. & Pub. Pol'y* 591 (1994).

Brent, Paul. "Voice Mail Can Do More Than Just Answer Phone." *Financial Post*, 1 April 1995, p. 28.

Byrne, John A. "Strategic Planning: After a Decade of Gritty Downsizing, Big Thinkers Are Back in Corporate Vogue." *Business Week*, 26 August 1996.

Conrod, Monique. "Business Urged to Safeguard Internal Information." *The Lawyers Weekly* 14, no. 48 (28 April 1995).

Culnan, Mary J. "An Issue of Consumer Privacy." *New York Times*, 31 March 1992, sec.3, p. 9.

Currie, Brainerd. "Notes on Methods and Objectives in the Conflict of Laws." 8 *Duke L.J.* 171 (1959).

Darr, Frank. "A Proposed Defamation Standard for Commercial Computer Information Systems." 18 *Hastings Comm/Ent L.J.* 267 (1996).

Davis, Simon. "Closed Circuit Television and the Policing of Public Morals." Advanced Surveillance Technologies Conference, Copenhagen, Denmark, 4 September 1995, records of which can be found at the Electronic Privacy Information Center (EPIC) @ http://www.epic.org.

"Does America Still Work? On the Turbulent Energies of the New Capitalism." *Harper's Magazine*, May 1996, 35.

Dyson, Ester. "Intellectual Value." *Wired* 3.07, 1994.

Estreicher, Samuel. "Employee Involvement and the 'Company Union' Prohibition: The Case for a Partial Repeal of Section 8(a)(2) of the NLRA." *N.Y.U.L. Rev.* 125 (1994).

Flint, Jerry. "The Company of the Year." *Forbes Magazine*, 13 January 1997.

Grodin, Joseph R. "Constitutional Values in the Private Sector Workplace." *Indus. Rel. L.J.* 1 (1991).

Handa, Sunny. "Copyright Liability When Browsing on the Information Highway." 29 *Law/Technology J.* 11 (1996).

______. "Reverse Engineering Computer Programs Under Canadian Copyright Law." 40 *McGill L.J.* 621 (1995).

Handa, Sunny, and Marc Branchaud. "Re-evaluating Proposals for a Public Key Infrastructure." 29 *Law/Technology J.* 1 (1996).

Hardy, Trotter. "The Proper Legal Regime for Cyberspace." 55 *U. Pitt. L. Rev.* 993 (1994).

Keegan, Victor. "How Digital Billionaires Altered the Meaning of Wealth." *Globe and Mail*, 10 August 1996, D4.

Klare, Karl. "The Labor-Management Cooperation Debate: A Workplace Democracy Perspective." 23 *Har. Civ. Rights-Civ. Liberties Rev.* 39 (1988).

Klein, Daniel B. "In Defence of the Credit Bureau." 12 *Cato J.* 393 (1992).

______. "Promise Keeping in the Great Society: A Model of Credit Information Sharing." 4 *Econ. & Pol.* 117 (1992).

Laperrière, René. "La protection des renseignements personnels dans le secteur privé et la loi québécoise de 1993." *La vie privée sous surveillance.* Cowansville: Yvon Blais, 1994.

Leroy, Michael. "Can Team Work? Implications of Electromation and Dupont Compliance Analysis for the Team Act." 71 *Notre Dame L. Rev.* 215 (1996).

Loundy, David. "E-Law: Legal Issues Affecting Computer Information Systems." 12 Computer/L. J. 101 (1993).

"McDonald's Snooping Too." *Privacy Journal 21*, no. 3 (January 1995) 3.

Nimmer, Raymond T., and Patricia Krauthouse. "Electronic Commerce: New Paradigms in Information Law." 31 *Idaho L. Rev.* 937 (1995).

O'Conner, Marleen. "The Human Capital Era: Reconceptualizing Corporate Law to Facilitate Labor-Management Cooperation." 78 *Cornell L. Rev.* 899 (1993).

Onyshko, Tom. "Information Technology Poses Threat to Personal Privacy. Canada Needs New Laws to Protect Privacy: Phillips." *The Lawyers Weekly* 14, no. 39 (24 February 1995) 39.

Peladeau, Pierrot. "Data Protection Saves Money." *Privacy Journal* 21, no. 8 (June 1995).

Pillar, Charles. "Bosses with X-Ray Eyes." *MacWorld*, July 1993.

Prosser, William. "Privacy." *Cal L. Rev.* 383 (1960).

______. "The Fall of the Citadel." 50 *Minn. L. Rev.* 791 (1966).

Prowda, Judith. "Privacy and the Security of Data." 64 *Fordham L. Rev.* 738 (1995).

"Racy Voice Mail Message Raise Concern over Privacy." *North Bay Nugget*, 16 December 1994, C5.

Rustad, Michael. "The Commercial Law of Internet Security." 10 *High Tech. L.J.* 213 (1995).

Samuelson, Pamela. "The Copyright Grab." *Wired* 4.01, 1995.

Solomon, Lewis D. "Perspectives on Human Nature and Their Implications for Business Organizations." 23 *Fordham Urb L.J.* 221 (1996).

Soma, John T., and Jay Batson. "The Legal Environment of Commercial Database Administration." *Jurimetrics Journal* 297 (Spring 1987).

Stelling, Susan. "Privacy in the Digital Age." *c!net news*, June 1996.

Stone, Katherine Van Wenzel. "The Legacy of Industrial Pluralism: The Tension Between Individual Employment Rights and the New Deal Collective Bargaining System." 59 *U. Chi. L. Rev.* 575 (1992).

"The Scary Prospect of Fast Information." *Globe and Mail*, 30 September 1996, A16.

"The Threat to British Liberty." *The Economist*, 15-21 February 1997, p. 16.

Uchitelle, L., and N.R. Kleinfield. "On the Battlefields of Business, Millions of Casualties." *New York Times*, 3 March 1996.

Voas, J.M., L.K. Voas and K.M. Miller. "A Model for Assessing the Liability of Seemingly Correct Software." Proc. of the IASTED Conference of Reliability, Quality Control and Risk Assessment, Tysons Corner, VA, 1992, pp. 32-35, reprinted at http://www.rstcorp.com/liability.html.

Volokh, Eugene. "Cheap Speech and What It Will Do." 104 *Yale L.J.* 1805 (1995).

Warren, Samuel, and Louis Brandeis. "The Right to Privacy." 4 Harv. L. Rev. 193 (1890).

Wein, Leon E. "The Responsibility of Intelligent Artifacts: Toward an Automation Jurisprudence." 6 *Harv. J.L. & Tech.* 103 (1992).

Wright, Tom. "Caller ID Guidelines." Toronto: Information and Privacy Commission, Ontario, 1992.

______. "Privacy Makes Good Business Sense." Toronto: Information and Privacy Commission, Ontario, 1994.

______. "Privacy Protection Models for the Private Sector." Toronto: Information and Privacy Commission, Ontario, 1995.

______. "Workplace Privacy: The Need for a Safety-Net." Toronto: Information and Privacy Commission, Ontario, 1993.

Yntema, Hessel E. "The Objectives of Private International Law." 35 *Can. Bar Rev.* 721 (1957).

Cases

Aetna Casualty and Surety Co. v. Jeppesen, 642 F.2d 339 (9th Cir. 1981).

Alberta Government Telephones v. CRTC, [1989] 2 S.C.R. 225.

American Civil Liberties Union v. Janet Reno, Attorney General of the United States, 929 F.Supp. 824 (E.D. Pa. 1996).

Apple Computer Inc. v. Microsoft Corporation, 759 F.Supp. 1444 (N.D. Cal. 1991).

Asahi Metal Industry Co. v. Superior Court, 480 U.S. 102 (1987).
Avrahami v. U.S. News & World Report, Petition No. 961837, S.C. Va., on appeal from the Cir. Ct. Of Arlington County (12 June 1996). More information can be found at http://www.epic.org.
Bank Leumi Trust v. Bally's Park Place, 528 F.Supp. 349 (S.D. N.Y. 1981).
Beloff v. Pressdram, [1973] 1 All E.R. 241 (Ch. D.).
Breen v. Hancock House Publishers Ltd. et al. (1986), 6 C.I.P.R. 129 (F.C.T.D).
Brocklesby v. Jeppeson,767 F.2d 1288 (9th Cir. 1985); leave for *certiorari* denied at 106 S. Ct. 882 (1986).
Burger King Corp. v. Rudzewicz, 471 U.S. 462 (1985).
Canadian Admiral Corporation v. Rediffusion Inc. (1954), Ex. C.R. 382.
Canadian National Railway Co. v. Norsk Pacific Steamship Co., [1992] 1 S.C.R. 1021.
Cartwright v. Wharton (1912), 25 O.L.R. 357 (H.C.J., Common Pleas Div.).
Central Trust Co. v. Raffuse (1986), D.L.R. (4th) 481 at 521-22 (S.C.C.).
Cianci v. New York Times Publishing Co., 639 F.2d 54 (2d Cir. 1980).
Clements Auto Co. v. Service Bureau Corp., 444 F.2d 169 (8th Cir. 1971).
Coastal States Trading Inc. v. Shell Pipeline Corp., 573 F.Supp. 1415 (S.D. Tex. 1983); aff'd 788 S.W.2d 837 (1990).
Compo Co. Ltd. v. Blue Crest Music Inc. (1979), 45 C.P.R. (2d) 1 (S.C.C.).
Cubby v. CompuServe, 776 F.Supp. 135 (S.D. N.Y. 1991).
Dodge v. Ford Motor Co., 204 Mich. 459, 170 N.W. 668, 3 A.L.R. 413 (S.C. Mich. 1919).
East River S.S. Corp. v. Transamerica Delaval, Inc., 476 U.S. 858 (1986).
E.I. du Pont de Nemours & Co., 311 N.L.R.B. 893 (1993).
Electromation Inc. v. NLRB, 35 F.3d 1148, 309 N.L.R.B. 990 (7th Cir. 1994).
Escola v. Coca Cola Bottling Co. of Fresno, 150 P. 2d 436 (S.C. Cal. 1944).
Feist Publications Inc. v. Rural Telephone Service Inc., 663 F.Supp. 214 (D. Kan. 1987).
Feist Publications Inc. v. Rural Telephone Service Inc., App. to Pet. for Cert. 4a, judgt. order reported at 916 F.2d 718 (1990).
Feist Publications Inc. v. Rural Telephone Service Inc., 499 U.S. 340 (1991).
Gibson v. Florida Legislative Investigation Committee, 372 U.S. 539 (1963).
Haig v. Bamford, [1977] 1 S.C.R. 466.
Hedley Byrne & Co. v. Heller & Partners Ltd., [1964] A.C. 465, [1963] 2 All E.R. 575.
Hubbard v. Vosper, [1972] 1 All E.R. 1023 (C.A.).
International News Service v. Associated Press, 248 U.S. 215, S.Ct. 68, 63 L.Ed. 211 (1918).
International Shoe Co. v. Washington, 326 U.S. 310 (1945).

Jefferys v. Boosey (1855), 4 H.L.C. 815.

Lasercomb America Inc. v. Reynolds, 911 F.2d 970 (4th Cir. 1990).

Lerman v. Chuckkleberry Publishing, Inc., 521 F.Supp. 228 (S.D.N.Y. 1981).

Lion Laboratories Ltd. v. Evans, [1985] Q.B. 526 (C.A.).

M'Alister (or Donoghue) v. Stevenson, [1932] A.C. 562 (H of L).

MacKenzie Patten & Co. v. British Olivetti Ltd., (1984) 48 M.L.R. 344 (Q.B.D.).

Moreau v. St. Vincent, [1950] Ex. C.R. 198.

Morguard Investments Ltd. v. De Savoye, [1990] 3 S.C.R. 1077.

Parke v. Daily News Ltd., [1962] 1 Ch. 927, [1962] All E.R. 929 (Ch. D.).

PEINET Inc. v. O'Brien (1995), 61 C.P.R. (3d) 334 (P.E.I. S.C.T.D.).

R. v. Butler (1992), 70 C.C.C. (3d) 129, II C.R. (4th) 137, [1992] 1 S.C.R. 452.

R. v. Cognos Inc., [1993] 1 S.C.R. 87.

R. v. James Lorimer & Co., [1984] 1 F.C. 1065, 77 C.P.R. (2d) 262 (C.A.).

R. v. McLaughlin (1980), 53 C.C.C. (2d) 417, [1980] 2 S.C.R. 331, 18 C.R. (3d) 339.

R. v. Oakes, [1986] 1 S.C.R. 103.

Rae v. T. Eaton Co. (1961), 28 D.L.R. (2d) 522 (N.S. S.C.).

St. Albans City and District Council v. International Computers Ltd. , [1996] 4 All ER 481 (C.A.).

Shea et al. v. Janet Reno, Attorney General of the United States, 930 F.Supp. 916 (S.D. N. Y. 1996).

Smyth v. Pillsbury Co., 914 F.Supp. 97 (E.D. Pa. 1996).

Steve Jackson Games v. United States Secret Service, 816 F.Supp. 432 (W.D. Tex. 1993).

Stevenson v. Crook et al., [1938] 4 D.L.R. 294 (Ex. Ct.).

Stratton Oakmont Inc. v. Prodigy Service Co. , 1995 N.Y. Misc. Lexis 229, 23 Media L. Rep. 1794 (S.C. N.Y., Nassau Co. 1995).

Talley v. California, 362 U.S. 60, 4 L. Ed. 2d 559, 80 S. Ct. 536 (1960).

Teck Corporation Limited v. Millar, [1973] 2 W.W.R. 385, 33 D.L.R. (3d) 288 (B.C. S.C.).

Téléphone Guèvrement v. Québec, [1994] 1 S.C.R. 878.

U&R Tax Services Ltd. v. H&R Block Canada Inc. (1995), 62 C.P.R. (3d) 257 (F.C.T.D.).

U.S. v. Thomas, 74 F.3d 701 (6th Cir. 1996).

Winnipeg Condominium Corporation No. 36 v. Bird Construction, [1995] 1 S.C.R. 85.

World-Wide Volkswagen Corp. v. Woodson, 444 U.S. 286 (1980).

Canadian Legislation

Act Respecting Access to Documents Held by Public Bodies and the Protection of Personal Information, R.S.Q. 1985, c. A-2.1.

Act Respecting the Protection of Personal Information in the Private Sector, S.Q. 1993, c. 17.

Broadcasting Act, R.S.C. 1991, c. 11 B-9.01.

Canadian Business Corporation Act, R.S.C. 1985, c. C-44.

Civil Code of Quebec, S.Q. 1991, c. 64.

Competition Act, R.S.C. 1985, c. C-46, as renamed and amended by S.C. 1986, c.26, Part II.

Constitution Act, 1982, being Schedule B to the *Canada Act 1982* (U.K.), 1982, c. 11.

Copyright Act, R.S.C. 1985, c. C-42.

Criminal Code of Canada, R.S.C. 1985, c. C-46.

Integrated Circuit Topography Act, R.S.C. 1985, c. I-14.6 [1990, c. 37].

Patent Act, R.S.C. 1985, c. P-4.

Radiocommunications Act, R.S.C. 1985, c. R-2.

Telecommunications Act, S.C. 1993, c. 38.

Trade-Marks Act, R.S.C. 1985, c. T-13.

U.S. Legislation

Arms Export Controls Act, 22 U.S.C. § § 2751 et seq. (1976).

Communications Decency Act, 47 U.S.C. § 223 (a)-(h) (1996).

Computer Fraud and Abuse Act, 18 U.S.C. § 1030 (1988).

Copyright Act, 17 U.S.C. §. 107 (1994).

Electronic Communications Privacy Act, 18 U.S.C. § § 2510-2711 (1988 & Supp. V 1993).

Encrypted Communications Privacy Act, S. 376, 105th Cong., 1st Sess. (1997).

International Traffic in Arms Regulation, 22 C.F.R. §§ 120-130 (1995).

National Labor Relations Act, 29 U.S.C. § 151 (1982).

Privacy Protection Act, 42 U.S.C. § 2000aa (1988).

Restatement (Second) of Torts, s. 402A (1964).

Restatement (Second) of Torts, s. 568 cmt. b (1989).

"*Team Act*," S. 295, 104th Cong., 1st Sess. (1995); H.R. 743, 104th Cong., 1st Sess. (1995).

Telecommunications Act, Pub L. No. 104-104, 110 Stat. 56 (1996).

Trademark Act ("Lanham Act"), 15 U.S.C. §§ 1051-1127 (1988).

Uniform Commercial Code, s. 2-201(1) (1991).

Utah Digital Signature Act, Utah Code Annotated Title 46, Chapter 3 (1996).

Wire Fraud Act, 18 U.S.C. § 1343 (1982).

Other Documents

Canadian Standards Association. *Model Code for the Protection of Personal Information*. Canada: CSA, 1996. CSA document no.: CAN/CSA-q830-96.

Commission of the European Communities. *Directive on the Protection of Personal Data and on the Free Movement of Such Data*, 1995 OJ2 281, 95/489/EC.

Information Highway Advisory Council (IHAC). *Privacy and the Canadian Information Highway*. Ottawa: Supply and Services Canada, 1995.

______. *The Challenge of the Information Highway: Final Report of the Information Highway Advisory Council*. Ottawa: Supply and Services Canada, 1995.

______. *Copyright and the Information Highway: Final Report of the Copyright SubCommittee*. Ottawa: Information Highway Advisory Council, 1995.

McBurnett. *PGP Web of Trust Statistics*, January 1996, http://bcn.boulder.co.us/~neal/pgpstat/.

Society of Management Accountants of Canada. *Electronic Commerce*. Management Accounting Issues Paper 9. Hamilton: SMAC, 1994.

Organization for Economic Cooperation and Development. *Guidelines on the Protection of Privacy and Transborder Flows of Personal Data*. Washington, D.C.: OECD Publications and Information Center, 1981.

UNCITRAL. *Model Law on Electronic Commerce*, U.N. Doc. A/51/17 (1996).

Index

Index

Index

Index